CW00551792

LANDMARK COLLECTOR'S LIBRARY

HISTORIC HALLAMSHIRE

History in Sheffield's Countryside

DAVID HEY

For
Hannah Clare Bentley,
born within Hallamshire,
30 October 2001.

LANDMARK COLLECTOR'S LIBRARY

HISTORIC
HALLAMSHIRE

David Hey

Landmark Publishing

Published by

Ashbourne Hall, Cokayne Ave
Ashbourne, Derbyshire DE6 1EJ England
Tel: (01335) 347349 Fax: (01335) 347303
e-mail: landmark@clara.net
web site: www.landmarkpublishing.co.uk

1st edition

ISBN 1 84306 049 3

British Library Cataloguing in Publication Data: a catalogue
record for this book is available from the British Library.

Printed by Bookcraft Bath Ltd

Designed by able design

Front cover and page 3
Ecclesfield Church: the south-west view of the church in the
mid-nineteenth century, from the Revd J. Eastwood's *History of Ecclesfield* (1862).

Back cover:
This print of High Bradfield appears at the beginning of the chapter on Bradfield, which
was written by the Revd Reginald A. Gatty for his father's *A Life at One Living* (1884).

CONTENTS

Acknowledgements

The photographs were mostly taken by the author or are part of his
collection of old photographs. He wishes to thank the following;
D. Crossley (Stumperlow cottage), C. Slinn (Ecclesfield church, finial and priory),
P. F. Ryder (Housley Hall and Green farm barn), Meridian Airmaps Ltd (Canyard
Hills aerial photograph) and B. Blanksby (map of grouse troughs).

When Horace Walpole passed through Sheffield in 1760 he described the place as 'one of the foulest towns in England in the most charming situation'. Two years later, Thomas Gray saw Sheffield 'by a pretty river's side, surrounded with charming hills', but thought that the Peak District was 'a country beyond comparison uglier than any other I have seen in England, black, tedious, barren, and not mountainous enough to please one with its horrors'. Sheffield's surroundings obviously provoked reactions that were as varied as those that were prompted by the town itself. But on the whole people agreed with the author of *The British Traveller, or Modern Panorama of England and Wales* (1819), who advised his readers that 'the environs of Sheffield are agreeable, and may even be characterised as romantic'.

Sheffield's countryside is also full of historical interest. We do not need to have the fertile imagination of Sir Walter Scott, who in *Ivanhoe* (1819) wrote of 'the fabulous Dragon of Wantley', 'desperate battles' and 'gallant outlaws', in order to appreciate the wealth of evidence on the ground. The local landscape has been shaped by man's activities since prehistoric times. The moors to the west of Sheffield owe their appearance to Bronze Age settlers, medieval cattle- and sheep-farmers, mighty lords who hunted deer, and the 'sportsmen' who shot grouse with fanatical enthusiasm. The local woods are not simply the parts of the landscape that could not be ploughed, but are the products of careful management for the production of charcoal, white coal, coppiced wood and timber for building. Some of the fields were shaped as medieval clearings, many of the roads and lanes go back well into the packhorse era, and the rough character of the gritstone edges owes much to the quarrying of millstones and the smelting of lead.

The local and family historian is concerned not just with the remaining visual evidence but with the people who have shaped the landscape. Medieval lords built castles and moated manor houses and fenced off deer parks nearby, gentry families erected the fine gabled halls that still adorn the countryside, and ordinary farming families have persisted in the same district over several hundred years in the small farms that are so characteristic of the Pennines. A surprising number of timber-framed farmhouses and barns survive from the Middle Ages or from the Tudor period. Minor place-names which were first recorded in medieval documents and local surnames which were formed seven hundred years or more ago unlock many secrets in the local landscape and help us to see how ordinary families moulded their environment in a less dramatic but more enduring way than the feudal lords and religious orders.

A sense of history enriches the pleasures of walking in the countryside by adding to the appreciation that can be obtained from the study of natural history and geology. Most of the topics that I have written about here were first explored with extramural students at the University of Sheffield and with local and family history societies. I was fortunate to be in the right place at the right time, when government funding was still available for extramural teaching. My job was hugely enjoyable and rewarding and I learned a great deal over the years from those who attended classes or lectures. I must make special mention of my Names Project group at the National Centre for English Cultural Tradition, whose members have contributed so much to the work on local surnames. The current members of the group are Denis and Florence Ashurst, Vera Edwards, Anne Giller, Julia Hatfield, Margaret Oversby,

June Royston-Tonks, Harold Taylor and Peter Wilkinson. I must also particularly acknowledge Stanley Jones and Peter Ryder, who have helped me over the years to understand our ancient local buildings.

The study of surnames is based on the pioneering work of PH Reaney, himself a Sheffield man. The acknowledged pioneers of the study of vernacular architecture – SO Addy and CF Innocent – also came from Sheffield. Joseph Hunter, Hallamshire's first historian, is remembered as one of England's greatest antiquaries and Alfred Gatty and Jonathan Eastwood, vicar and curate of Ecclesfield Church, were in the same tradition. In the twentieth century TW Hall performed the invaluable service of transcribing, translating and cataloguing manorial records, deeds and charters and numerous contributors to the *Transactions of the Hunter Archaeological Society* have continued this task and have published their interpretations of the evidence. All students of the local history of the Sheffield district are indebted to them.

The staff of Sheffield Archives and of the Local Studies Department at Sheffield Central Library have been unfailingly helpful over the forty years or so that I have been using their services. Many of the topics that I have written about here first interested me as a young school teacher at Ecclesfield, Colley and Holmfirth before I acquired a proper training as a postgraduate student and research fellow under William Hoskins, Alan Everitt and other members of the 'Leicester School' of English local historians. The opportunity to take early retirement has given me the time to reflect on these topics anew and to write up my conclusions. An earlier version of *The Dragon of Wantley* appeared in *Rural History*, 4, 1 (1993), pp. 23–40 and I am grateful to the editors of this journal for permission to reproduce it.

David Hey

Hallamshire is an ancient name for Sheffield and the villages, hamlets and farmsteads in the surrounding countryside. It is a name that everyone knows, for the Hallamshire Hospital is the largest building in the city, the Hallamshire Golf Club have a course at Lodge Moor, high above the Rivelin Valley, and the local telephone directory lists over thirty organisations, ranging from the Hallamshire Harriers and Hallamshire Opticians to Hallamshire Pest Control. The shortened version of the name has as many entries in the directory, extending from the Hallam Carpet Company and Hallam Kitchens to Hallam Office Supplies, the Hallam School of Motoring and the Hallam Veterinary Centre. The city's newer university has taken the name of the University of Sheffield Hallam, one of the largest hotels is known as Hallam Towers, the local commercial radio station is Hallam FM, and the western parliamentary constituency is that of Sheffield Hallam. Yet few people seem to know where Hallamshire starts and ends. I have heard speeches where Hallamshire has mistakenly been thought to extend so far as to include Rotherham, Barnsley and Chesterfield. In fact, it covered much the same area as the present Sheffield Metropolitan District. It has persisted as a recognisable unit for well over a thousand years.

Hallamshire is first recorded by its full name in a charter of 1161, though it was undoubtedly much older than that.[1] The Domesday Book of 1086 uses the shortened version, which the Norman clerk wrote as *Hallun*.[2] Much earlier, the Anglo-Saxon kingdom of Northumbria had been divided into units known as shires for military, administrative and ecclesiastical purposes. Confusingly, the word also became used for counties, but in the north it was applied originally to districts such as Allertonshire, Blackburnshire, Howdenshire, Mashamshire, Richmondshire, Riponshire and Sowerbyshire. All these names survived long after the Norman Conquest and some have been revived in recent times, but Hallamshire is unique in the way that the name continued in common speech for hundreds of years. It was the most southerly of all the Northumbrian shires, for it shared a border with the kingdom of Mercia. To the south lay the county of Derbyshire, the diocese of Lichfield and Coventry, and the province of Canterbury. This southern boundary was a firm one, with no detached parts of parishes and manors lying on the other side. It may already have been ancient by Anglo-Saxon times, for the parallels between the Northumbrian shires and medieval Welsh lordships hint at a Celtic origin for both institutions.[3]

An early origin for Hallamshire is also suggested by the place-name Ecclesfield, whose first element implies the existence of a Christian community back in the Romano-British period.[4] The Anglo-Saxons used the Latin word *eccles* to name places that already had a church when they arrived. The Welsh *eglwys* derives from the same source. Ecclesfield church, which became known locally as 'The Minster of the Moors', once served the whole 71,526 acres of Hallamshire, for, as we shall see in chapter two, Sheffield was once a mere chapel-of-ease, like Bradfield. In a charter of 1268 Hallamshire was said to cover just Sheffield, Ecclesfield and Bradfield within its 'metes' or boundaries.[5] Confusion arose later when the lords of Sheffield acquired neighbouring manors, particularly Handsworth. But as late as 1642 a local surveyor was certain that, strictly speaking, Hallamshire contained only Sheffield, Ecclesfield and Bradfield.[6]

The old parish of Sheffield covered the same area as the borough that was created in 1843 and the city fifty years later and the parish of Ecclesfield remained intact until Victorian times. We can therefore

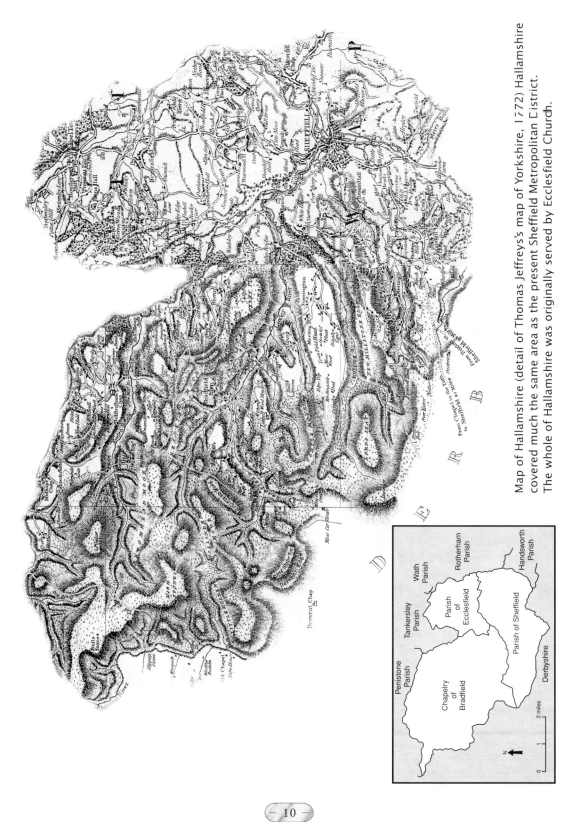

Map of Hallamshire (detail of Thomas Jeffreys's map of Yorkshire, 1772) Hallamshire covered much the same area as the present Sheffield Metropolitan District. The whole of Hallamshire was originally served by Ecclesfield Church.

trace the boundaries of Hallamshire confidently with the aid of eighteenth- and nineteenth-century maps and by the study of significant place-names. The moorland boundary in the west, which was marked on Jeffreys' map of Yorkshire (1767–72) and Burdett's map of Derbyshire (1763–68), remains intact to this day.[7] Starting at Swains Head, high above the Longdendale valley, it descends the deep valley of the River Derwent and the Howden reservoir as far as Abbey Brook. Here, just on the Derbyshire side of the boundary, stood a grange of Welbeck Abbey which was acquired by the Cavendishes of Chatsworth upon the dissolution of the monasteries. The boundary leaves the river at this point to climb steeply to the south-easterly skyline, which is marked by a series of dramatic rocks known as Lost Lad, Back Tor, Cakes of Bread and Dovestones Tor. Its course is marked by a wall that stands on the top of an earthen bank that has been thrown up from a ditch. What was once merely a medieval farm boundary within the Howden part of Hallamshire became accepted as the county boundary, where previously the general direction towards the rocks on the skyline was thought sufficient. Looking back from the ridge, Howden Edge frames the view, curving five miles to the north as far as Swains Head and forming a classic Pennine 'den' that opens out of the river valley on to the moors. The first element of the name, meaning 'hollow', is strikingly apt.[8]

Watercourses and groups of rocks twisted into grotesque shapes by wind, rain and ice have so far been our boundary points, but now we proceed across boggy moors to Moscar Cross, before climbing to another gritstone edge at Stanage End. We shall look at the boundary disputes between Hallamshire and Hathersage in this area in chapter six. Stanedge Pole rises from angular rocks and on the horizon the Ox Stones attract the eye at the highest point on an otherwise featureless moor. Here we part company with the present Sheffield boundary, which has been extended to include moors and settlements that were once part of Derbyshire. The original line continued to Limb Brook, whose attractive descent through Whirlow to Ecclesall Woods and its confluence with the River Sheaf now forms part of the Sheffield Round Walk. Two mounds, which were probably Bronze Age burial sites that have since been obliterated, once marked this part of the border. In 1574 a party perambulating the boundary noted 'a great heape of stones called Ringinglawe', a name which is derived from words describing a ring-shaped mound or Bronze Age ring cairn. Whirlow's name simply means 'boundary mound'.[9]

So far we have been following a well-defined, largely natural boundary which was probably the one that separated Northumbria from Mercia. The *Anglo-Saxon Chronicle* twice suggests that Dore formed the southern boundary of Northumbria. In a symbolic gesture in 828 the Northumbrians crossed their frontier to agree terms with the victorious army of Egbert of Wessex. In 942 Edmund, son of Edward the Elder, conquered the Danes of Mercia and became the ruler 'as far as where Dore divides'. The place-name means 'a narrow pass', or literally a door.[10] The township of Dore extended up to the Limb Brook and the River Sheaf, whose Old English name means 'boundary'.[11] This river has given Sheffield its name. The boundary between Hallamshire and Derbyshire followed the Sheaf for about two-and-a-half miles before taking a right-angled turn up the Meersbrook (the 'boundary stream').[12] It then skirted Sheffield Park and followed the Car Brook around the commons of Darnall and Attercliffe to the River Don. Wherever possible, water courses were used to mark the boundary, which then turned north-west up the Blackburn Brook as far as Thundercliffe Grange, where it climbed a stream to the ridge at Thorpe Common before pursuing a winding course to take in Cowley and Chapeltown. Heading west along Warren Lane, it sought the Storrs Dyke, so as to include High Green, and the Mark Brook (another name for a boundary stream)[13] up to Hazelshaw. Here it zig-zagged over the ridge and descended to the River Don down the side of Wharncliffe Woods. The Don and the Little Don then formed a clear boundary for several miles, as far as Langsett Moors, where the Hoar Stones (a name signifying a boundary but now corrupted to Horse Stones)[14] pointed the way along Howden Edge and over Featherbed Moss to Swains Head, the staring point of our perambulation.

So Hallamshire was a well-defined district in the south-western corner of Northumbria that has retained much of its identity. The meaning of its name is much more of a problem. The technical explanation offered in the English Place-Name Society's volume is that it is a dative plural meaning

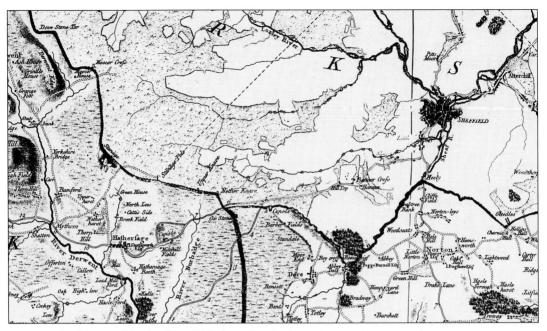

Peter Burdett's map of Derbyshire (1767) marks the boundary as it crosses the moors past Moscar Cross and Standedge Pole.

These rocks known as Ox Stones rise dramatically from an otherwise featureless landscape and so were chosen as natural markers of the south-western boundary of Hallamshire.

'at the rocks'. Place-names were commonly formed in this manner and rocky outcrops are prominent features of the local landscape. But another possibility is that the name is derived from *halgh*, denoting a separate portion of land in a border position.[15] The shortened form of the name has caused much confusion. Two of the townships of the parish of Sheffield were known as Upper and Nether Hallam and within Upper Hallam the name of the small settlement of Hallam Head has led to persistent but misguided claims that here was the original centre of Hallamshire, the place where Earl Waltheof's hall stood before the Norman Conquest. Hallam Head stands high above the Rivelin Valley, alongside the ancient track known as the Long Causey and next to Burnt Stones Common. In 1931 T Walter Hall claimed this name as evidence that the hall had been destroyed during William the Conqueror's infamous 'harrying of the north'.[16] It is now known that the harrying did not extend to South Yorkshire; indeed, Waltheof retained his possessions until much later. The stones must have been burnt in some other way. Hall's view that Hallam Head marked the site of a lost village is also mistaken, for it was never more than a hamlet. The small 'townfields' that were divided into strips were no different from those of all the other hamlets of Hallamshire and several places had a building known as the Hall. The documentary and the topographical evidence does not distinguish Hallam Head from its neighbours. The Anglo-Saxon building that was discovered during excavations at Sheffield Castle is the most likely candidate for the hall of Earl Waltheof that was recorded in Domesday Book.[17]

The Norman lords retained the name of Hallamshire for their lordship and administered it from their motte-and-bailey castle at the confluence of the Sheaf and the Don. This early centre was replaced in the 1270s by Thomas de Furnival's enormous stone castle, which survived until the 1640s. Another motte-and-bailey castle was erected by the Norman lords on a dramatic site at High Bradfield, but this was abandoned early in the Middle Ages. For administrative purposes the lordship was divided into four 'sokes': Sheffield, Ecclesfield, Bradfield and Southey (which extended over the southern part of Ecclesfield parish and that part of Sheffield which lay north of the River Don).[18] As we shall see in chapters two and three, the Norman lords created several sub-manors for their leading followers: at Bolsterstone, Cowley, Darnall, Ecclesfield, Midhope, Owlerton, Shirecliffe and Wadsley, but these estates remained dependent on Sheffield Castle. The cutlery trades for which Hallamshire became famous throughout the world were regulated through the manor courts which were held at the castle until the death of Gilbert Talbot, seventh earl of Shrewsbury, in 1616. The lordship then passed through the marriage of Gilbert's daughter, Alathea, to the Howards, Dukes of Norfolk. They were absentee owners and so, in 1624, the cutlers acquired an Act of Parliament to form their own organisation, 'The Company of Cutlers in Hallamshire', with jurisdiction throughout Hallamshire and within six miles of its borders.[19] The success of the cutlery trades meant that the name of Hallamshire was preserved, even after the importance of the old lordship faded. When Joseph Hunter published his monumental history of the district in 1819 his natural choice of title was *Hallamshire*.

The Domesday Book entry for Hallamshire is tantalisingly brief. Sheffield and Attercliffe were mentioned and small Anglo-Saxon estates were recorded at Ecclesfield, Grimeshou [thought to have been near Grimesthorpe], Holdworth, Onesacre, Ughill and Worrall, but sixteen other outlying settlements were grouped together as unnamed *berewicks*. Some of these were probably already several centuries old. Anglo-Saxon place-names such as Dungworth and Hawkesworth show that Hallamshire families were farming land right up to the edge of the moors long before the Norman Conquest. The most important change was the creation of an urban centre alongside the castle. The Norman lords laid out a large, rectangular market place and gave the leading inhabitants some independence as burgesses. The pattern of the central streets, the elevation of the chapel to parish church status, the building of the town mill at Millsands, the hospital on Spital Hill, and Lady's Bridge across the Don all date from the time of the Louvetots, Hallamshire's first Norman lords. The power of the Louvetots and their successors – the Furnivals and the Talbots – was evident not only from the mighty castle but from the enormous hunting park, which stretched from the back gardens of the High Street burgesses across the River Sheaf as far as the county boundary at Gleadless. Beyond the park lay the villages of Attercliffe and Darnall, which were probably laid out anew by the Norman lords.[20]

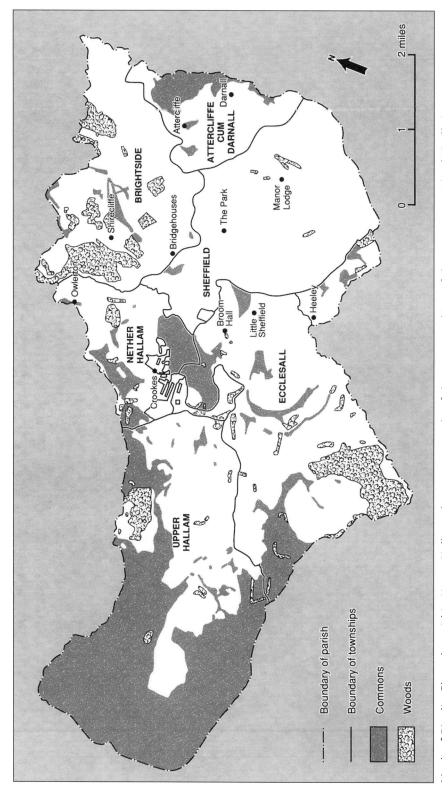

Much of Rivelin Chase lay within Upper Hallam, the most westerly of the six townships of the ancient parish of Sheffield.

Boundary of parish

Boundary of townships

Commons

Woods

The springwoods of Brightside Bierlow. This detail of William Fairbank's map of Sheffield parish in 1795 shows some of the carefully-managed coppice woods to the north of the town, such as Cook Wood, Burnt Greave and Shirecliff Park.

Hunting

At the *Quo Warranto* enquiries in 1281 Thomas de Furnival claimed that his ancestors had enjoyed hunting rights within Hallamshire since the time of the conquest.[21] The park was probably created by the Louvetots but was not recorded until two fourteenth-century *inquisition post mortems* of the Lords Furnival.[22] When John Harrison surveyed the manor for the Howards in 1637[23] the park covered 2,641 acres and was enclosed within a ring fence eight miles in circumference. Harrison observed that, 'This parke is very well adorn'd with great store of very Stately Timber and not meanly furnish'd with fallow Deare, the number of them at present is one Thousand, whereof Deare of Auntler is two hundred'. The lord kept 1,491 acres under his own control and let the other 970 acres to fifteen tenants-at-will. The fields within the park were considerably larger than the closes found elsewhere in Hallamshire. They made a sharp contrast to the strips in the townfields of the adjoining villages of Attercliffe, Darnall and Heeley and were farmed mostly as pasture. The Manor Lodge had been a medieval hunting lodge within the park, but in the sixteenth century successive Talbot lords extended it into a splendid country house. The absentee Howards failed to maintain it, however, and it was reduced to its present ruinous condition in 1708. The deer had long since been removed from the park.

John Harrison concluded his survey of the manor in 1637 by remarking that:

> This mannor is not only profitable but for pleasure also, being furnished with red deare and fallow, with hares and some rowes, with pheasante and great store of partridges, and moore game in abundance, both blacke and red, as moorcocks, moorehenns, and young pootes upon the moores, as also mallard, teale, hearnshawes, and plover. The chiefest fishinge within this mannor is the rivers that passeth through the same, wherein are great store of salmons, trouts, chevens [i.e.chub], eeles, and other small fish.

The Norman lords had set aside large tracts of the Hallamshire moors on which to hunt: Loxley Firth or Chase, Hawkesworth Firth, and particularly Rivelin Chase (the subject of chapter six), a total of 10,767 acres if we include the associated woodland at Stannington and Loxley. These adjoining territories stretched across the Loxley and Rivelin valleys and beyond Bradfield Dale as far as Hallamshire's western boundary. Deer were hunted here during the time of the Louvetots, Furnivals and Talbots, but in the seventeenth century the absentee Howards showed little interest. Hawkesworth and Loxley Firths may no longer have been used for hunting by the time that Harrison made his survey in 1637. He noted the two keepers who still lived at Redmires in Rivelin Chase, but the deer were removed from there a generation or two later.

The lords of the sub-manors of Hallamshire also set aside land in which to hunt. Elias de Midhope had hunting rights on Midhope moors in the late thirteenth century and the lords of the sub-manors of Ecclesall, Shirecliffe, Cowley and Wadsley had their well-defined deer parks, some of which made a permanent impact on the local landscape, as we shall see in chapter three.

Woods

The great woods that the lords of Hallamshire owned within their hunting districts were felled in the late seventeenth century at the same time as the removal of the deer. The woods of Rivelin and Loxley were mentioned in the *inquisition post mortem* of Lord Furnival in 1332, when a value was given to the rents obtained from the grazing of pigs there. Three centuries later, John Harrison and John Evelyn enthused about the oak timber that grew in Haw Park on a steep, rocky slope, covering seventy-five acres on the Stannington side of the Rivelin valley. These famous trees were tall and straight and reached sixty feet in height before branching out. Travellers remarked that they had 'not seen such Timber in Cristendome'. In 1662 Evelyn claimed that the timber in Haw Park was all that remained in the district, but it too was felled during the late seventeenth century, about the same time as the deer were removed from the chase.[24]

Ditches and earthen banks still mark the old divisions between cattle heys and sheep pastures in this moorland part of Hallamshire at Howden boundary ditch.

Abbey Clough. The wild terrain of the Hallamshire moorlands was fit only for grazing and the digging of peat. Welbeck Abbey had a grange just beyond the Hallamshire boundary, where Abbey Brook flowed into the River Derwent.

Coppicing had become far more lucrative than the long-term management of timber. During the sixteenth century the demand for underwood to make charcoal for the iron masters, white coal for the lead smelters or for fencing, handles and numerous other purposes, together with the production of 'punch wood' to make pit props for the coal mines ensured that former deer parks and medieval wood pastures were converted into 'springwoods', which were felled at regular intervals. In 1637 Harrison noted '2 thousand acres of wood and timber (besides Sheffield Parke) whereof there are above 16 hundred acres of spring woods besides great store of old trees fir for noe other purpose but for the making of Charkehole'. On the north side of the River Don the springwoods on the slopes of Brightside Bierlow – Cook Wood, Burngreave, Shirecliffe Park, Hall Carr Wood, Wincobank Wood, etc. – formed a sharp contrast to the tree-less open fields and commons of Attercliffe and Darnall in the low-lying lands across the river. Some trees were left three decades or more until they were thick enough to make pit props, but most were felled at much shorter intervals. The woods were carefully managed and divided into sections to ensure a regular cropping rotation. A survey in 1642 measured Greno and Hall Woods at 566 acres in the northern part of Hallamshire and Beeley Wood at eighty acres.[25] Ecclesall Woods remain a permanent reminder of how the lords of the sub-manor there converted their deer park into a springwood during the sixteenth century, then turned much of it into 'high forest' during Victorian and Edwardian times when coppicing paid less well. After World War I these old deciduous woods became less of an economic asset and were felled only at irregular intervals.

Moorland Pastures

The lords of Hallamshire adopted a variety of policies on how best to farm their moorland pastures. They kept some as their demesne lands on which they reared deer, cattle and sheep, granted others to Beauchief Abbey and Worksop Priory, and took rents on the rest from tenants-at-will. Like other great landowners on the Pennines, they reared young cattle at two special farms known as 'booths' (from the Viking word), or as 'vaccaries' (the Latin word used in the documents). In 1181, for instance, Fulwood Booth and Old Booth, Bradfield, were restocked with forty cows, four bulls and eight oxen.[26] Young cattle were still reared at Fulwood Booth in Elizabethan times and in 1637 this farm covered 123 acres, next to the Beauchief abbey grange and the deer keepers' residence at Redmires. By then, the 429 acres of Auley Meadows, now known as Hollow Meadows, had been converted to pasture and the 347 acres of Agden sheep pasture were tenanted at the will of the lord by Richard Broomehead and Edmund Hobson. Harrison described this stretch of moorland as 'A Sheep pasture called Agden lying betweene Agden Common called Cowell' on the north east and the 346 acres of Hawksworth Firth to the south and west. Other sheep pastures belonging to the lord lay above the cattle enclosures at Howden.

Howden is divided by numerous ditches and banks similar to the one that forms the county boundary. Some are just earthen banks, others are surmounted by dry-stone walls. Several stretch across the moors without obviously forming enclosed fields. They demarcate the various cattle 'heys' [hedged enclosures], sheep walks, 'outpastures' and 'turbaries' [for the digging of peat] of the medieval lords of Hallamshire and their tenants. William Senior's early seventeenth-century maps of the nearby moorland properties of the Cavendish family show similar boundaries which divide the sheep walks of the different farms in the Hope Woodlands and numerous holloways can be followed on the ground from the places where peat was dug for use as winter fuel.[27]

Harrison's survey records the tenants-at-will of the various cattle heys and sheep pastures at Howden, measuring their lands in acres, roods and perches. William Greaves had

> *a dwelling house of 5 bayes a peate house of 2 bayes a stable of 2 bayes a Barne of 3 bayes another barne 8 bayes & a Kilne of one bay a fold and the nether field (meadow) lying next Darwin water west 13.1.16 … the Abby lane.*
> *… nether hey and hey banke lying in 2 parts between the over hey $ the Cow hey in part & sheep pasture called the Dayne in part North & the nether Houlden in the use of Ann*

Churt Clough. The thick layers of peat on Hallam Moor were formed in prehistoric times. For the last two hundred years the clough has formed part of a grouse-shooting moor.

Margery Hill is the highest point in Hallamshire. The trigonometrical point stands at 1793 feet.

Morton South & the next part of little Houlden in the use of Robert Barber east .... 470.0.24.

... Calfe Hey (pasture) lying next the Over Hey or the Cowhey North & next the nether Hey or the Hey Bank South East ... 9.3.12.

... the Over Hey & the Cowhey lying betweene the sheep pasture called the Dayne north & east

... an out pasture for sheep being moorish Ground called the Dayne lying betweene a parte of little Houlden ... & Wigtwisell Common in parte & Boulsterstone Lordshipp also north & Darwin water & the Dutchey land South & next a Manner of the lords Called Glossop Dale in some little parte alsoe South or else the boundary of these out Grounds may be expressed thus, from Cromwithey Yate Following the brooke to Swane grave head & to Certaine Lands belonging to Glossop Dale & so to the uttermost Edge on the bank of Dean head Stones & to 3 Gate stones without Couldwell Clough head & so to the uttermost Crowstone Edge end & so Crossing the Black Dike to Margery Beardlesse to the High Stone & so to Greave sicke .... 2267.0.31.

This boundary can still be traced along Howden Edge.

Nicholas Bray tenanted

A Close Called Holden Greene with a Peat house (pasture & arable) lying betweene Holden Banke north & nether Houlden South & abutteth upon the Abbey Lane west ... 3.0.23.

At 'nether Houlden' Annis Morton tenanted 915 acres of moorland, comprising a pasture Called nether Holden lying betweene nether Hay & Hey Banke north the Lordship of Hathersedge South & South West ... 617.2.37.

the Out pasture of little Houlden for Sheep lying betweene Hawkesworth Firth East & the last pieces ... & abutteth upon the two white stones in Crosse Hill north & the Lordship of Hathersedge south west ... 297.1.25.

Finally, Roger Barber held at will

An Out pasture for Sheep being parte of little Houlden lying betweene the last piece East & South East & Wigtwisell Common North & North east & the Dayne in parts & nether hey or Hey Banke in part West & the nether Holden South West ... 648.2.25.

Tenant Farmers

Unlike these graziers on the wild, western edge of the moors, most of the Hallamshire farmers were smallholders. Local medieval records do not give precise measurements of land, but describe a farm in general terms as 'a messuage with one bovate', which is as vague as saying 'a farmhouse and a farm'. In Yorkshire a bovate (or oxgang) could vary in size between as few as four acres and as many as twenty-eight, but the normal range was from eight to fifteen acres.[28] The first definite information about the size of farms in Hallamshire comes from John Harrison's survey of 1637,[29] when most farms were less than ten acres, but those of the yeomen were larger; twenty-six households farmed between twenty and fifty acres, and twenty-two farmed between fifty and a hundred acres. A few farms were larger still, but they included extensive stretches of woodland and most of them were divided between different tenants. The pattern of small farms that still characterises the Pennine foothills is an ancient one. Farming families were able to survive because they had generous grazing and other rights on the numerous greens and extensive commons. A jury of the manor court in 1650[30] declared that copyholders had the right to fell and use any wood that grew on their own lands, to dig and sell any coal, slate or stone that lay under their lands and to get stone, turf, clods, earth and clay from the commons. Further income came from dual occupations. The cutler-farmer or nailer-farmer was a typical figure in rural Hallamshire until well into the nineteenth century[31] and many other crafts were pursued in combination with agriculture.

In the Middle Ages most occupiers of small farms in Hallamshire held their property from the lord by copyhold tenure, so called because tenants kept a copy of the relevant entry in the manor court rolls. The copyholders had rights which were enshrined in the customs of the manor and their tenure was as secure as that of a freeholder. Most importantly, they could bequeath their property to their heirs upon payment of an entry fine, the level of which had often been fixed generations ago. The Hallamshire manor court rolls contain a great deal of evidence to show that by the late Middle Ages entry fines were fixed 'according to the ancient custom'. Their value to the lord was therefore diminished during the periods of inflation that characterised the Tudor era. During the mid-seventeenth century it became estate policy in Hallamshire to offer 21-year leases to tenants and to let the lord's demesne lands, such as Howden or Agden on yearly tenancies whose renewal was at the will of the lord.[32] Only then did the older method of holding land by copyhold start to fade away.

Often a farmer would hold some of his land by copyhold and the rest by freehold. The Hallamshire manor court rolls[33] describe the tenures of the copyholders as either 'hastler' land or 'mattock' land. For example, in 1380 Isola, the wife of Adam Lynott, took half a bovate of 'hastler' land and two acres, one rood of 'mattock' land in Fulwood for the term of her life. Whole farms, or half or quarters of such, were held by hastler tenure. In 1324, for instance, William de Tinsley was admitted by the court to a bovate of hastler land in Dungworth. By contrast, mattock land usually referred to small portions (measured in acres and roods). Exceptions, such as an entry in the court rolls of 1392 whereby John, the son of Thomas Rawson surrendered 'one messuage and one bovate of land called mattock land in Fulwood' to John Lynott, are rare. The newly-cleared 'assarts' or 'intakes' of various small sizes were described as mattock land because a mattock was an agricultural tool used for grubbing up land. The term was used to distinguish such clearings from the older farms which were held by hastler tenure. It is more difficult to explain what was meant by 'hastler'. The word was probably derived from the Latin *hasta*, meaning a spear. The *Oxford English Dictionary* notes that a hastler was an officer of the kitchen, but in Hallamshire (and nearby in the manor of Eckington) the term seems to have been synonymous with that of grave or greave, which was used in other manors, such as the huge manor of Wakefield. The hastler tenants were the ones from whom the various officers such as the constable were chosen. In 1441 the jury of the manor court fined 'the hastler tenants of Ecclesfeld 'because they had not chosen a collector of estreats of the court there'.[34] The hastler tenants were the occupiers of the ancient farms.

A person who held 'hastler' land of the lord of Hallamshire seems to have been liable for military service when called upon. This explains a colourful custom which survived until 1715. The lords enforced petty law and order through a 'Great Court Leet with a View of Frankpledge', which was known locally as the Sembly Quest. Every Easter Tuesday a large and ragged army of freeholders and tenants assembled in front of the manor court house in the Wicker and afterwards paraded through the main streets of Sheffield. The Quo Warranto Rolls of 1293–94 record Thomas de Furnival's claim 'to be able to call a meeting of all his men of Hallamshire once a year ... in place of the great tourn'. The assembly was also mentioned in the *inquisition post mortem* of William, Lord Furnival in 1383. Thomas Creswick of Owlerton Hall, yeoman, who took part in the Easter Tuesday Sembly Quest in 1601, said that he provided 'a horse or gelding and a man well armed and arrayed for the warres'.[35] The custom was still going strong in 1637, when John Harrison observed that:

upon every Sembly Tuesday is assembled upon Sembly Green, where the court is kept and near unto the castle, at the least 139 horsemen with horses and harness provided by the freeholders, copyholders, and other tenants, and to appear before the lord of the manor or the steward of the court to be viewed by them, and for confining the peace of our sovereign lord the king.

Joseph Hunter saw an older list of only ninety-six men and noted that by the end of the seventeenth century the numbers varied between sixty and eighty. The custom came to a sudden end in 1715, when the Duke of Norfolk decided that the recent Jacobite rebellion had made it impolitic for the leading Catholic nobleman to parade a private army. Meanwhile, the term hastler had faded away. It was still known in the early seventeenth century but John Harrison did not use it in his survey of 1637.

Townfields and Intakes

Harrison's survey of the manor in 1637 shows that most of the agricultural land was divided into small closes which had been cleared from the woods and moorland edges over the centuries. Farmers could also graze their livestock on the commons, greens and vast moors, and at certain times in some of the woods. But he also showed that numerous villages and hamlets still had their communal 'townfields' where cereals (mainly oats) were grown in strips.[36] Two- or three-field systems were operated at Attercliffe, Darnall, Crookes, Ecclesfield and Chapeltown, elsewhere the strips formed a single townfield. Evidence of such fields can be found in Sheffield parish at Hallam Head, Heeley, Pitsmoor and Sharrow, and in the chapelry of Bradfield at Bradfield, Brightholmlee, Dungworth, Midhope, Onesacre, Stannington, Ughill, Wadsley, Wigtwizzle and Worrall. Hamlets such as these were the basic farming units, whose communal decisions were confirmed by the manor court. The extent of their territories was still known in Victorian times and was marked on the first edition of the six-inch Ordnance Survey map in the 1850s. From the sixteenth century onwards local farmers began to agree on piecemeal enclosure schemes, which replaced the old arrangements. The Midhope townfield, for example, was enclosed by agreement in 1674.[37] Other townfields survived, at least in part, until they were enclosed by Acts of Parliament in the late eighteenth and early nineteenth centuries at the same time as the commons and wastes.

As hunting was only an occasional activity, the more fertile lands in the Rivelin and Loxley valleys were farmed in much the same way as in the neighbouring hamlets. Dungworth, Hallam Head and Stannington each had their townfields and commons, as well as newly-won fields of various shapes and sizes that were often known as intakes ('intacks') or stubbings. The term 'royd', which was very common further north, was little used in Hallamshire. The present pattern of farms and fields along Bradfield Dale, as far as Hawkesworth Head, is similar to that depicted by Harrison in 1637 and is probably little different from the one which was created in the thirteenth and fourteenth centuries. The earliest manor court rolls, from 1277 to 1288, record farmers clearing small pieces of new land at Hawkesworth Head. These intakes were typically between half an acre and two acres in size, for which the tenant paid a small entry fine and an annual rent, but some of the new clearances from the woods and the moors were tiny. In 1284, for example, Adam Hawkesworth took an eighth of an acre of new land in Hawkesworth. In the previous year he paid 2s.6d. for admission to half an acre of land in Thornsett, at an annual rent of three pence. We see here a farmer who was gradually creating a farm on the edge of the moors and who took his surname from the place where he lived. Gaps in the manor court rolls prevent our continuing the story until 1417, by which time the records speak only of transfers of land, not of new intakes. In 1427, for instance, John Hawkesworth surrendered a messuage and six acres of cultivated land in Hawkesworth to John Tompson, perhaps the man who gave his name to Thompson House. The present pattern of fields and farms seems to have been created in the Middle Ages, before the Black Death reduced population pressure and brought the period of expansion to a sudden end.[38]

The early manor court rolls provide ample evidence of an active land market in Hallamshire during the late thirteenth century. By 1277, when the rolls begin, some families had already moved from the place whence their surname was derived. The terse entries in the manor records show that although some families stayed at the same farm for generation after generation through the Middle Ages and beyond, other properties were sold, mortgaged and sub-divided and fresh land was cleared from the edges of the commons and wastes. The dramatic fall in population levels that occurred all over the country in the fourteenth century provided opportunities for the fortunate and the energetic to thrive. An *inquisition post mortem* for the lord of Hallamshire in 1332 referred to the decay of population and an inability to find tenants.[39] The Black Death of 1348–50 and the heavy mortalities of 1361–2, 1369 and 1375 reduced the national population by more than a third. Unfortunately, the manor court rolls for Hallamshire do not survive between 1348 and 1377, perhaps because of all this turbulence, so we do not have a clear picture of the effects of endemic plague. Some surnames which appeared in

The original cruck frame of this cottage at Stumperlowe was revealed upon demolition. Most of Hallamshire's cruck-framed cottages and barns date from the fifteenth to the seventeenth century.

thirteenth- and early fourteenth-century documents disappeared and in other cases brothers, sisters or more distant kin inherited the family farm far more frequently than had been usual in normal years. By the mid-fifteenth century the national population was back down to its Domesday Book level. It did not recover until the reign of Queen Elizabeth.[40]

It was against this background that families such as the Shirecliffes and Steads were able to grasp the opportunities to prosper. Extra land was acquired and younger sons were able to move into untenanted property nearby. Land which had fallen out of cultivation was brought back into use, right to the edge of the moors, usually as pasture. In 1440–41, for example, Edward de Ryles, Agnes his wife, and Richard their son, were given permission 'to pluck up by the roots and clear away, in all lands that could be ploughed, thorns, brambles and thicket'.[41] Late-medieval Hallamshire benefited from the growth of rural industry and the development of pastoral farming that raised levels of prosperity in some parts of England. In common with many other places, by the late fifteenth century Hallamshire had achieved a new stability, with families settled for generation after generation at the same farm and their cousins living close by. We shall explore this continuity in some detail in chapters three and five.

Wood Pastures and Commons

Some tenants had grazing rights in the lord's woods and others rented woodland as part of their farms. In 1442, for instance, twenty shillings was 'received from the grass of the pasture in Bylleywode thus let to the tenants of the lord there this year'.[42] In 1637 the 'herbage' of Greno and Wincobank woods belonged to tenants and the wood of Scraith Bank 'belongeth to the Lord but the feed to the tenants'.[43] A survey of 1611 shows that in the Grenoside-High Green district farmers often rented some woodland as well as pastures, meadows and perhaps a little arable land. Amongst the tenants in this area, Thomas Richardson rented $11^1/_2$ acres of meadow, $55^3/_4$ acres of pasture and $49^1/_2$ acres of wood, Richard Wilson rented 30 acres of meadow, just over 51 acres of pasture and 79 acres of wood, and Thomas Slater rented $11^1/_2$ acres of meadow, $43^1/_4$ acres of pasture and 130 acres of wood.[44] Other tenants rented special 'haggs' of holly to feed their sheep in winter, just as the lord's officers fed holly leaves and branches to the deer. In 1441–42 the accounts of the forester of Bradfield included: 'For holly sold there for the fodder of the animals in winter'. John Harrison noted several 'hollin rents' in his survey of 1637 and leases show that the practice continued well into the eighteenth century. The last one was dated 1737, by which time the deer had been removed from the parks and chases and new winter fodder crops were available for the sheep.[45] Holly trees are still abundant in parts of the Rivelin valley and farm names such as Hollin House, Grenoside, and Bell Hagg in the Rivelin valley commemorate this ancient custom.

The tenants of the lord of Hallamshire were dependent on their rights to graze cattle and sheep over the numerous greens, commons and wastes. Shiregreen and High Green lay on the eastern and northern borders of Hallamshire and many other greens were marked on eighteenth-century maps before they disappeared at the time of parliamentary enclosure. Bents Green, Nether Green and Newfield Green are amongst some of the names which survive. The villages with two or three open fields had commons that were much larger than these greens, such as Attercliffe Common, Ecclesfield Common and Crookesmoor, names which are still in use though the commons were divided up in the closing years of the eighteenth century. The shopping district known as The Moor in Sheffield was once the common of Little Sheffield beyond Moorfoot. Pitsmoor, Ranmoor and Shalesmoor remain other well-known names within the city of Sheffield. Well away to the west and the north west, the most extensive commons and wastes covered thousands of acres of heather moors and mosses in the highest and bleakest parts of Hallamshire, alongside the lord's hunting chases, cattle pastures and sheep walks. The commons of the various hamlets were separated by deep boundary ditches. That which runs along Cartledge Stones Ridge and which now marks the boundary of the National Trust's High Peak estate once divided the lord's pastures in Howden from the commons of Wigtwizzle and Cowell. To the west of Cowell House the boundary ditch that separated the commons of Cowell and Wigtwizzle is marked on Ordnance Survey maps in italic letters as Bar Dyke.[46] This has always been assumed to be an ancient linear earthwork, comparable with the Roman Rig in South Yorkshire and the Grey Ditch in Derbyshire, though it does not fit into a wider system of defences. Perhaps the commoners simply used an ancient ditch as their boundary on the brow of the hill, but as no firm evidence of its antiquity has been found we should consider the possibility that the Bar Dyke does not date from the Dark Ages but was dug to mark a medieval boundary between two commons.

The sub-manors of Ecclesall, Bolsterstone and Midhope also had extensive commons and wastes on the high moors. The regular pattern of the fields on either side of the straight road to Ringinglow dates from the enclosure of the Ecclesall commons in 1779–88. The upper and nether commons of Bolsterstone, together with Whitwell Moor, were enclosed in 1778–82 and the commons and wastes of Midhope were divided by new dry-stone walls in 1818–23. The wastes could not be improved and so went mostly to the lords of the sub-manors to be used for the shooting of grouse. The enclosure surveyor thought that the 1,240 acres of Bolsterstone's upper commons were 'so bad in nature as in our opinion they will not at present answer the expenses of fencing and inclosing. Therefore we do allot the same to be an open pasture for the use of ... Lord Melbourne only'; they now form part of

Cartledge boundary ditch was probably dug in the Middle Ages to separate the lord of Hallamshire's cattle and sheep pastures at Howden from the commons of Agden and Wigtwizzle.

Broomhead Moor, once the greatest grouse-shooting moor in the Peak District. Upon the division of Midhope's commons and wastes Godfrey Bosville received 2,080 of the 3,332 acres that were enclosed. The Duke of Norfolk received a similar giant's share of the Bradfield and Upper Hallam moors. The rest was allotted to the tithe owners, freeholders and tenants in proportion to the value of their previous grazing and other common rights. Many a Pennine farmhouse and its field walls date from the period immediately after the signing of the enclosure award.[47]

Cutlery

In the wider world Hallamshire was associated with cutlery.[48] 'Hallamshire cutts' were referred to in the Chester port books in Elizabethan times, long before the formation of the Company of Cutlers in Hallamshire in 1624. The making of knives and scissors was a medieval craft in Sheffield and Attercliffe that gradually spread into the rural parts of Hallamshire. By 1540, John Leland, the first man to give a brief description of places throughout England and Wales, could observe, 'Ther be many smithes and cuttelars in Hallamshire'. The cutlery trades expanded considerably in Elizabethan times under the patronage of four generations of Lords Talbot, Earls of Shrewsbury, who dominated Hallamshire from the great country house that they built on the site of the old hunting lodge in their park. Although London remained the leading centre of cutlery manufacture until well into the eighteenth century, Hallamshire triumphed over its provincial rivals, such as Thaxted and Salisbury. It had the great advantage of water power for grinding. The rivers Don, Sheaf, Porter, Loxley and Rivelin are modest in size, but they fall quickly from the Pennines and could be dammed at frequent intervals. By 1660 at least forty-nine sites were occupied by water mills of various sorts and by 1740 the number had risen to ninety; two-thirds of these mills were used for grinding cutlery. Meanwhile, the local sandstone proved ideal for grinders' wheels. Sheffield acquired a reputation as a smoky, industrial town long before the Industrial Revolution and many of the farmers in the rural parts of Hallamshire earned extra income as part time cutlers or part-time nail makers. In a few places, such as Rock House, Stannington, the former cutler's smithy can still be recognised among the outbuildings of the farm. But the most evocative remains of the rural cutlery industry are found in the Rivelin and Loxley valleys, where many more grinding wheels were erected on new sites during the first half of the eighteenth century. The surviving goits and dams and the overgrown ruins of former wheel pits and buildings speak of a prosperous era that lasted for the best part of two centuries. As we shall see in chapter seven, industry has played a crucial role in shaping the Hallamshire countryside.

These seventeenth-century knives were amongst those that were recovered from mud banks in the River Thames in the 1980s. They can be recognised as Hallamshire knives from their marks.

By the 1930s Nether Cut Wheel was the only grinding wheel still at work in the Rivelin Valley. Known as Marshall's Wheel in 1726, it was long concerned with the grinding of scythes. Water was channelled from the dam into a pentrough and on to an overshot water wheel, which was geared to several grindstones inside the 'hull', as the building was called.

In a secluded position behind the magnificent late-medieval church at Ecclesfield stands one of the most unusual and intriguing buildings in Hallamshire. It is generally agreed that Ecclesfield Priory was built sometime in the second half of the thirteenth century and that after the dissolution of religious houses by Henry VIII it was converted into a superior farmhouse with the name of Ecclesfield Hall. In 1736 a new Georgian hall was built alongside it to the west, possibly destroying some of the medieval work. The older building assumed the name of Ecclesfield Priory again when it was carefully restored in 1866. Much has been written about it, particularly by the Revd Jonathan Eastwood in his *History of the Parish of Ecclesfield* (1862), where he transcribed and studied the documents that were then available, but the exact history of this tantalising place remains elusive. Another attempt to unravel the story is overdue.

Before the Norman Conquest Hallamshire had formed part of the extensive estates of Waltheof, Earl of Huntingdon, who for the most part must have been an absentee landlord. Waltheof survived the early years of the Conquest and his position must have seemed secure when he married Countess Judith, the niece of William the Conqueror, but in 1076 he was beheaded after he had been involved in a fresh revolt. Ten years later, Domesday Book placed Hallamshire amongst the possessions of Roger de Busli, or Builli, the lord of the great, new Norman honour of Tickhill and one of the largest landowners in the north of England until his death at the end of the eleventh century. Roger took his name from what is now the small town of Bully-le-Vicompte in Normandy, near Neufchâtel-en-Brai. Towards the end of the reign of William I he celebrated his rise to fame and power by founding Blyth Priory on the opposite side of the great swamp from Tickhill. The original nave of the impressive priory church survives, with severe arches forming an arcade, clerestory and triforium that reach up to the plain rib vaulting of the ceiling. In his foundation charter Roger stated that forty shillings of English money should go each year to the Benedictine abbey of the Holy Trinity at Rouen, a monastery which he had patronised before the Conquest. Blyth was therefore one of the 118 'alien priories' in England, forty-three of which were large institutions with cloister, refectory and all the other buildings that one associates with a monastery. The other 'alien priories', including Ecclesfield, were small, often little more than cells, their priors and monks owing complete allegiance to the abbot or prior of the foreign house which had sent them across the Channel to act as stewards of their English possessions.[1]

Roger de Louvetot, who seems to have been the person described in the Nottinghamshire part of Domesday Book as Roger, the man of Roger de Busli, took his name from Louvetot, a small place in Normandy to the west of Rouen. Modern Louvetot is a single-street village with several timber-framed buildings but with no evidence of a former manor house or castle; its church was rebuilt at the end of the Middle Ages. It is not known whether Roger de Louvetot fought at Hastings, but he soon possessed far greater estates in Yorkshire, Nottinghamshire and Huntingdonshire than he had held in his native land. His fortunes improved considerably after the deaths of Roger de Busli and Eustace the sheriff of Huntingdonshire and the lordship of Hallamshire became his prized possession. Roger was still alive in 1109 and was succeeded by his nephew, Richard, who died about 1116. Richard's son, William de Louvetot was largely responsible for building a castle at Sheffield and developing a market

Above: A view of the Ecclesfield Priory from the church tower, showing the thirteenth-century building and the Georgian hall of 1736.

Right: Fourneville Church in Normandy retains much of the character that would have been familiar to the Furnivals, lords of Hallamshire, who took their name from the village, near Honfleur.

town alongside it. He and his wife, Emma, also founded a priory for Augustinian canons at Radford on the southern edge of Worksop during the third and fourth decades of the twelfth century. Their priory church is one of the finest medieval buildings in Nottinghamshire, fronted by twin Norman towers, which were heightened in the later Middle Ages. Excavations have shown that the surviving Norman work is from a late twelfth-century rebuilding of the original church. The residential buildings of the priory were destroyed not long after the Dissolution, but the impressive late-medieval gatehouse survives. William and Emma were buried at Worksop Priory and were succeeded by their son, Richard, and then by their grandson, another William. Between 1171 and his death in 1181 this second William gave the canons at Worksop the substantial gift of the small tithes (one third of the whole) of Bradfield and Sheffield, the two chapelries within the parish of Ecclesfield, on the understanding that they would provide pastoral care. The canons also received valuable property on the north side of Sheffield's High Street, which Ralph Gosling marked as Prior Gate on his map of the town in 1736. They continued to present vicars at Sheffield until the Dissolution.[2]

William de Louvetot II's daughter Matilda (who was commonly known by the pet form Maud) was only seven when he died. Hallamshire eventually passed to her husband, Gerard de Furnival, who came from Fourneville, a village gathered around a small, twelfth- and thirteenth-century church that lies a few miles south-west of Honfleur, in Normandy. Gerard was lord of Hallamshire until he died at Jerusalem on crusade in 1219.[3] Thirty years later (when she was 75) Maud confirmed to the canons of Worksop all the gifts of William, her father, and Richard, her grandfather, and Gerard, her husband.[4] The male line of the Furnivals continued in Hallamshire until the later fourteenth century. The great timber-framed long barn at Whiston (another manor that Maud had inherited) was erected during their time.

St Wandrille's Abbey

The foundation of new priories at Blyth and Worksop is only an introductory part of the story. The warriors who accompanied William the Conqueror in 1066 and the adventurers who followed them retained their estates in Normandy and often presented Norman abbeys with the tithes and other possessions of the churches on their new manors in England. Long before the Conquest, Louvetot church had been given to the Abbey of St Wandrille, which lies about four or five miles south-east of the village, near one of the great loops of the River Seine. The abbey was Benedictine, the first of the great monastic orders, and had been founded by St Wandrille in the mid-seventh century on the banks of the Fontenelle stream, which flows into the river Seine, about three miles away. It had been rebuilt in the early eleventh century by Richard II, Duke of Normandy, the grandfather of William the Conqueror, and had become famous throughout his territory. The Dukes of Normandy were great benefactors. After the Conquest, Countess Judith (William I's niece) endowed it with her manor of Boughton in Northamptonshire, but she does not appear to have been the person who granted the church and a manor at Ecclesfield to the monks. Other grants of English properties followed quickly. Domesday Book records St Wandrille's English possessions in 1088 as the manor at Boughton and a church (meaning revenues such as the tithes) at Towcester (Northamptonshire), a manor at Wandsworth (Surrey), the churches of Rushall, Sherston and Upavon (Wiltshire), the manor of Wareham and the churches of Bridport, Burton Bradstock and Whitchurch Canonicorum (Dorset), and the manor of Dullingham and land at Stetchworth (Cambridgeshire). William the Conqueror himself had donated the churches at Burton Bradstock, Sherston, Towcester and Whitchurch Canonicorum. But no mention was made in Domesday Book of the abbey having any possessions at Ecclesfield. The grant must therefore have been made after 1086.[5]

St Wandrille's Abbey lies deep in the wooded and peaceful Fontenelle valley, enclosed by a high wall and dominating a small village that stands on the hill to the west. Local limestone was used as the building material throughout, with good-quality ashlar stone masking rubble interiors. A visitor's first impression is of seventeenth- and eighteenth-century buildings in a grandiose, classical style, much adorned with heraldic devices, but something of the medieval past is captured by scattered, timber-framed farm buildings in the meadows across the Fontenelle stream. On entering the abbey one sees the ruined church, which is nowhere near as dramatic as that of the famous Norman monastery of Jumièges, a few miles up the Seine, but which is sufficiently imposing to suggest former grandeur. The church was rebuilt in the thirteenth and fourteenth centuries, partly out of the tithes of the parishioners of Ecclesfield. Its nave walls survive to medium height and the bases of the piers of the former arches are still in place. These give a good idea of the original plan of the west end, with had plain walls and no chapels. It is much more difficult to get a sense of the east end, which would have been more elaborate. The only substantial remains of the church are in the north transept, whose Gothic arches still reach to roof height, with some faint evidence of coloured paintings.

A Benedictine monk, with close-cropped hair and traditional black habit, guides tours every day at 3.30 pm. Entering the residential and working part of the monastery, we immediately see how it occupies a spacious site, with large workshops and other buildings standing in the distance on the north side of the stream. The cloister was completed about 1510, with fine windows in the Flamboyant style. On the north side of the cloister, normally out of bounds to the visitor, a long building contains traces of eleventh-century windows. This is the refectory, which claims to be the oldest in Western Europe and which is now the only surviving Romanesque part of the abbey. On the south side of the cloister are defaced images of the Virgin and Child and other decorated stonework that was spoilt by a Calvinist mob that sacked the monastery in 1562. A few medieval stones and some floor tiles survive, but no tombs. The monastery went into long decline and in 1631 the central tower collapsed, so that the four great bells are now housed in a cage north-west of the church. But in 1636 new enthusiasm was injected by a young Counter-Reformation body, the Congregation of St Maur, who set out to rebuild the abbey in the style which we see today. The Abbey of St Wandrille found new fame under the Maurists and flourished until the French Revolution forced its closure in 1790. The following year the buildings were declared the property of the nation and much of the stone of the church was sold. In 1863 the Marquis de Stacpoole bought the monastery and transformed it into a stately home. This was not the end of the story, however, for in 1894 monastic life recommenced and has continued to the present day. In 1992 the resident community of Saint Wandrille comprised forty-six Benedictine monks. They have taken over the old buildings and have created a new church from a medieval timber-framed barn which they moved from a farm across the River Seine.

St Wandrille's Abbey. The ruins of the north transept of the thirteenth-century abbey church stand within the precinct of the present Benedictine monastery. The tithes of the people of Hallamshire helped to finance this work.

Ecclesfield Church

The gift of Ecclesfield was certainly a prized one, for the parish was huge and the revenue substantial. The first element in Ecclesfield's place-name implies that a Christian community had been established here before the Anglo-Saxons arrived, centuries before the Norman Conquest, but no early architecture has survived the various rebuildings of the church. The only Anglo-Saxon work to remain is a poor-quality cross shaft which was dug up outside the west door in 1893 and which now stands just inside the south door of the chancel. The late–Norman nave piers and a contemporary arch in the porch indicate that a substantial aisled building had been erected by 1200. A new campaign was started just

Roger Dodsworth, the seventeenth-century antiquary, said that Ecclesfield church was known locally as 'The Minster of the Moors'. Its external appearance dates largely from the period, 1480-1520.

The chapel of the Priory occupied the upper floor of the thirteenth-century building. Many of its original features were preserved in the Victorian restoration.

over a hundred years later and a final great rebuilding took place between 1480 and 1520. The early fourteenth-century crossing piers were re-used in this last mighty effort. Inscriptions on the woodwork (and formerly on the glass) show that the chancel and chantry chapels were rebuilt *c*.1502–05, about the same time that the parishioners were remodelling their parts of the church. A distinctive feature is the porch, which has half-detached buttresses and pinnacles connected to the body of the church by flying buttresses, as at Silkstone. Externally, the church is all of that final period, except that in 1823–25 the nave aisle walls were heightened to accommodate a gallery. Internally, the church is the product of the High Church Movement of Victorian times, though a little medieval glass has been re-assembled in windows in the north aisle and in the vestry and the carved finials on the stalls in the chancel and chapels, together with some benches and misericords, date from the sixteenth century. In 1620 Roger Dodsworth, the great Yorkshire antiquary, visited Ecclesfield and wrote, 'This church is called (and that deservedly) by the vulger the Mynster of the Moores, being the fairest church for stone, wood, glase, and neat keeping, that ever I came in of contry church'.[6]

The Minster of the Moors was an apt title for Ecclesfield church, for its enormous parish originally covered the 71,526 acres of the whole of Hallamshire. In 1268 Hallamshire was defined as covering the territory served by the churches of Ecclesfield and Sheffield and the chapel of Bradfield. In 1291 two-thirds of the tithes and other dues of the church of Sheffield were said to go, via Ecclesfield, to St Wandrille's Abbey (the other third and the right to present vicars going, as we have seen, to Worksop Priory). In 1376 an inquisition found that the parish church of Sheffield, formerly a chapel of Ecclesfield, was still amongst the possessions of the abbey.[7] Sixty years later, the successors to St Wandrille's Abbey, the Carthusian Priory of St Anne, Coventry, leased the tithes, offerings and other revenues of their church at Sheffield to the rector of Treeton and the vicar of Sheffield.[8] The Carthusians retained their rights in Sheffield until the dissolution of religious houses in the reign of Henry VIII. Meanwhile, the church at Bradfield, which was referred to in papal bulls of 1142 and 1146, remained a chapel of Ecclesfield until Victorian times.[9] The church at Whiston was also listed as a chapel of Ecclesfield in 1188, but by 1236 it had become independent.[10] As lords of the manor, the Furnivals presented rectors to the living at Whiston, but two-thirds of the tithes were still being paid to St Wandrille's Abbey in 1267. Somehow the connection was weakened, for in 1324 Whiston was not included in an inventory of the abbey's possessions. However, the link was not completely severed, for in 1376 a yearly pension was still paid by the parishioners on the feast of All Hallows to the Abbey of St Wandrille.

St Wandrille's Abbey and the agreement of 1161

When did St Wandrille's Abbey receive this substantial grant? And when was the priory founded at Ecclesfield? As the priory was simply a cell of the Norman abbey, no foundation charter was required, and as the original gift is not recorded in the abbey's archives, we have to search for other evidence. In 1235 Maud de Louvetot, in a deed of confirmation to St Wandrille's Abbey of the right to the patronage of the church of Ecclesfield and to an estate known later as the 'Rectory manor', said that the monks had these 'of the gift of her ancestors'.[11] In 1323 the register of Archbishop Melton noted the claim of Robert de Bosco, the prior of Ecclesfield, that Roger de Louvetot, former lord of Hallamshire, gave the church of Ecclesfield to St Wandrille's Abbey, and that this gift was confirmed by King Henry I.[12] As Henry came to the throne in 1100 and Roger died before 1109, the grant must have been made between those two years, if the claim was correct. We have no reason to doubt it.[13] In a papal bull of 1142 Pope Innocent II confirmed that St Wandrille was in possession of Ecclesfield church, its chapels at Sheffield and Bradfield, two-thirds of the tithes of Hallamshire and a mill at Ecclesfield.[14] All the evidence points to a grant made in the early years of the twelfth century.

Pope Innocent II's confirmation of the possessions of the Abbey of St Wandrille mentions the English estates that had been recorded in Domesday Book (which we have noted above) and the later gifts of the churches and tithes of Wilsford and Manningford, near Upavon (Wiltshire), the church and tithes of Boughton (Northamptonshire), and the various properties and rights at Ecclesfield.[15] The abbey did not erect a cell or priory on any of their other English possessions. Ecclesfield was probably their most valuable foreign property, as well as being the only one that lay north of the Trent. It would have been in the monks' interest to build there almost straight away, but no firm documentary evidence for a priory exists before 1273. We shall see, however, that monks were certainly here at various times in the twelfth century.

The restoration of Ecclesfield priory in 1866 revealed the remains of an outer wall, at the west end of the chapel, which the architect suggested might have been a relic of buildings erected in the twelfth century, but this speculation has not been investigated by modern archaeological methods.[16]

The monks of St Wandrille were responsible for divine worship at Ecclesfield, the canons of Worksop Priory for services at Sheffield and Bradfield. The first mention of clergymen at Ecclesfield comes between 1150 and 1160, when Robert *decanus de Ecclesfeld* and his brother, Roger the priest, witnessed a charter of Richard de Louvetot.[17] An agreement made between Richard de Louvetot and the Abbey of St Wandrille in 1161 provides clearer evidence of who such clergymen were, for it mentions 'the monks of Ecclesfield'.[18] This agreement was concerned not with the grant of Ecclesfield church and the tithes but with the 600 acres of land and wood that formed the Rectory Manor. Perhaps the original grant of Roger de Louvetot had been one or more of the six pre-conquest manors of Ecclesfield within the lordship of Hallamshire. This might explain why the Hundred Rolls of 1277 named Thomas de Furnival as lord of the manor of North Ecclesfield, territory that was apparently distinct from the Rectory Manor.[19]

Richard de Louvetot and the monks agreed that the assarts (clearings) on the right hand side of the way which led from Sheffield to Ecclesfield, as far as Blackburn Brook,

The Birley Stone. The base of this cross may well be medieval, though the shaft is later. In 1161 it was an agreed boundary point between lands belonging to the lord of Hallamshire and the abbey of St Wandrille.

'as the hedge was anciently before the burning' belonged to the Abbey of St Wandrille and that the assarts on the left hand side of the way were in the possession of Richard, 'as the hedge was anciently before the burning'. The way referred to is Sheffield Lane, the route that was made into a turnpike road from Sheffield to Barnsley, Wakefield and Leeds in 1758, and which is now the A6135. This was the ancient route out of Sheffield in a northerly direction and a natural choice of boundary. The clearings between this road and Blackburn Brook formed the 300-acre estate that was farmed by the monks from their grange at Woolley. The clearings on the other side of the road formed the core of the lord's estate that was centred on Southey Hall. When writing his *Hallamshire* in 1819, Joseph Hunter

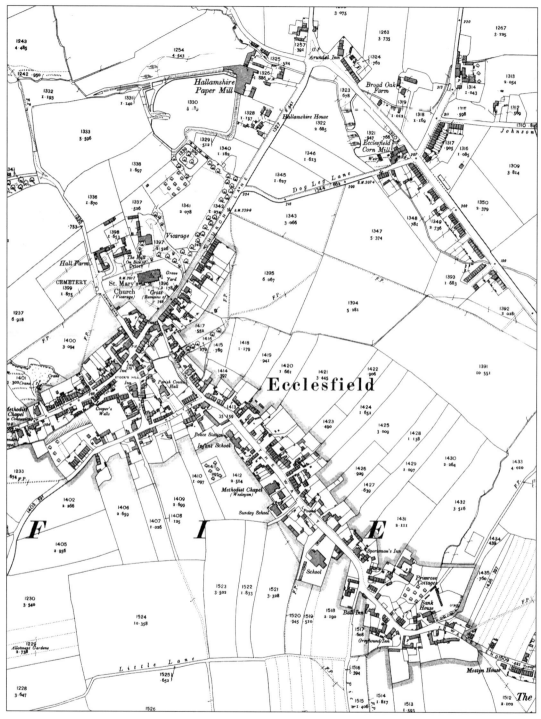

Ecclesfield in 1901. The six-inch Ordnance Survey map marks the Priory behind St Mary's Church. The fishponds occupied field number 1341. The Hallamshire Paper Mill was the successor to the Priory's corn mill.

St Wandrille's Abbey. The eleventh-century refectory range is the oldest building of its kind in western Europe. The cloister was re-designed in Flamboyant style about 1510.

wondered whether the tantalising reference to 'the hedge as it was before the burning' referred to the destruction of 1069–70, known as the 'Harrying of the North', in which William the Conqueror devastated large tracts of northern England in order to subdue a revolt. If the 1161 confirmation charter was using the words of an earlier agreement between the Lord of Hallamshire and the monks, then such a burning would have been a fresh memory. But there is no evidence to show that South Yorkshire was laid waste in this horrific campaign. Earl Waltheof, Lord of Hallamshire, remained loyal to William until a further revolt in 1075. The burning must have some other explanation.

The agreement of 1161 demarcated other properties of the lord and the monks and left in joint possession 'the wood, as the way goes from the Church of Eglesfeld, as far as Burleyestan to the left, and another from Burley to the assarts of Wereldesend to the left'. This way can be identified as Wheel Lane and its continuation over Jaw Bone Hill and down to Oughtibridge. 'Burleyestan' is the Birley Stone, a medieval boundary marker which still stands (albeit with a later shaft in the original socket) on the top of Jaw Bone Hill, near a modern direction finder. It also served in later times as the division between the Grenofrith and Southey quarters of Ecclesfield parish. 'Wereldsend' was literally 'World's End', a nickname for a settlement on the edge of the parishes of Ecclesfield and Sheffield, now known as Wardsend. The agreement mentions other assarts in this part of the parish that are difficult to identify, but one large clearing that belonged to the monks took the name Prior Royd, a name which survives to this day on the parish boundary next to Wharncliffe Woods. By the seventeenth century this medieval clearing had reverted to woodland. The farm on the edge of this wood, which became known later as Hunter House, may well have been the one from which the monks worked their lands and pastured their sheep and pigs in this wood pasture district on the north-western boundary of Ecclesfield parish.

The agreement of 1161 did not need to specify the core of the monks' estate around their priory in Ecclesfield. The extent of this property is evident from a survey of the former Rectory Manor in 1637, which we shall examine later. This part of the manor included the corn mill that was mentioned in a papal bull of 1142. The nearest mill to the priory lay just down the hill at the edge of the common, where a large and deep dam survives. Its description in the survey of 1637 and in the enclosure award of 1789 leaves no doubt that this was the ancient corn mill. By 1794 it was being used as a cotton mill and in 1848 it was converted into a paper mill; finally it got burnt down. The earthworks of the monks' fishponds can still be traced on the flat ground between the mill and the church. Fishponds are, of course, features that were commonly associated with monastic sites.

The monks attracted some other, much more modest, gifts from the inhabitants of Hallamshire. In 1286, for instance, Robert le Rous of Onesacre gave an annual rent of 12d from two acres of land at Onesacre.[20] The surviving court rolls of the Rectory Manor show that grants of land were received at Creswick, Nether Hartley, Shiregreen, Bradfield and Oughtibridge.[21] No grants were received from the villagers of Ecclesfield, however, and it is noticeable that the priors rarely appeared as witnesses to local deeds. Were they regarded suspiciously, perhaps even with hostility, as foreigners to whom tithes and other dues had to be paid and from whom little was received in return? We can only speculate about this, but the silence of the documents may be revealing.

Priors, Vicars and Disputes

After 1161 our information about the monks comes mainly from disputes, a fact which may in itself be significant. From time to time the Abbey of St Wandrille adopted the common practice of leasing or farming out the manor and the collection of tithes and of appointing a vicar to fulfil their pastoral duties. A dispute of 1187–8 suggests that the monks had withdrawn, for the priest Jeremiah of Ecclesfield claimed that the full rectorial tithes should have been paid to him and that he had an hereditary right to the Rectory Manor. An agreement was made in 1188 whereby Jeremiah (who was referred to as 'our cleric') was made perpetual vicar with a third of the tithes and the farmer of the other two-thirds at the rent of twenty marks (£13 6s 8d) for his life.[22] No mention was made of the Rectory Manor, however. It is perhaps significant that at this very time open conflict had broken out between the Duchy of Normandy and the Kingdom of France, which was to end with the absorption of Normandy into France in 1204, after which many Anglo-Norman lords abandoned their estates across the Channel. The political situation is known to have influenced elections to key posts at religious houses in Normandy from 1187 onwards.[23] Jeremiah may have tried to take advantage of this troubled situation or perhaps to have exaggerated his claims in order to get his position at Ecclesfield formalised. He died not long after agreement was reached in 1188.

The situation after Jeremiah's death is not at all clear. Eastwood claimed that Jeremiah was succeeded by his brother, Ralph, and subsequently by Robert, Ralph's son, both of whom were witnesses to the 1188 agreement.[24] However, Ralph and Robert were popular Norman names and it is not certain that Ralph, the parson of Ecclesfield, who was involved in a dispute over the Rectory Manor in 1199–1206, was the brother referred to in 1188. Eastwood also claimed, without quoting any supporting evidence, that Ralph's son, Robert, was succeeded by three generations of sons, Thomas, Roger and Thomas, and that this last Thomas was still making claims to the Rectory Manor in 1279.[25] This is an unlikely succession, for by the thirteenth century a ban on clerical marriages (except for those in minor orders) was strictly enforced.[26] The normally meticulous Eastwood confuses the matter by dating some of these clergymen from a confirmation made by the dean and chapter at Rouen in 1245 and not from the agreement of 1188. The Robert, clerk of Ecclesfield, who witnessed Thomas de Furnival's confirmation charter to the Abbey of St Wandrille in 1258, must have lived to a ripe old age if he was indeed the nephew of Jeremiah. The claims of an hereditary succession do not stand up to close investigation. There is little evidence that any of the various clergymen who were named in twelfth- and thirteenth-century documents were related.[27]

The Abbey of St Wandrille was caught up in further political events beyond their control during the middle decades of the thirteenth century. In 1235 the abbey presented to the rectory of Ecclesfield a certain Rufinus, who was described as the son of a nobleman from Versailles and the nephew of a cardinal.[28] Rufinus held numerous benefices in Europe and never set foot in England. He simply took the rent that he was able to get from the farmer of the Rectory Manor and the collector of the tithes and he appointed a vicar to serve in his place. Eastwood quotes letters which were written between 1236 and 1244 by the Archbishop of Rouen to the Archbishop of York, in which he says that the monks of St Wandrille, yielding to the

South-east view of the priory. An engraving from Eastwood's *Ecclesfield*, taken not long before the Victorian restoration of the building.

importunities of certain powerful nobles of the district, had conferred the church of Ecclesfield against their will and had leased the Rectory Manor on bad terms. He begged the Archbishop of York to see that they were not defrauded of their rights.[29] The appeal seems to have been made in vain, for the Archbishop of York could do little about it.

In 1246 Rufinus was succeeded by another absentee, Hugh Rubeus, the nephew and chaplain of Pope Innocent IV. He appointed proctors to farm out his Ecclesfield possessions during his life at a yearly rent of 170 marks (£113 3s 4d).[30] In 1267, as rector, he appointed Robert the clerk of Ecclesfield to act on his behalf at an enquiry. This Robert was presumably his vicar. Whether Robert was a monk of St Wandrille or a local man we cannot say. Soon afterwards, however, the Abbey of St Wandrille recovered control of its affairs. In 1278 brother Peter de Sancto Romano, described as prior and proctor of St Wandrille, was in charge of the administration of all the goods of the church of Ecclesfield.[31] It is tempting to ascribe the building of Ecclesfield Priory as we know it to these years. The evidence of the style of architecture certainly points to the late thirteenth century as the period of building.

A papal bull of Clement IV in 1267 confirmed the possessions of St Wandrille's Abbey, including those at Ecclesfield, Sheffield, Bradfield and Whiston. The arrangement of 1188 by which the abbey claimed only two-thirds of the tithes, with a third going to the vicar was still accepted. In 1273 a similar confirmation by Pope Gregory X made the first mention of a priory at Ecclesfield. It is possible, therefore, that the present priory was built between 1267 and 1273, but it is also possible that an older, twelfth-century building was still in use and that the present building is a little later. The Abbey of St Wandrille's recovery of the manor and the advowson was confirmed in 1279. Twelve years later, the abbey held the manor, a grange at Woolley, tenements in Bradfield and the church of Sheffield.[32] However, the situation changed again soon, for in the early fourteenth century a John de Louvetot and his son farmed the Rectory Manor and the monks were found to be neglecting their pastoral duties.[33]

The return of foreign monks to Ecclesfield must have affected the responsibility for the provision of divine services, for a vicar was no longer needed to act on their behalf. But the monks were not

An engraving from Revd A. Gatty, *A Life at One Living* (1884), showing the chapel before the Priory's restoration.

assiduous in the pursuit of their duties. In 1308 Archbishop Greenfield noted that Robert de Bosco, a monk of St Wandrille, was in residence as prior and proctor but that no vicar had been appointed for some years. Two years later, he ordered the Abbey of St Wandrille to appoint a perpetual vicar, with a parsonage-house, and to pay two chaplains (one at Ecclesfield and one at Bradfield) to assist the vicar. He did not query the right of the abbey to present a vicar to the living when a vacancy occurred.[34] The archbishop was tightening up on similar cases elsewhere at the time, e.g. at Bawtry and Austerfield. It is not certain that the instruction to build a parsonage-house was ever carried out, for in April 1311 Robert de Bosco himself was presented as both vicar and prior. Archbishop Melton's register (1317–40) notes that de Bosco was called *prior de Eglesfeld*. If the prior and the two chaplains lived in the priory, a new parsonage-house would not have been necessary. In 1376 the situation was said to be that 'there is a vicarage [i.e. the office, not a building] at Ecclesfield, to which when vacant the abbot should appoint one of his monks,' and that 'these possessions have always been occupied by a single monk of the abbot called there the prior of Ecclesfield, who had with him two or three monks.'[35] The number of people living in the priory could never have been very large, though we probably need to add living-in servants.

The Fourteenth Century

A view of the economy and the internal arrangements of the priory can be obtained from surveys taken by royal agents on the outbreak of war between England and France in 1324 and again in 1337, when the assets of alien priories were seized for the king's use. In 1324 the priory was staffed by the prior and a companion, two chaplains, and another clergyman who served as proctor for the collection of offerings and other sources of income. Three poor persons were said to be 'daily sustained by the Prior's alms'. An inventory of goods and chattels was valued at £30.17s.1d.[36] The monks' possessions at Ecclesfield included a saddle horse for the prior, a packhorse blind of one eye, three cart horses, six plough-bullocks, a bull and six cows, a boar, three sows and ten porkers. At Woolley Grange they owned six bullocks, a little wheat, some rye and a considerable quantity of oats. The bullocks were used for cultivating the land. The monks were assisted by a servant at each place and by three ploughmen and a reaper who was in charge of the arable lands and woods.

The 1324 inventory was compiled at a time when the country was just emerging from several years of bad harvests, cattle plague and sheep murrain. The next inventory, which was taken in 1337 in more settled times, gives a better picture of the monks' activities. The six cows were now twelve, the pigs now numbered thirty, with two porklets, and 100 sheep with 160 wethers were kept. Seventy stones of wool were laid in store and large amounts of rye, barley, oats and peas had been harvested. The prior still had his saddle horse but the half-blind packhorse had died. Three cart horses and sixteen plough-bullocks provided power to pull two ploughs – 'the worse for wear both in wood and iron' – and three wains. The household utensils at the priory included a dish (with a cover), a dish for washing, four brass pans, four porringers, four dishes worse for wear and other small utensils for use in the kitchen and cellar. The vestments and accessories in the prior's chapel included a cope, alb, girdle, stole and maniple, a chalice, and a small figure of a saint, whose name is illegible in the document but which was possibly that of St Wandrille. In the prior's chamber (the first floor of the adjoining north-south range) were beds for the prior and his companion, and six beds for visitors. The total value of the inventory was £46 1s 4d, a sixty-one per cent increase since 1324. The monks therefore seem to have been in day-to-day charge of their farms at Ecclesfield and Woolley during those years, but the account of debts due to the monks mentions several people who leased the right to collect the tithes in various parts of the chapelry of Bradfield and of Attercliffe.[37]

We are provided with other brief glimpses of life at the priory during the fourteenth century. In 1315 a commission of oyer and terminer investigated claims that persons who,

pretending that they were the King's ministers and held commissions under the great seal to take the King's treasure to a certain place, with a great multitude, horse and foot, entered the priory of Ecclesfield and assaulted Robert the prior, his men and servants, maimed them, carried off his goods, and committed other acts to the injury of the liberty of the church.[38]

This prior was Robert de Bosco, who resigned in 1328, on account of old age and ill health, and who was succeeded by a succession of monks from St Wandrille.[39] Most of these men are merely names to us. John de Fauvel or Favell (1328–49) was described as prior, rector or vicar of the church of Ecclesfield. His successor, Robert Gullielmi, the prior from 1349 to 1369, does not fit our conception of the pious monk. In 1357 the abbey ordered two messengers, with letters, to bring him, by force of arms if necessary, back to St Wandrille, because he had taken no notice of a summons to answer serious charges about his 'evil life and embezzlement of the priory's goods'. He nevertheless received leave of absence in 1360–1 and 1362–4 and In 1367 licence to pass from Dover to France, and he remained in post at Ecclesfield until his death. He was followed by Magister[40] William Fulmere (1369–71), who was presented by the Crown during another war with France. Fulmere's appointment was revoked in 1370 when the Archbishop of York ruled that the custom which excluded secular persons from the vicarage had been breached. The Crown then presented brother John Burdet (1371–72), monk of St Wandrille, in his place, but Fulmere contested the new appointment. The peace was shattered by a violent argument and Burdet was committed to Newgate prison for threatening William Fulmere in life and limbs. He was eventually set free, but only after a long drawn out dispute with Fulmere. Meanwhile, in 1372 the Crown had presented Sir[41] Henry de Medbourne, chaplain to Lord Latimer, as the new prior. A complaint from Burdet against Medbourne was heard in Parliament in 1376. Ecclesfield Priory was once more caught up in the consequences of far-away political struggles.

During this period, if not before, the monks leased their estates to local men. At the time of the poll tax return of 1379 Richard de Wentworth was the farmer of Woolley Grange and John Spencer held a lease of the rest of the Rectory Manor.[42] In 1377 the Abbey of St Wandrille tried to appoint James Pseaulme, one of their monks, as prior, but Henry Medbourne seems to have remained in post until 1385 when, with the Crown's blessing, he and Nicholas Shirbourn exchanged Ecclesfield for the church of Fordingbridge (Hampshire).[43] This sorry tale of wrangling came to an end in 1386, when all the possessions of the alien priories, including those of St Wandrille's Abbey, were confiscated by the Crown during yet another war with France. In 1386 the right to present vicars to the church of Ecclesfield and to collect the tithes in Hallamshire was granted to the new Carthusian Priory of St Anne, Coventry, and soon afterwards they received the Rectory Manor also. The Abbey of St Wandrille continued to try to present their nominees to Ecclesfield for some years after their loss, but this time they failed to regain their possessions. Their long connection with Hallamshire was finally severed.

The Priory of St Anne, Coventry

The Carthusian Priory of St Anne, Coventry, had been founded in 1385 by William, Lord Zouch, who gave fourteen acres of land in the suburb of Shortley. King Richard II laid the foundation stone. The Poor Brothers of God of the Charterhouse, to give the Carthusians their full title, were the most ascetic order of monks in the late Middle Ages. They lived a solitary life in their cells, observing a vow of silence. Their numbers were restricted at each monastery to a prior and an 'upper house' of twelve monks and a 'lower house' of eighteen lay brothers, in deliberately modest buildings. The remains of Mount Grace Priory in north Yorkshire (founded in 1398) provide the best idea of the lay-out of a Carthusian monastery; nothing survives of St Anne's Priory at Coventry. The Carthusians were the only monastic order to retain their enthusiasm and to attract patronage after the Black Death. Even so, their endowments were mostly those which the Crown had confiscated from alien priories, such as St Wandrille's. The Priory of St Anne, Coventry, started with three monks from the Charterhouse, London, three monks from Beauvale monastery (Nottinghamshire) and four new monks.[44]

The Carthusians, being an order dedicated to a solitary existence, never sent monks to live in the priory at Ecclesfield. Instead, they appointed vicars and chaplains to see to the pastoral care of the parish and they farmed out their Rectory Manor to tenants. Manor courts were held in the old hall of the Priory under a steward. The earliest surviving records of these courts date from 1425. The usual formula at the start of proceedings was to record a meeting 'At the court of the prior of the house of saint Anne next Coventry'. When John, the younger son of Henry Shirecliffe, was described as being of 'le Hall' in Ecclesfield in 1476 he was presumably leasing the Rectory Manor and living in the old priory. The vicar must have been living in a parsonage-house by then. From before 1526 the Shirecliffes were also sharing in the profitable venture of collecting the tithes.[45] The *Valor Ecclesiasticus* (1535), drawn up for the Crown shortly before the Dissolution, noted that St Anne's Priory received a rent of £60 13s 4d from the 'rectorial farm' of the parish church of Ecclesfield and the chapel of Bradfield, and that the monks paid a vicar the yearly stipend of £2 13s 4d. The *Valor* also referred to the 'dwelling house' of the vicar.[46] In John Harrison's survey of the Rectory Manor in 1637 this building was described as 'a dwelling-house ... lying on the north side of the churchyard, between Ecclesfield Hall, west, and a lane east'. This old vicarage has been replaced on three occasions since.

Eight of the vicars presented to the living at Ecclesfield by St Anne's Priory are known by name.[47] In 1394 William Bryan, 'Vicar of the Church of Ecclesfield' was recorded as a trustee.[48] Later references to vicars name Arnald Wyke (1401–9), Robert Normanton (1424), Thomas Swyft (died 1478), Thomas Clark (1478),[49] Magister John Talbot (1518), Magister William Holme (1519–24) and Edward Hatfield (1534–5).[50] The present appearance of the parish church dates from the incumbency of Thomas Clark. Whilst most of the church was the responsibility of the parishioners, the Priory of St Anne joined the rebuilding programme enthusiastically. In 1498 Thomas Ricard, Prior of St Anne's, inscribed his name on the great east window of Ecclesfield church, which the monks paid for, and in 1505 Vicar Clark joined with Henry Wrastler in providing a new window in the north side of the north quire.[51] A carved finial on one of the stalls, which seems to depict the Virgin and Child, may be reasonably interpreted as St Anne (the mother of the Virgin) with her child, for St Anne was the patron of the priory at Coventry and the parish church was dedicated to St Mary.

After the Dissolution

The Carthusian Priory of St Anne, Coventry, surrendered to the Crown commissioners in January 1539.[52] In 1542 Francis Talbot, fifth Earl of Shrewsbury, exchanged a Buckinghamshire manor for the right to present vicars and collect the tithes at Ecclesfield. In 1544 he presented Magister Charles Parsons and in 1549 John Tyas as vicars. In 1549 Edward VI granted the Rectory Manor to the Countess of Northumberland for life. Upon her death in 1572 the rights passed to her nephew George,

The west end of Ecclesfield Church seen from the Victorian lychgate at the entrance to the churchyard.

A carved wooden finial on a bench end in the eastern part of Ecclesfield Church, once the responsibility of the Carthusians of St Anne's monastery, Coventry. St Katherine is shown carrying her wheel of martyrdom.

the sixth earl of Shrewsbury. The Shrewsburys leased the Rectory Manor to the Shirecliffes of Ecclesfield Hall, the existing tenants, and farmed the right to the tithes to the Shirecliffes and other Ecclesfield parish gentry.[53] The Shirecliffes converted the hall in the early seventeenth century by inserting a huge fireplace, rows of mullioned windows and other features, though the chapel and the room underneath were left unaltered.

The fullest information that we have about the Rectory Manor comes from a survey made by John Harrison in 1637, a century after the monks had lost possession.[54] The old estate was intact, though it was leased in parcels to different tenants. Harrison started with:

The scite of the mannor, or mansion house called Ecclesfield-hall with all the Out-houses there to belonginge some of them beeing in decay and some fallen downe. Also the orchard, gardens, yard, the conney-greave and the Intack (arable) lyinge next unto Ecclesfeild Churchyard towards the south and the Vicarage south east and containeth 6ac.1ro.32$^{1}/_{2}$p. – Item, a water Corne Mill with a cottage lyinge on the west end of Ecclesfeild Moore and next unto the Lee bottome.

This is the corn mill that was referred to in 1142 and 1451.[55] The land belonging to the hall (including Prior Royd) amounted to 336 acres 1 rood 13$^{8}/_{10}$ perches; it was let to various tenants at a rent of £295 2s 8d. Mr Shirecliffe, at the hall, paid £70 per annum and £6 10s 0d for 'the rents of the Coppiholders and Customary Tennants within the said Mannor'. Mr Thomas Shirtcliffe, Mr Freeman and others paid £200 p.a. for the right to collect the tithes that had formerly gone to the monks. By

Prior Royd stood 'a dwellinge house of three bayes and a barne of one bay and a close lyinge next to Grano more east' with other land amounting to 73 acres 1 rood 16 perches and a wood of 52 acres 0 rood 20 perches. Eastwood thought that the dwelling house was most likely that known as Hunter House, 'where there are still some old buildings, which may be the remains of the ancient grange'.[56] Prior Royd Wood stretches down to Hunter House, which is in effect the northern terminus of Birley Edge. In 1637 a 'Priory Wood' joined the northern side of Beeley Wood, south of Oughtibridge Hall and east of the river Don. This name has disappeared but it seems to have been one of the woods mentioned in the agreement of 1161.

Harrison also noted:

the Capitall Messuage, Tenement, and farme called Wolley Grange alias Oakes-farme (belonging to Ecclesfeild hall and the Rectory), lyinge at Shiregreene within the parish of Ecclesfeild aforesaid and Soake of Southall, and in the occupacion of severall men.

The original grange buildings took up nearly an acre of ground, on the opposite side of Shiregreen to Raynaldthorpe (later, Hatfield House). The farm land went as far as Woolley Wood and the Blackburn Brook and amounted to 297acres 3roods 1perch. The property was let at £64 6s 8d per annum. Sited on high ground on the edge of the present Concord Park, the old grange commanded a view of the church and priory, nearly two miles away.[57] An old cruck-framed barn on the site of the former grange, which is now used as an implement store for the maintenance of Concord Park, may have been erected during the later stages of the monks' ownership, but only a dendrochronology date can tell. Three bays long, it was originally at least a bay longer to the west. The truss in the wall at the

present west end retains part of its infill of studs, laths and plaster-daub.

The priory, by now known as Ecclesfield Hall, was the home of a branch of the Shirecliffe family from the fifteenth to the seventeenth century. They were responsible for much of the building's present appearance. By 1672 Mr Robert Greene of Thundercliffe Grange, who had married the Shirecliffe heiress, was living there.[58] When his widow, Alice Greene of Ecclesfield Hall, died in 1691 an inventory of her personal estate listed the rooms as follows: hall, little parlour adjoining to the hall, milk house, kitchen, brewhouse, oxen house, dining room, closet, buttery, cellar, Chappel parlour, passage, Chappel Chamber, Greene Chamber, passage, Servants Chamber, boulting house, hay lath, fold, stable, and Old Chappell (which was used as a store for '2 harrowes and Some old things, 2s. 6d., Certaine Tinn

Concord Park cruck barn. Only the technique known as dendrochronology can resolve the question: was this barn erected when Woolley Grange belonged to Ecclesfield Priory or from not long after the Dissolution?

Things and the huslement in and about the house, 3s. 4d.').[59] As the arrangement and dimensions of the rooms were not given in this inventory, it is difficult to say whether the building of a new Georgian farmhouse, which can be dated to 1736 by an inscription over front door, destroyed some older work. It depends on whether or not some of the service rooms were contained in outbuildings to the rear. The old priory could never have been much larger than the present building, which may well preserve the original shape, though the internal arrangements and the structural detail owe much to the major restoration which was carried out in 1866 by M E H Hadfield, the Sheffield architect, for Bernard Wake.[60] From then onwards, the Priory and the Hall became separate dwellings.

The present priory consists of a two-storeyed rectangular block, arranged north-south next to the 1736 hall, and a smaller section in the south-

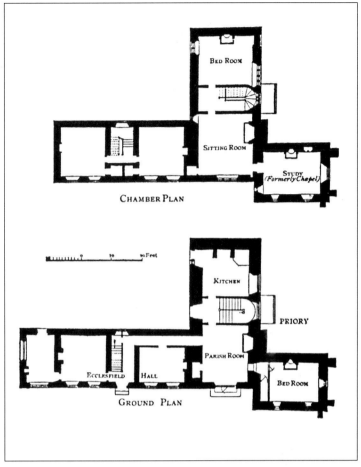

A plan of the ground floor and upper rooms of the Priory, drawn for Revd Alfred Gatty, vicar of Ecclesfield from 1839 to 1903.

east corner, containing the chapel. Both parts stand on the bedrock and are built of local coal-measure sandstone, with millstone grit dressings. The north-south range was altered in the seventeenth century and again in 1866, so its original arrangements are difficult to reconstruct. The windows on its east side are mostly seventeenth-century work, but the large mullioned-and-transomed window in the south gable is Victorian.

The drawings of the priory in Eastwood's *History of the Parish of Ecclesfield*, made a few years before the 1866 restoration, show that Hadfield did not alter the external appearance of the chapel wing.[61] The door to the basement is spanned by a two-centred, chamfered arch. Tiny windows provide light from the south and the east into the basement and the chamber above, and buttresses give support where the ground dips away. The chapel is the best preserved room in the building. Only the roof is not original thirteenth-century work. The trefoil-headed lancets of the large east window are convincing evidence that the building dates from the later part of the thirteenth century. The chapel is lit further by double lancets, a single lancet, and a small square-headed window. The piscina on the south wall is original and the aumbry, with wrought iron hinges and oak doors in the opposite wall, also looks medieval. The whole of this part of the Priory remains much as it was when the black-habited Benedictine monks from Normandy ordered its erection more than 700 years ago.[62]

THE HALLAMSHIRE GENTRY AND THEIR HALLS

3

The medieval halls of the knightly families who owned sub-manors within Hallamshire under the Louvetots and Furnivals of Sheffield Castle have disappeared with hardly any trace, though in some cases their sites are known. The families which had occupied these halls had all died out in the senior line by the end of the Middle Ages. They were gradually replaced by another group of families that often had deep roots within Hallamshire at a more modest social level. By the seventeenth century this new group were prosperous enough to build the sturdy, gabled halls which still adorn the Hallamshire countryside.

The Mounteneys

The most substantial medieval hall was Cowley Manor, which for centuries belonged to the Mounteney family. In 1637 the manor of Cowley covered 1,053 acres on the northern border of the parish of Ecclesfield.[1] The chapel that served this manor is thought to have stood a short distance to the west of the manor house, at a place that was still called Chapel in the seventeenth century but which, with the growth of industry, has become modern Chapeltown. In 1619 Roger Dodsworth, the Yorkshire antiquary, was informed that at Cowley the Mounteneys had once had 'great woods, and abundance of redd deare, and a stately castle-like house moated about, pulled down, not long since by the Earl of Salop [Shrewsbury] after he had purchased the land'.[2] The woods still stretch up the hill from Cowley as far as the M1 motorway, but the medieval manor house and its moat have gone completely and the site of the chapel is unknown.

The Mounteneys were the most prominent and the longest surviving of the knightly families of Hallamshire. Several places in France are called Montigny, but our family probably took their name from Montigny, near Rouen, in Normandy, not far from Louvetot and the Abbey of St Wandrille. Today, this Montigny is a large and prosperous village with some old timber-framed houses. The small, simple parish church, dating from the twelfth and thirteenth centuries, stands at the south-western edge of the settlement, near a high brick wall which encloses the extensive grounds of the fine seventeenth- or eighteenth-century hall that is probably the successor of a medieval manor house. During the thirteenth century the Mounteneys became lords of the sub-manors of Cowley and Shirecliffe within the lordship of Hallamshire. Before them, Jordan de Reineville (a member of another family who had taken their name from an estate in Normandy) had been Lord of Cowley. The De Reinevilles were leading tenants of the De Lacis, lords of Pontefract, from immediately after the Norman Conquest, at Campsall, Badsworth and elsewhere. Adam de Reineville had four sons: William, Adam, Swein and Jordan, but it seems that these four failed to produce sons of their own. Jordan de Reineville's daughter, Margaret, married Sir Robert de Mounteney, who thus acquired Cowley. Jordan's other daughter, Alice, married Thomas de Bella Aqua (another Norman family, also known as Belheu in the Norman French form of the name, which means fine water), who acquired properties in Bolton-upon-Dearne and Rawmarsh.[3]

Sir Robert de Mounteney, the husband of Margaret de Reneville, was the son of Arnald de Mounteney, who had married a daughter of Gerard de Furnival and Maud de Louvetot, the lord and lady of

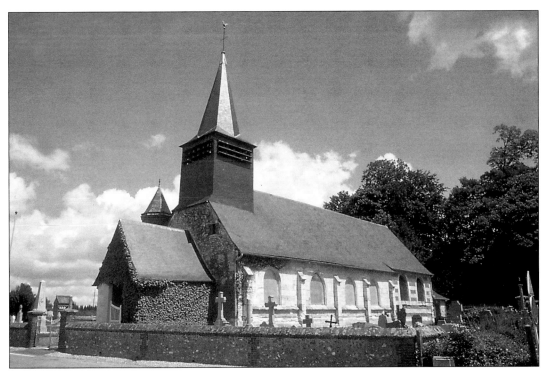

The medieval church at Montigny in the Seine valley, from where the Mounteneys took their name.

Hallamshire. The Mounteneys perhaps acquired the sub-manor of Shirecliffe through this marriage. They were clearly the second most important family in Hallamshire at that time. Sir Robert de Mounteney (who went on crusade with Lord Furnival) was a witness to various local charters in the thirteenth century and Alice de Mounteney was prioress of the Benedictine nunnery at Wallingwells on the Yorkshire-Nottinghamshire border. In 1297 Thomas de Mounteney was taxed on his properties in the parishes of Sheffield and Ecclesfield,[4] which implies that by then he owned the sub-manors of both Shirecliffe and Cowley. The poll tax returns of 1379[5] do not record the Mounteneys at Cowley or Shirecliffe, but John Mounteney, 'armiger' (a man with a coat-of-arms), paid 40d tax (ten times the rate paid by most people) at Whiston, another manor of the Furnivals. In or about 1390 this John Mounteney, described as 'chevalier' or knight, acquired a royal charter that allowed him to hunt in Cowley, Shirecliffe (where he had a park), Ecclesfield, Rotherham and Wath. In 1520 an *Inquisition Post Mortem* taken at Rotherham after the death of Robert Mounteney, esquire, reported that he had held the manors of Cowley and Shirecliffe and that he had granted his son, Robert, the manor of Hesley 'being a parcel of the manor of Cowley'.[6] The Mounteneys had by that time been a major local landowning family for the best part of four centuries.

As Cowley was their chief residence, the Mounteneys were usually buried in Ecclesfield church. In 1620 Roger Dodsworth noted that the east window of the south quire of the church contained the images and shields of arms of the Mounteneys, beginning with Arnald and proceeding with Robert, Thomas, Thomas, John, Thomas, Robert and Nicholas. The Mounteney arms were also displayed in a north window. Late-medieval woodwork that can still be seen in the eastern part of the church includes that of the oratory of John Mounteney, the last of the male line at Cowley. Dodsworth noted that it was erected so that prayers could be said for the souls of Robert Mounteney of Cowley, armiger (1519), and John Mounteney of Cowley, armiger (1536). John's daughter, Barbara, married Thomas Thwaites, esquire, of Marston, near York. In 1572 John Thwaites, the brother of Thomas, sold Cowley,

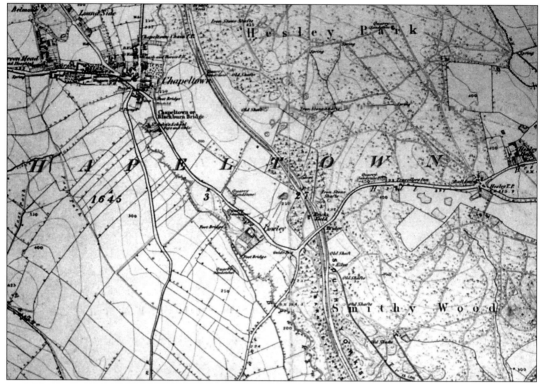

The sub-manor of Cowley occupied the northern part of Ecclesfield parish, between the Blackburn Brook and Hallamshire's boundary with Wentworth and Tankersley.

Hesley and Shirecliffe to George Talbot, the sixth Earl of Shrewsbury, and so the sub-manors returned to the lordship of Hallamshire. The manor house at Cowley was pulled down and replaced by a farmhouse, which was described by John Harrison in 1637 as 'the scite of the Mannor of Cowley called Cowley hall with a dwelling house of two bayes, a cowhouse, a heyhouse, and a close'. The Guest family were farmers there throughout the seventeenth century. Cowley Manor and Hesley Hall were both rebuilt in a Georgian style, five bays wide and two storeys high, during the eighteenth century. The moat which enclosed the earlier Hesley Hall was still in use when Harrison surveyed the property in 1637, but no traces of it survive. Shirecliffe Hall remained a desirable residence in the seventeenth century, when it was the home of the Dissenting minister, Rowland Hancock, and then of Joseph Banks, Sheffield's leading attorney, but the deer were removed from the surrounding 143-acre park, which was converted into a coppice wood.[7] Shirecliffe Hall has gone completely and much of the park now serves as a dry ski-slope.

Meanwhile, younger branches of the family earned their livings in Sheffield, where in 1379 John Mounteney was taxed as a butcher and his namesake was a smith. Some later branches acquired gentry status. A family of Mounteneys who were lawyers settled at Wheatley, beyond Doncaster.[8] Thomas Mounteney of Wheatley, esquire, a barrister-at-law and JP, was buried at Doncaster in 1616. His son, Thomas Mounteney of Wheatley, esquire, had two sons and two daughters, but the male line withered soon afterwards. The Rotherham branch lasted longest. Richard Mounteney, esquire, lived in the largest house in town, where High Street joined Wellgate. Nicholas Mounteney, gentleman, and his son, Francis, were the leading townsmen for much of the seventeenth century. In 1656 Charles Tooker of Moorgate Hall enhanced his social standing by marrying Anne Mounteney. The Rotherham list in the 1672 hearth tax returns for south Yorkshire was headed by Francis Mounteney, esquire, with nine hearths.9 The surname has survived elsewhere, but Francis seems to have been the last of the south Yorkshire Mounteneys, a family that had prospered for over five hundred years, far longer than any of the other Hallamshire families of knightly rank. They are commemorated in Ecclesfield by Monteney Road and Monteney Crescent.

Other Knightly Families

The next most important sub-manor within Hallamshire was the lordship of Ecclesall. Ralph de Ecclesall, who witnessed a grant from Gerard de Furnival to Kirkstead Abbey which can be dated before 1219, appears to have been the same man as Ralph, the son of Ralph, the son of Gilbert, who witnessed another grant to these Cistercian monks.10 The family therefore did not take an hereditary surname until they acquired their manor of Ecclesall from Gerard de Furnival, even though they were previously of local importance and perhaps of Norman origin. Their sub-manor, which was held by military service, had its own court and copyholders, and its hall, chapel and deer park. The family were benefactors to their neighbours, the canons of Beauchief Abbey, who in return for generous grants took services at the chapel at Ecclesall. The descent of the family can be traced through Ralph to Sir Robert, to Sir Ralph, and to another Sir Robert (a witness to Sheffield's town charter in 1297). In 1329 Sir Robert de Ecclesall was said to hold the manor of Ecclesall and lands in Sheffield, Broom, Crookes and Aldwark. He died before 1342, without male heirs, and the manor eventually passed to the Scropes of Masham (north Yorkshire), who held it until 1517, when it passed to the Strelleys of Nottinghamshire and eventually to the Brights of Whirlow. Upon the marriage of Mary Bright to Charles Watson-Wentworth, second Marquis of Rockingham and owner of the Wentworth Woodhouse estate, the lordship of Ecclesall passed to the Rockinghams and then to their successors, the Fitzwilliams. Nothing survives of the old manor house or its chapel (which stood near the top of Carter Knowle Road, not far from the present Ecclesall church). The name Parkhead is, however, a reminder of the old deer park, which stretched down the hill to the River Sheaf. In the sixteenth century the park was converted into a coppice wood. Seventeenth- and eighteenth-century maps show that it was the same size and shape as the present Ecclesall Wood.11

The sub-manor of Wadsley was probably identical with the Anglo-Saxon estate that was recorded in Domesday Book. Here the family of De Wadsley had a hall, park, manorial rights and a chapel within the parish of Ecclesfield. Their surname was first recorded in 1227, when Hugh de Waddislay witnessed a deed. During the course of the thirteenth, fourteenth and fifteenth centuries various other deeds name members of this family at Wadsley and nearby at Worrall.12 The family also had interests outside Hallamshire. The Hundred Rolls of 1274–75 name Edmund de Wadsley as farmer of the manor of Rotherham (which was held by Rufford Abbey) and in 1307 Sir Robert de Wadsley received a royal grant of a weekly market and an annual fair there. In 1379 John de Wadsley, 'chivaler', headed the list of poll tax payers in Ecclesfield parish and Thomas de Wadsley was taxed in Sheffield parish. In 1452 Edmund de Wadsley was said to hold the manor of Wadsley of the Earl of Shrewsbury at the fourth part of a knight's fee (the same tenure by which the Mounteneys held Shirecliffe). The De Wadsleys were clearly an important family in south Yorkshire for two or three centuries but the male line ended with this Edmund and a William, who held land at Woodsetts, near Grenoside. Before the end of the fifteenth century the manor of Wadsley passed by the marriage of an heiress to Henry Everingham of Stainborough, whose descendants held it until 1557. The manor of Wadsley changed hands frequently in later centuries and all evidence of the medieval arrangements was gradually destroyed. The deer had been removed from the park by 1621, the hall was rebuilt in 1722, and the chapel was replaced by a new church in 1833–34.13

The manors of Bolsterstone and Midhope lay within the Waldershelf quarter of the chapelry of Bradfield, the remotest part of Hallamshire. Their early lords were wealthy knights who failed to

The medieval deer park of the lords of Ecclesall stretched down the hillside from Parkhead to the River Sheaf. In the sixteenth century it was converted into a coppice wood and was managed as such until the First World War.

Bolsterstone Castle. The name is misleading, for this medieval building was not a castle, but the manor house of the lords of the sub-manor of Bolsterstone within Hallamshire.

This medieval chapel-of-ease of the lords of the sub-manor of Midhope within Hallamshire was rebuilt in 1705 by Godfrey Bosville of Gunthwaite, using much of the old material.

establish dynasties. In the thirteenth century Ralph de Sheffield, whose principal residence was at Braithwell, a few miles to the east of Hallamshire, acquired Bolsterstone through his marriage to an heiress, Dionysia. Their elder son, Thomas, inherited Braithwell and their younger son, William, became Lord of Bolsterstone, and later of Midhope and Langsett. The Bolsterstone branch of the family continued with John and his son, Thomas de Sheffield, but then failed in the male line. Thomas' daughter married Sir Robert de Rockley, whose family held the manor of Bolsterstone until it reverted (before 1442) to the lords of Hallamshire.[14] Some walls of the late-medieval manor house at Bolsterstone that is known locally as Bolsterstone Castle remain standing. We lack firm evidence as to whether the building was erected by the Rockleys or by the Talbots, lords of Hallamshire.

The earliest reference to the De Midhope family is to John de Midhope in 1227. In 1243 this John was described as the seneschal (the leading officer) of Hallamshire. Nine years later, his son, Elias de Midhope, held the manor of Langsett (otherwise known as Penisale), just across the northern border of Hallamshire. Elias prospered and enlarged his domains, partly through his marriage to Dionysia, the widow of Sir Ralph de Sheffield. In 1306 James de Midhope granted to John, his son, his estate in Midhope, Over Midhope, Langsett, Swinden and Hordern, but when John de Midhope died between 1327 and 1337 without children the estate passed via his widow to her brother, Sir Thomas de Barnby, who lived at Barnby Hall near Cawthorne.[15] Sir Thomas built a chapel-of-ease at Midhopestones, which he dedicated to St James. This chapel owes much of its present charm to the restoration in 1705 by Godfrey Bosville of Gunthwaite, who had purchased the manor of Midhope in 1690 and whose coat-of-arms is displayed on the porch, together with his initials and those of his wife, Bridget, but the medieval roof truss and much of the original walls survive. The eighteenth-century building is the same shape and size as its fourteenth-century predecessor. Fragments of Sir Thomas de Barnby's hall at Midhope also remain, notably the wooden frame of a window in a building which is now a barn. Hall Farm was once known as the Court House, for this is where meetings of the manor court were held.[16]

Timber-Framed Halls

The visual evidence on the ground is a poor indicator of the past importance of these knightly families. Their residences have been swept away as completely as Sheffield Castle, which was demolished in 1649–50 at the end of the Civil War. Even less is known about the other medieval sub-manor of Hallamshire, at Darnall. Better evidence from the Middle Ages survives further down the social scale. The outstanding building is Housley Hall, Chapeltown. At first sight the house is an eighteenth-century structure with sash windows and a door surround in Georgian style, but the stone cladding masks a timber-framed interior that is undoubtedly medieval. A drawing and plan of 1867 suggests that the original building was L-shaped and that it faced at right angles to the present house. Two stone cross-wings were added in the late sixteenth or early seventeenth century, perhaps when the property passed upon the marriage of an heiress to Gerard Freeman.[17] Many another timber-framed house survives behind later stone cladding in south-west Yorkshire, but Housley Hall is rare in that its roof trusses are supported not by the typical king posts and cruck frames of the district but by a crown-post structure. This type of roofing is superior in its carpentry techniques. We associate crown posts with the magnificent Wealden houses of Kent and with the town houses of York, notably the fourteenth- and fifteenth-century examples in the Shambles. Such carpentry methods were rare in south Yorkshire. The only other examples known to survive are at Castlegate (Tickhill) and Walesker Lane (Woodall), though perhaps Oughtibridge Hall once had one. The surviving crown-post roofs of gentry houses in west Yorkshire have been dated to before 1450.[18] Such buildings are amongst the earliest timber-framed structures in northern England and pre-date houses framed with king-post roofs or with crucks.

Housley Hall has not been dated by the new technique of dendrochronology (or tree-ring dating). If it dates from the late-fourteenth or early-fifteenth century, like its counterparts in York and west Yorkshire, it must have been built for the family which took their name from the place. The Housleys of Housley and their descendants through a female line were here for about five centuries. The first record of the surname is from 1297, when John de Houselay was one of the better-off parishioners who paid the tax known as the lay subsidy.[19] The name had become hereditary by 1320, when Henry, the son of John de Houseley, acquired land nearby. A Richard de Housley witnessed deeds in 1343 and 1348, and in 1359 John, the son of Richard de Houseley, acquired lands in Mortomley. In the poll tax return of 1379 for the parish of Ecclesfield John de Houselay, a beast merchant, paid two shillings tax; another John and a Laurence de Houselay were each taxed at the lowest rate of fourpence They were the only people bearing this surname in south Yorkshire at that time. Housley has remained a very local name. The family farmed land in Chapel, Mortomley and Whitley as tenants of the lords of Hallamshire. In 1415 John Housley, junior, took from the lord's waste a parcel of land at Chapel Green for making a granary there, forty feet in length and forty feet in width, and another parcel of the lord's waste for making a fold. The brothers William de Housley and John de Houseley were named in deeds and court rolls of 1436–41 and in the 1451 Book of Feudal Aids, when John farmed in Chapel and William held property in Chapel, Whitley, Birley and Grenoside. One of these Housleys may have been responsible for building the surviving hall. As beast merchants they would have been able to afford a more substantial house than their neighbours. Stanley Jones, whose views command respect because of his wide knowledge of medieval buildings throughout the country, thinks that a late fourteenth-century date for Housley Hall is not unreasonable.

By a series of complicated transactions, which ended in 1485, the Housley estate was bought by Thomas Rotherham, Archbishop of York and Lord Chancellor of England. The archbishop was born a Scott but he followed the same practice as the monks in taking the name of his birthplace as his surname. He mentioned Housley Hall in his will of 1498, when he left it to his cousin, John Scott, but in 1500 Thomas Housley married Alice Scott and the hall returned to the original family. Thomas Housley of Housley, who died in 1601, was the last of the male line at the hall, which passed to his daughter and heir, Anne, the wife of Gerard Freeman, the first of several generations of this gentry family to live at Housley. The last three were each named Housley Freeman, esquire. The male line of the gentry Housleys died but junior branches preserved the old surname. Numerous Housleys were recorded in the sixteenth-century parish registers of Ecclesfield and Sheffield and many later Housleys appeared in the Cutlers' Company freedom and apprenticeships lists. The Sheffield hearth tax returns of 1672 name Robert and Thomas Howsley, each with a smithy. These cutlers had long ceased to have any connection with the place from where their surname originated, though they lived only a short distance away.

A few years before he bought Housley Hall Archbishop Rotherham had purchased a nearby estate at Barnes, a hamlet which still bears the names of Barnes Hall and Barnes Green. During the thirteenth and fourteenth centuries the family that lived there were known as Barnes. The estate then passed through marriage to the Bromleys, who came from the hamlet of that name two miles away in the township of Wortley. They held it until 1442 when William Bromley sold it to Robert Shatton, who kept it until 1477 when he sold it for £140 to Thomas Rotherham. Upon his death in 1500 the archbishop bequeathed Barnes (and, as we have seen, Housley Hall) to his relative, John Scott, whose ancestors had farmed in the parish of Ecclesfield since the thirteenth century. In 1379 four John Scotts paid poll tax in Ecclesfield parish; one was an arrowsmith, another a tailor. The manor court rolls of 1440–41 record the Scotts at Hartley and Birley and mention William Scott of Rotherham in connection with Ecclesfield.

It was probably Archbishop Rotherham's relations who converted Barnes Hall into one of the leading gentry residences in Ecclesfield parish. Before it was pulled down in 1824 to make way for a new structure the building consisted of an open hall, which was entered through a large Gothic door, and two-storeyed cross wings in a late-medieval style. The line of Scotts that became established at

A rare example in South Yorkshire of the queen-post style of roof trussat Housley Hall. The medieval timber framing is not seen from outside as the hall was clad with stone and re-styled in the eighteenth century.

An old drawing of the late-medieval Barnes Hall, from Eastwood's *Ecclesfield*. It was demolished in 1824 to make way for a new hall.

Barnes Hall were descended from the archbishop's brother. They ended with Sir Richard Scott, who died in Ireland in 1638 while acting on behalf of Sir Thomas Wentworth's Council. His striking alabaster monument is the finest memorial in Ecclesfield church. It was engraved by William Wright of Charing Cross, London, using 'the purest and best white allibaster' and aiming at a true likeness.[20] Sir Richard bequeathed Barnes Hall to his half-brother, Richard Watts, whose descendants held it until 1823, when it was bought by William Smith of Cowley Manor.

Oughtibridge Hall has recently been identified by Stanley Jones as another medieval house that once bore a crown-post roof. The interpretation rests on the evidence of original mortises in the altered roof truss. The building is T-shaped, with an elongated hall and east wing; the west wing was added in the late sixteenth century by a younger branch of the Wilsons of Broomhead Hall. Some of the timbers are exposed externally. Oughtibridge Hall appears to be contemporary with Housley Hall, though it is a little smaller. It stands just inside the ancient parish of Ecclesfield, on a bank east of the river Don. The family that took their surname from this place are recorded locally from 1277 to the later fifteenth century, but as they were assessed at the lowest rate of poll tax in 1379 they cannot have been the builders of the hall. They seem to have moved up the hill to Birley. The poll tax returns name Richard de Leghston, a beast merchant who paid two shillings like John de Houselay, in this part of Ecclesfield parish, close to people with the surnames Birley and Oughtibridge. He, or a descendant, seems a possible candidate for the builder of the hall. His surname was perhaps derived from Laughton-en-

The Scott memorial. The finest monument in Ecclesfield Church is that commemorating Sir Richard Scott of Barnes Hall. Made in 1640, of the 'purest and best' white alabaster, it was brought from London via Hull and Bawtry.

Oughtibridge Hall. The earliest part of this timber-framed building was erected in the same style as Housley Hall. It may have been built for a beast merchant, John de Leghston, or his successor, John, the son of Thomas Scott.

le-Morthen (which is spelt in a similar manner in early forms). The Leghstons were at Ughill in 1295 and 1340, and in 1364 Richard de Leghston joined with Henry de Birley, franklin, to grant land to a Worrall man. In 1388 John, the son of Thomas Scott, was admitted by the manor court to 'all lands in Ecclesfield that had descended to him upon the death of John de Leghston'. The Scotts therefore gradually acquired Housley, Barnes and Oughtibridge and became leading gentry in the parish of Ecclesfield.

The Rise of the Shirecliffes

Several other local families rose in status over the centuries, though in less dramatic ways than the Scotts. It is sometimes difficult to pinpoint the individuals who were responsible for the changes in a family's fortune. Often it was a case of slow advance over the generations. But the descendants of ordinary farming families in the Middle Ages were more often than not the ones who built the gabled halls of Hallamshire in the seventeenth century and who were able to style themselves gentlemen, even if they did not always possess a coat-of-arms.

The Shirecliffes were one of the families that rose from the ranks of the local husbandmen. They took their name from their point of origin in the northern part of the parish of Sheffield but by the 1370s they had moved a short distance across the border into Ecclesfield parish. The first reference to the surname is in 1335 when Nicholas de Shercliffe paid an entry fine to the Lord of Hallamshire to hold a small amount of new land there. As we have seen, Shirecliffe was a sub-manor held by the

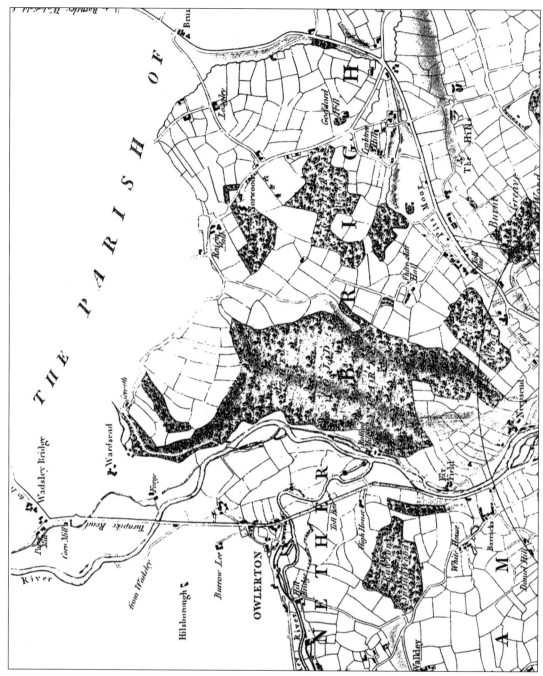

The Shirecliffes or Shirtcliffes were a prolific and successful Hallamshire family who took their name from this small settlement on the hillside north of the River Don.

Mounteneys, who lived at Cowley, but Nicholas de Shirecliffe apparently held land in Shirecliffe that lay outside this manor. As the Mounteneys were absentees, Nicholas may have been the sub-tenant of the manor or perhaps even a younger or an illegitimate son of the Mounteneys. This conjecture might help to explain the family's rise in status during the following century, but the supposed connection is pure speculation. The Shirecliffes (whose name became spelt in a variety of ways, e.g. Shirtcliffe, when they became prolific) soon moved from their place of origin to neighbouring parts of Hallamshire. Four households of De Shirclyf (a John, two Roberts and a Thomas) were taxed in the parish of Ecclesfield in 1379, all at the basic rate of fourpence. In the manor court rolls of 1440–41 William and Henry de Shirclyf were jurors for the soke of Ecclesfield and in 1442 Henry was the rent collector for Southey soke. The rise in the family's fortunes appears to have begun about this time or within the next generation. In 1476 John, the younger son of Henry Sheircliffe, was described as being of 'le Hall' in Ecclesfield, the adaptation of the old priory behind the parish church, which had been confiscated from St Wandrille's Abbey in 1386 as an alien priory and granted to the Carthusian monastery of St Anne, Coventry. Perhaps at that time the Shirecliffes were leasing the Rectory Manor from the monks like John Spencer had done in 1379? After the Reformation they certainly did so and from before 1526 they shared in the profitable venture of collecting the tithes of Ecclesfield parish.[21]

Meanwhile, William's son, Thomas, had become Master of Game in Hallamshire, an important manorial office. The family's improved social status was confirmed when Thomas' son, Alexander, married Isobel Mounteney of Cowley. Roger Dodsworth, the Yorkshire antiquary, noted in 1620 that in the south quire of Ecclesfield church an inscription read: 'Here lyeth Thomas Shercliffe, In Halamshire Master of Game ... Alexander, his son and heire, Lies here hard by, Who languish'd in sorrow By his mistris' cruelty'. The family figure in numerous land transactions at the manor courts of Sheffield, Ecclesfield and Cowley during the later Middle Ages. William's younger son, John, was the head of the line that eventually acquired Whitley Hall, less than a mile away, and by 1482 a branch had been established at Butterthwaite, where they were still resident a century later. By 1510 William Sheircliffe of Ecclesfield Hall was being described as 'gentleman', though a coat-of-arms and a crest were not granted to the family until 1614. The rising status of the Shirecliffes was signalled in 1577, when Nicholas Sheircliffe of Ecclesfield Hall, gentleman, married Barbara Wombwell, the eldest daughter and heiress of a branch of a medieval gentry family who were living at Thundercliffe Grange on the north-eastern border of Hallamshire. During the early seventeenth century Ecclesfield Hall was converted into a modern dwelling, suitable for the leading family in the village. The male line ended later that century. Mr Robert Greene of Thundercliffe Grange married Alice, the heiress of the Shirecliffes and was living at Ecclesfield Hall by 1672.

Meanwhile, Robert Shirecliffe (the second son of Richard) of Ecclesfield, had bought Holehouse, near Whitley, and in 1616 his son, Thomas, had bought the main estate at Whitley from the Parkers, a family of scythe-makers from Norton parish. In 1584 William Parker had built a new Whitley Hall, the first Elizabethan stone residence in Ecclesfield parish. Most of the present building dates from the seventeenth century, however, from the time of the Shirecliffes. It was the finest and most up-to-date gentry residence in the parish and the home of the Shirecliffes until the late eighteenth century. The Shirecliffe memorials in Ecclesfield church date from Thomas Shirecliffe of Whitley Hall (who died in 1628) up to 1789, when the male line of the gentry family at Whitley failed.[22]

Meanwhile, younger branches of the family had moved into Sheffield, where they earned their living as cutlers. Three Shirtcliffes were named in a list of Hallamshire cutlers drawn up in the first few years after the creation of the Cutlers' Company in 1624.[23] In 1672 sixteen householders named Shirtcliffe were taxed in south Yorkshire; Mr Shirtcliffe paid for nine hearths at Whitley Hall, three men were taxed in Sheffield, two in Brightside bierlow, and others were scattered further east at Adwick-le-Street, Arksey, Brearley (2), Brodsworth, Conisbrough, Harthill, Pickburn, Stainton and Ulley. The Nottinghamshire and Derbyshire returns each list just one Shirtcliff household.[24] The family had spread beyond Hallamshire but were still living within twenty miles of their place of origin.

The Steads

The rise of the Steads was as spectacular as that of the Shirecliffes. Their surname has been thought to have two sources in the West Riding, both of them derived from farmsteads. Most bearers of this surname are descended from a family that had settled at Stead on Bolton Priory lands near Burley-in-Wharfedale by the thirteenth century, but the south Yorkshire Steads came from just north of Hallamshire, from Stead Farm on the edge of Hoyland Common and Wentworth. The farm is now approached through a housing estate along Stead Lane. George Redmonds points to circumstantial evidence that the two families might have a common origin, for part of Wentworth lay in the honour of Skipton and was granted to Bolton Priory. The Knights Templar also owned properties at both Steads.[25] In 1379 the poll tax return for Wentworth named John del Stede (smith), John, his son, Richard del Stede, Peter del Stede and Peter del Stede (shoemaker). The surname had already begun to ramify, but the Steads were of low social status compared with that achieved by their descendants.

A marriage settlement of 1386 provides evidence of when and how the Steads moved to Onesacre: John de Stede gave to Joan, the daughter of Peter Atkinson of Chapel, for his life and then to any children they might have, all right in the property which he had inherited after the death of Alice de Stede in Onesacre; Peter del Stede was a witness. This marriage to Joan Atkinson was John de Stede's second wedding, his first having been to Alice Rous, the heiress of the Onesacre estate. In 1402 John del Sted, who (in the words of the court roll) held of the lord half of certain lands and tenements in Onesacre for the term of his life, as of right of Alice Rous, his former wife, paid to the lord 3s 6d yearly and worked at the mill of Bradfield and went to the lord's hunting for three days, and did suit at the lord's court and other services according to the custom of the manor; after his death John del Sted, the son and heir of John and Alice, inherited these freehold lands and tenements. No other local court roll or deed mentions hunting; its inclusion in this instance seems to indicate the rise in status of the Steads through their marriage to the Rous heiress. Rous, meaning red, was a Norman French name. It is likely that the family acquired what had been (according to Domesday Book) the small pre-conquest estate of Onesacre as favoured tenants of the Norman lords of Hallamshire. In 1286 Robert le Rous gave an annual rent from some lands in Onesacre to the Abbey of St Wandrille in Normandy. The Rous family are well-recorded at Onesacre and at nearby Spout House for much of the fourteenth century until the male line failed.

Further evidence of the Steads' move from Wentworth to Onesacre comes from an agreement of 1409 between John de Steyd of Wentworth and Joan, formerly the wife of Peter de Steyd of Onesacre, whereby John was to have the part of the buildings, orchards and gardens, which were formerly held by Robert Rous in Onesacre, situated on the north side of the road from Wigtwizzle to Oughtibridge, and Joan had the part, with the buildings, orchards and gardens, that lay on the south side; William de Steyd acted as witness. In 1419 Joan, formerly the widow of of John de Stede of Wentworth, granted to Richard de Stede, her son, all her property in Onesacre, which John de Stede, her husband, had inherited after the death of Alice de Stede, his mother.

The move was a momentous one for the Steads. The Onesacre estate descended within the family over the next four hundred years. A direct line can be traced from the late fifteenth century when Thomas Stede was succeeded by John, who in turn was followed by three Nicholases, Thomas, Nicholas and four more Thomases. The family gradually acquired considerable property in the neighbourhood and in the middle years of the seventeenth century Nicholas Stead (1583–1639) and his son, Thomas (1619–86), built the imposing gabled and mullioned Onesacre Hall, which dominates the hamlet. According to John Wilson, the eighteenth-century antiquary of Broomhead Hall, the master mason who built Onesacre Hall and Spout House was John Hawley of Thorn House, with his son and namesake.[26]

'Mr Stead' was taxed on six hearths at Onesacre in 1672. Three other Steads were living in Bradfield, Stannington and Wortley, but the five others living further east in south Yorkshire had long lost any family connection they might once have had. The Steads had not spread into Derbyshire or even into

Onesacre Hall. Nicholas Stead and his son, Thomas, built this fine, gabled hall in the middle years of the seventeenth century, nearly three hundred years after their ancestors had acquired the property through marriage.

Sheffield. Part of their increased wealth came from marriages to heiresses, notably in 1696 when Elizabeth Creswick married Thomas Stead of Onesacre, gentleman (1672–1739) and added Burrow Lee and Hillsborough to the family's possessions. Their grandson, Thomas Stead (1728–93) married Millicent, the daughter of Strelley Pegge of Beauchief Hall, in 1768 and built Hillsborough House in Georgian style and surrounded it with a park. At his death, the Stead estate covered nearly 2,000 acres, with sixteen properties in Onesacre, Worrall, Stannington, Bentyhough, Moor Hall, Holdworth, Bradfield, Loxley, Oughtibridge, Wadsley, Ingbirchworth and Sheffield. When his widow, Millicent, and their eldest son, Thomas, sold the estate in 1794, a party to the sale was Sir John Rous, baronet, of Dennington (Suffolk). The two families must have preserved a connection over the four centuries since the marriage of Alice Rous to Peter de Stead or have become aware of it through an interest in genealogy. No other links between the two families are recorded in the numerous documents that survive concerning the Steads. We must draw the surprising conclusion that Sir John Rous was brought in to give his blessing to the severing of the family's ancient connection with Onesacre. Another son of Thomas and Millicent, Benjamin Broughton Stead of Beauchief Hall, changed his name in 1836 to Pegge Burnell, having inherited the Beauchief estate of his uncle, Peter Pegge Burnell.[27] The Steads had risen from modest status in the Middle Ages to the leading ranks of local society, but had finally abandoned their ancient surname.

The Brights and the Wilsons

A few other long-established farming families – the Brights, Wilsons, Greaveses, Moorwoods, Marriotts and Parkins – also rose to the ranks of the gentry in the post-medieval period. Their advance up the social scale could not have been predicted in the Middle Ages when they were little different from their neighbours.

Bright is a nickname derived from an Old English word meaning 'bright, beautiful, fair'.[28] The local Brights were living in Hallamshire in the early fourteenth century, though they were not recorded there in the poll tax returns of 1379. John Bright was at Whirlow Hall by 1410, from where he farmed lands at Whirlow and Fulwood. He was succeeded there by eight generations of direct descendants, mostly yeoman farmers, who in the Elizabethan period became lead smelters and traders and were thus able to acquire sufficient wealth to extend their estate. At that time the Derbyshire lead field was the most important in Europe and rich profits could be made by smelters and merchants. Many of the seventeenth-century halls of north Derbyshire were built out of profits from the lead industry. In or about 1619 the Brights built a new stone hall at Whirlow, with a central block, projecting gabled wings and large mullioned windows. The hall remained with the family until about 1720, when Henry Bright, who had a notorious reputation as an extravagant liver, had to sell the estate to avoid bankruptcy. It was replaced by a more modest hall in 1843.

Meanwhile, in the early seventeenth century Thomas Bright, a younger son of John Bright of Whirlow, moved across the parish of Sheffield to the timber-framed Carbrook Hall. There in 1623 his son, Stephen (1583–1642), who had prospered as a lead merchant and as bailiff of Hallamshire, added a stone parlour block. Stephen was able to afford craftsmen who had worked for the Earl of Shrewsbury and the Cavendishes and who were masters of the new designs, using strapwork patterns and naturalistic foliage. They provided plaster ceilings, wooden panelling and a carved oak fireplace which still adorn the surviving wing in what is now a pub. His hall was the finest and most up-to-date residence in Hallamshire. He became Lord of Ecclesall in 1638 and acquired a coat-of-arms just before his death. His son, John Bright, was the leading figure in Sheffield parish during the Civil War, a prominent puritan and a colonel in the Parliamentary army. Upon the Restoration John was made a baronet and moved well north of Hallamshire to Badsworth Hall. His grandson, John, inherited his Hallamshire estates, including the lordship of Ecclesall, which eventually passed to this younger John's daughter, Mary, the wife of Charles Watson-Wentworth, second Marquis of Rockingham, of Wentworth Woodhouse, the leader of the Whig Party and briefly Prime Minister. The Brights had advanced far up the social scale.[29]

In the meantime, John, the younger brother of Henry of Whirlow and Thomas of Carbrook, had purchased Banner Cross, Ecclesall, where he was followed by three generations of direct descendants, and Thomas Bright, a younger son of the Whirlow branch in the next generation, had moved to Greystones, where he was succeeded by his son and grandson. The Brights had become a prolific gentry family in four different parts of the parish of Sheffield. By the end of the eighteenth century, however, all the gentry lines had disappeared. The surname was perpetuated by junior members of the family who had moved into Sheffield and Rotherham; for example, three Brights were named in the earliest records of the Cutlers' Company. Their standard of living was much lower than that of their prosperous namesakes.

In contrast, the Wilsons of Broomhead are still a well-known local family. They were farmers on the same scale as most of their neighbours until the reign of Elizabeth, when their fortunes began to rise. Their descent has been traced from William, the father of John de Hunshelf or de Waldershelf (born *c.*1320), but this is not the William from whom the surname was derived. The name did not become hereditary until two generations later, when the Wilsons were settled at Broomhead. They were first recorded with their surname in the 1379 poll tax return for the chapelry of Bradfield, when John Weleson paid fourpence tax. In 1398 John Wilson de Bromhead was referred to as John, the son of William, the son of John de Waldershelf. Thirty years later, another deed named 'John Willeson of

Carbrook Hall. In 1623 Stephen Bright, bailiff of Hallamshire and a prosperous lead merchant, built the stone range alongside the old timber-framed hall. At the time, the Brights were the leading gentry family in Hallamshire.

Bromehede the elder'. Christopher Wilson, who inherited the farm at Broomhead about 1454 and who lived until 1492, was the first to bear a Christian name which became very common in the family. He married Ellen Leigh of Padley, the first marriage by a Wilson to someone outside the near neighbourhood of Broomhead. Christopher's son, John, held land in Derwentdale, in the manor of Hathersage, on the western side of Broomhead Moor, which he left to his younger son, Arthur, a member of the Earl of Shrewsbury's household. In 1536 the Broomhead estate passed to thirteen-year old Christopher, the son of Arthur's deceased elder brother. Later, Christopher's brother, Thomas, moved to Oughtibridge Hall, where his descendants continued for a few generations. He may have been the builder of the timber-framed west wing, which still survives. The Wilsons of Broomhead and Oughtibridge were both prominent in the struggle against the Wortley family's extension of their hunting chase on Wharncliffe, just up the hill from Oughtibridge, an act of aggression which was satirised in the scurrilous ballad, *The Dragon of Wantley* (see chapter 9).

In the late sixteenth century the Wilsons were still ranked as yeomen but Christopher Wilson's eldest son, Christopher, prospered as a member of Sir Thomas Wentworth's household at Wentworth Woodhouse and was styled gentleman. Thomas Wentworth's rise in fortune came shortly after the death of Gilbert Talbot, the last Earl of Shrewsbury to be resident in Sheffield. The young men of the neighbourhood were fortunate to have this new opportunity for social advancement. In 1640 Christopher Wilson built Broomhead Hall, a substantial stone structure which was pulled down and rebuilt in 1831. This hall, at the very edge of the moors, had several features that were fashionable at the time, both in planning and ornament. Christopher's great-grandson was John Wilson of Broomhead Hall, a noted antiquary. The family continued at Broomhead until the death of Henry Wilson in 1819, when the estate passed to his nephew, James Rimington, esquire. James' descendants, the Rimington-Wilsons, lived there well into the twentieth century.[30]

Other Gentry Families

Another fine seventeenth-century hall in the chapelry of Bradfield is tucked away at Hallfield, just below the road across the Strines. It was built by the Greaves family, who are another example of a family that rose from modest beginnings. Numerous groves of brushwood or thicket in various parts of the country gave rise to the common surname Greaves, but some of the local Greaveses have been in Hallamshire since the Middle Ages. In 1379 Robert Grayff paid poll tax in the parish of Ecclesfield, in 1417 John Greve succeeded his father, William, in a share of a farm at Westmondhalgh, and in 1427 he inherited a farm at Holdworth. Later manor court rolls mention property at Hawkesworth, Fulwood and Ughill that belonged to the Greaves family. In 1439 Agnes de Greve surrendered a farm at Hawkesworth to John Greves, junior. This was probably the farm known as Hallfield, which the Greaves family continued to hold as tenants of the lords of Hallamshire for several generations. Other branches farmed at Sheephouse and elsewhere within the parish of Penistone and at Wincobank.

Ralph Greaves, who died in 1565, was succeeded at Hallfield by his son, John Greaves, yeoman, and then by his grandson, another John Greaves, who was described as yeoman in 1623 but as gentleman upon his death in 1631. The basis of his prosperity is not known. The farm at Hallfield consisted of forty acres of land, twenty acres of meadow and twenty acres of pasture, with common rights on the adjacent moors. John also leased a farm nearby at Woodhouse and others at Wincobank, High Burton and Hunshelf. His elder son, Thomas, had no children, so the estate passed to his younger son, Nicholas, and in turn to Nicholas' son, John. Either Nicholas or John was responsible for building the tall gabled hall that shares some similarities of style with the contemporary Onesacre Hall of the Steads. This new house was in effect a large wing added to the old hall block, which was converted into a kitchen. 'Mr Greaves' was taxed on six hearths here in 1672. The inventory of personal estate that was made upon the death of John Greaves in 1692 depicts Hallfield simply as a superior farmhouse. Most of his wealth was invested in his livestock, especially his 337 sheep.[31]

The Moorwoods, neighbours of the Greaveses, rose from relatively humble beginnings in the thirteenth century to gentry status four hundred years later. Their surname is derived from a farmhouse to the west of Stannington and to the south of Dungworth, overlooking Rivelin Chase. Thomas de Morewood was a witness to a Sheffield deed dated before 1270 and in 1295 Andrew and Thomas de Morewood were witnesses to a deed at Ughill, close to Moorwood. In 1316 Jordan and Robert del Morwode were witnesses at Moorwood and in 1340 John del Morewode was a witness at Ughill. The Moorwoods were not rich enough to be taxed for the 1297 lay subsidy but during the fourteenth century the family's fortunes improved considerably. In 1379 John de Morewod, marshal, paid a shilling, one of the highest rates in the chapelry of Bradfield, and Agnes de Morewod, William de Morewod (chapelry of Bradfield) and John de Morewod (parish of Ecclesfield) each paid the basic rate of fourpence. A marshal was a man who tended horses, a combination of a farrier and an early veterinary surgeon. William de Morwod was described in 1383 and 1406 as 'of Westmondhalgh' and in 1416 as 'of Fayrhirst'. He held land in Dwarriden and Wigtwizzle and in 1411 a John de Moorwood held land in Holdworth Bank. The descent from these early Moorwoods is not clear but the main line became established at the Oaks (known later as Oaks Farm) in the Loxley Valley, two miles north of their ancestral home. The manor court rolls of 1440-41 name Thomas, William and (at the Oaks) John de Morewode. The Moorwoods continued at the Oaks (which is now on the south bank of Damflask reservoir) for over three centuries. In 1507 another John Morewood surrendered property in Dungworth and Bradfield to Rowland Morewood, who in 1548 passed these properties on to John Moorwood, perhaps the John who was at the Oaks in 1539. This John's son, Rowland Moorwood of the Oaks (died 1619), was the first to be described as gentleman. The heralds included him in their list of gentry at their visitation in 1584.

The rise of the Moorwoods to a leading position amongst the gentry of north Derbyshire and south-west Yorkshire during the seventeenth century came about through their success in trade. It is not known whether Rowland acquired wealth in the same way that his adventurous descendants were

Hallfield House. The Greaves family rose from modest status in medieval Hallamshire to gentry in the seventeenth century. Either Nicholas Greaves or his son, John, built this hall in similar style to that at Onesacre.

The Moorwoods were Hallamshire farmers who rose to gentry status through their success in trade during the seventeenth century. Andrew Moorwood built The Hallowes in 1657 in the parish of Dronfield.

to make their fortunes but he was prosperous enough to marry Catherine Stafford, the daughter of an Eyam gentleman, by whom he had four sons; John, the eldest, inherited the Oaks, Rowland moved to Castleton, Gilbert became a London merchant, and Anthony moved first to Hemsworth, in the parish of Norton, and then in 1629 to a large estate at Alfreton. Anthony had twin sons, Rowland (who died unmarried) and Anthony of Hazlebarrow (Norton) and Alfreton. This younger Anthony was Sheriff of Derbyshire in 1649, two years before he died without male heirs. His uncle, John (who died at the Oaks in 1647), had nine sons and seven daughters. Three of the sons moved to London, one settled in Selby, another was killed in Barbados, one died as an infant, Andrew married a daughter of William Spencer of Attercliffe, gentleman, and in 1657 built The Hallowes, the gabled hall that is now a golf club in Dronfield, and Gilbert became a lead merchant in Dronfield. The eldest son, Rowland Moorwood of the Oaks and Norton (1613–58) married Mary, the daughter of Leonard Gill of Norton, gentleman, and had three sons to succeed him. The south Yorkshire hearth tax returns of 1672 name only Mr [Samuel] Moorewood with five hearths at the Oaks, but ten Moorwoods were recorded in Derbyshire, including Mr John Moorwood, who paid tax on twelve hearths at Norton, and Mr Anthony Morewood, who paid on ten hearths at Hallowes. Alfreton Hall (sixteen hearths) had passed through the marriage of Anthony Moorwood's eldest daughter, Anne, to Alexander Stanhope, esquire, son of the Earl of Chesterfield. Rowland Moorwood's sons carried the line on into the eighteenth century. Joseph, the youngest, lived at Hemsworth; Samuel, the second son, lived at the Oaks, where he was succeeded by his son, John (1689–1771), who sold the Oaks upon moving to London; and John, the eldest son (1642–80), was granted a coat-of-arms in 1671 and inherited the estate at Alfreton. He served as Sheriff of Derbyshire, as did his son Rowland, and his grandson, George, but when George died in 1792 all the male lines that descended from his grandfather became extinct. The family's story over the previous two centuries had been a remarkable one.[32]

One more family in this part of Hallamshire is worthy of note. The name Marriott, which was a pet form of Mary, has multiple origins. The local Marriotts settled at Ughill, high on the hills in the chapelry of Bradfield, where they eventually rose from modest status to the ranks of the minor gentry. In 1379 John Mariot (chapelry of Bradfield) and Thomas and Richard Mariot (Handsworth) each paid the lowest rate of poll tax. The name does not appear again in local records until 1440–41, when John and William (soke of Sheffield), and Agnes and William (soke of Handsworth) were recorded in the manor court rolls. In 1442 John Dungworth of Carbrook surrendered a farm which he held in the low-lying part of Ughill, to John Marriott, senior, of Onesacre. This seems to have been the occasion when the Marriotts moved to Ughill. In 1468, 1477, 1500, 1546, 1590 and 1621 the farm passed to successive generations of John Marriotts. Other branches of the family farmed in Bradfield and Ecclesfield.

The Marriotts do not appear in the early records of the Cutlers' Company, though at least two were Sheffield filesmiths in the second half of the seventeenth century. In the 1672 hearth tax returns for south Yorkshire Marriotts were recorded at Bradfield, Dungworth (2), Handsworth, Sheffield (2), Stannington (2), Upper Hallam (2), and further east at Adwick-upon-Dearne, Hickleton, Hooton Pagnell, Ravenfield and Rawmarsh. They may not all have been connected. Thomas Marriott, who was taxed on six hearths in Sheffield in 1672, was a church burgess and therefore a man of some importance in the parish. His nephew, Thomas Marriott (1679–1754), the son of a Sheffield filesmith and himself a filesmith until his uncle died, inherited Ughill, where he was styled Mr Marriott of Ughill Hall. In 1743 he built the substantial Dissenting chapel at Underbank, Stannington, and bequeathed the fifty-seven acres of Spout House farm for the use of a minister. He was succeeded by his brother, Benjamin, but the male line then failed. The Marriotts had been at Ughill for over three hundred years.[33]

The remaining Hallamshire family that rose from the ranks of the ordinary farmers to gentry status were the Parkins of Mortomley. Parkin is a pet form of Peter. The surname has multiple origins but is found particularly in the north of England. No Parkins were recorded in 1379 poll tax returns for Hallamshire. They first appear in local records in 1416, when Joan Parkin was a witness to a deed at

Thomas Marriott of Ughill Hall built this distinguished dissenting chapel at Underbank, Stannington, in 1743. It is still used by a Unitarian congregation.

Wigtwizzle, and soon afterwards they acquired a foothold in the northern part of Ecclesfield parish. The Richard Parkin and John Parkin who were recorded at Mortomley in the Hallamshire manorial court rolls in 1440 were named in the 1451 Book of Feudal Aids; Robert Parkin held a farm with thirty acres of land in Mortomley, two acres nearby in Chapel and a farm in Staniforth, and John Parkin held another small farm in Mortomley. A direct line can be traced through the sixteenth and seventeenth centuries from Robert to Peter, John, Thomas, Zachariah and John, who built Mortomley Hall on the site of an earlier house in 1703. The building of the hall signalled the completion of the rise of the senior branch of the Parkins to parish gentry status. The Parkin name ceased to be attached to Mortomley when John's granddaughter, Catherine, married John Jeffcock of Cowley Hall, esquire.

Meanwhile, the Staniforth farm had passed to Richard Parkin, then in 1475 to his younger son, John, in 1500 to John's son and namesake, in 1539 to Nicholas Parkin, the brother and next heir of John, and in 1541 to Nicholas' young son and heir, another John. The Parkins were still there as cutler-farmers in the seventeenth century. Another branch of the family moved to Wadsley, where in 1531 John Parkin, senior, rented a water wheel called the South Wheel, in Wisewood. The Parkins were much involved in the cutlery trades. The 1614–15 list of Hallamshire cutlers included John Parkin of Wadsley and John Parkin of Southey (both of whom were members of the first jury), and George, John and Thomas Parkin. The hearth tax returns of 1672 recorded ten households of Parkins in Ecclesfield parish: John Parkin of Hazelshaw (4 hearths), Richard (1 and a smithy), Widow Parkin of Brook (1), Widow Parkin of Green (1), Thomas (2 and a smithy), John (5), Widow Parkin of Lane End (1) and Thomas (1), all in Grenofirth quarter in the northern part of the parish, and George

Parkins (2) and John Parkins (1) in Southey quarter. They were not then resident in other parts of Hallamshire, but by the early eighteenth century Thomas Parkin had established one of the two earliest steelmaking businesses in Sheffield. His granddaughter, Elizabeth Parkin, inherited his estate and became the wealthy owner of Ravenfield Park, a country estate some ten miles to the east of Sheffield. The fortunes of the eighteenth-century Parkins bore little resemblance to those of their medieval predecessors.[34]

By the middle of the seventeenth century a new breed of gentry families that had long been resident in Hallamshire as husbandmen or yeomen had become the leaders of local society.[35] The Dukes of Norfolk were absentee landlords, their castle had been demolished, and within two generations the Manor Lodge would be dismantled too. The Mounteneys, the last of the medieval knightly families, had almost come to the end of the line, and little remained of the old manor houses. Handsome stone halls with mullioned windows and fashionable gables had taken their place. They were the proud symbols of a new group of wealthy families. In time these families too would lose their dominance, just as the Mounteneys, Ecclesalls, Wadsleys, Midhopes and Sheffields had, but unlike the medieval knights some of the new gentry have left strong visual reminders of their presence.

The earliest written record that we have of Hallamshire is the entry in the Domesday Book of 1086.[1] This is a baffling record that confuses rather than enlightens us, but it does prove that permanent settlement had reached the very edge of the local moors by the eleventh century and possibly long before. Because it was concerned with tenure, and therefore with estates rather than actual places, Domesday Book does not record all the minor settlements that were in existence by the time of the Norman Conquest, but it does name Holdworth, Onesacre, Ughill, Wadsley and Worrall. If families had settled in such places as these, high on the hills and close to the moors, others had no doubt chosen more favourable sites in the sheltered valleys. But Domesday Book is the only record that we possess for the eleventh century and very few documents survive from the twelfth. Most of our local farmsteads and hamlets are not named in deeds or manor court rolls until the thirteenth century or later. By then, some of them might have been hundreds of years old. Judging by later experience, a few of these minor settlements might also have changed their names even before local records began.

Changing Place-Names

The modern names of our farms and hamlets are not much help when it comes to dating settlements with any degree of precision. Many of them end in -ley ('woodland clearing') or -thorpe ('outlying farmstead'), words which were formed by the Anglo-Saxons and Vikings but which passed into common speech and continued in use after the Norman Conquest. These names could have been fixed at any time between the ninth and twelfth centuries. We have to go back to the earliest recorded spellings of names to get a sense of their meaning, for they have often changed over the centuries. Sometimes the change is a minor matter, such as the development of Greno into Grenoside, Winco and Winkley into Wincobank, and Orepittes into Pitsmoor, but other changes are less obvious. The most spectacular change in Hallamshire was from Brekesherth to Brightside. The earliest recorded spelling of the place was Brichesherd in the 1170s but the name was written in numerous ways before it changed to Brightside during the sixteenth century, for it was difficult to pronounce and spell.[2] It is far from clear what the name means, but the first element may be an Old English personal name and the second seems to denote a smith's hearth. The change to Brightside appears to have been an attempt to make sense of an old name whose meaning was no longer apparent. In 1587 the place was described as Brixharth alias Brightsyde. The modern form of the name gradually became accepted and during the seventeenth century the old one disappeared. The surname which had been derived from the place-name went earlier. The first person of this name to be recorded in surviving documents was Adam de Brikesherd, who witnessed a deed at Barnes in 1267.[3] The surname was written in a variety of ways before it fell out of use in the mid-fifteenth century. It never took the form of Brightside.

This example alerts us to the fact that names might have changed dramatically over the centuries and that when we speak of 'lost place-names' we may be looking for places which still exist under other names. We shall find that this was quite a common process. Unlike some other parts of the country, in Hallamshire it is rare to find a settlement, as distinct from a place-name, which has

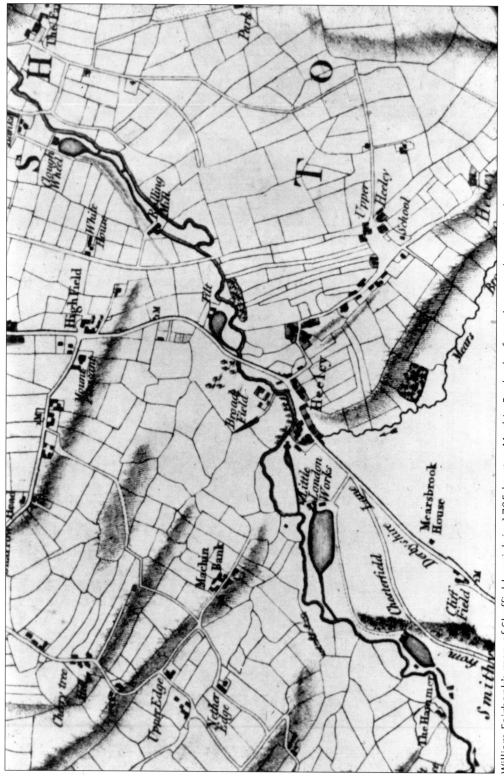

William Fairbank's map of Sheffield parish in 1795 locates Machin Bank, the farm that was known in the Middle Ages as Hauselin Bank after a family that came from Normandy.

disappeared from the map completely, though it is of course possible that the sites of abandoned farms were re-occupied after a long gap in time.

A clear example of a name change is provided by a farm near Sharrow Vale and Nether Edge which acquired the name of Hauselin Bank from a Norman family who were the principal tenants of the lords of the sub-manor of Ecclesall. The Hauselins and their lords were benefactors to nearby Beauchief Abbey. Hauselin has the literal meaning of 'householder', i.e. the owner of a house that was smaller than a manor house. The surname is still in use in parts of France.[4] The last known member of the local family to live in Hallamshire was John Hauslyne, who was recorded in or near Ecclesfield in 1440. Soon afterwards the Hauselins moved a little further north to Harley Hall, near Wentworth; Robert Hauslyn was described as 'of Wentworth' in 1477. After 1567, when Thomas Hauslin sold Harley to Thomas Wentworth, nothing more is heard of the family.[5] By 1613, Hauselin Bank, their original home in the manor of Ecclesall, had taken the name of the new owners and had become Machon Bank. It was marked as such on William Fairbank's map of the parish of Sheffield (1795). The name Machon Bank survives as a street name.

A good illustration of the process whereby a place-name changed under new owners is provided by the lost place-name Raynaldthorpe, which appears in numerous local deeds and manorial records during the thirteenth and fourteenth centuries in the parish of Ecclesfield. The name described the 'outlying farmstead' of a man with a Viking personal name.[6] Raynaldthorpe was a large farm of 220 acres that stretched up the hill from Hartley Brook to beyond Hatfield House Lane and Sheffield Lane Top. A stretch of common land known as Shiregreen separated Raynaldthorpe from Woolley Grange, the other large farm in that district and a possession of the Benedictine monks who were based at Ecclesfield Priory. In the Middle Ages part of the farm at Raynaldthorpe was reserved as a small park and some of the land was granted to the Knights Hospitallers of St John of Jerusalem.[7] By the mid-sixteenth century Nicholas Hatfield was in residence there. His family came from Hadfield, near Glossop, but the surname had softened to Hatfield. Nicholas was the first of three generations of Hatfields to live at Raynaldthorpe before the family moved twelve miles east to Laughton-en-le-Morthen, where they became prominent puritan gentry. Their timber-framed house at Raynaldthorpe survives in part; the central block has gone but the two cross-wings have been turned into separate dwellings.[8] During the time of the Hatfields the old name of the farm was dropped in favour of the family name. John Harrison's survey of the manor of Sheffield (1637) described it as 'Renalthorp Hall alias Hadfield Farme'.[9] In time, it became known as Hatfield House. The busy road that passes it bears the name of Hatfield House Lane.

Three other 'outlying farmsteads' that were distinguished by Viking personal names form a cluster a mile or two south of Raynaldthorpe. Grimesthorpe remains a well-known place-name on the northern bank of the river Don, but nearby Grimeshou has long since gone. Grimeshou was a small manor that was mentioned in Domesday Book. It took its name from the burial mound of the person called Grim whose name was attached to the 'outlying farmstead' that grew into a hamlet and which in the nineteenth century was engulfed by terraced houses alongside the new steelworks.[10] Osgathorpe and Skinnerthorpe are less well-known. A John de Schinarthorp was taxed in 1297,[11] but the surname did not survive and the place-name is commemorated only by Skinnerthorpe Road in Fir Vale. Osgathorpe is still a local surname, which was first recorded in 1267 when Roger de Osgathorpe witnessed a deed at Grenoside. (Some other Osgathorpes may have taken their name from Osgathorpe in Leicestershire.) The place-name survives as Osgathorpe Road, Pitsmoor, but the Cutlers' Company apprenticeship and freemen records[12] show that the name of the adjacent hamlet of Osgathorpe Hills had been shortened to The Hills by the seventeenth century. The only other 'outlying farmstead' in Hallamshire to be distinguished by the suffix -thorpe was Hoperthorpe in north-west Sheffield. The first element of this place-name was a Middle English surname derived from the occupation of cooper. Hoperthorpe became Upperthorpe and a later, lower settlement then took the name of Netherthorpe.[13] This new name is now one of the best known local place-names that end in -thorpe, though it is of much later origin than the medieval 'outlying farmsteads'.

Surnames from Ecclesfield Parish

A farm that once lay close to Raynaldthorpe but which has long since been destroyed by modern development provides another striking example of a 'lost place-name' which was replaced by another name. Staniforth is one of the most distinctive surnames in Hallamshire, a name which was coined locally and which is still concentrated in this district. The Staniforths come from a farm whose name meant 'the stony ford'.[14] The surname had been created by 1239, when a Robert de Stanford was named in a local document. In 1297 Matilda de Staniforthe was a taxpayer in the parish of Ecclesfield. The link between the surname and the place-name is proved by a deed of 1433 whereby John de

The hamlet of Creswick to the south-west of Ecclesfield village was the source of another prolific Hallamshire surname. Between 1630 and 1667 six Creswicks served as master of the Company of Cutlers in Hallamshire.

Staniforth is one of Sheffield's most distinctive surnames comes from 'the stony ford' at Low Wincobank. The surname had become hereditary by 1433, when the farm at Stanyford passed from John de Stannyford to his son, Richard de Stannyford.

Stannyford surrendered a farm in Stanyford to Richard de Stannyford, his son and heir. It is clear from deeds and manorial records that the stony ford was near Wincobank, just within the southern border of the parish of Ecclesfield. The ford crossed either the Blackburn Brook or the stream in the steep gully which descends to that brook. The exact position of the farm can be deduced from deeds and maps belonging to the Greaves family which form part of the Wheat collection at Sheffield Archives.[15] A map drawn by John Greaves in 1692 can be compared with the six-inch Ordnance Survey map of 1850 to prove that his farm was known in the mid-nineteenth century as Nether Wincobank. Nether and Low are interchangeable and the district is now known as Low Wincobank. The farm was close to the present church dedicated to St Thomas. The 1692 survey measured it at $27\frac{1}{4}$ acres, with a springwood of seven acres. The Greaves family became owners of this property in the seventeenth century. The earliest deeds in their possession (dating from 1523) show that what became known as Low Wincobank was originally called Staniforth. The early references to 'Staneford next Wyncobank' gradually give way to 'Winkoebanke'. The 1692 map and survey is labelled 'A Plot of Sertaine Lands, at Wincobanke, belonging to John Greaves'. The Greaves family came from Sheephouse (Penistone) and Hallfield (Bradfield Dale), and so perhaps were less concerned than the original inhabitants to preserve the old name. People bearing the surname Staniforth had by this time moved into Sheffield, Darnall and other parts of Hallamshire. Staniforth Road in Darnall is named after the family who built Darnall Hall in the seventeenth century but it does not indicate the whereabouts of the 'lost' place-name; the original 'stony ford' was two miles to the north.

Creswick is another distinctive local surname which was derived from a minor place-name in the parish of Ecclesfield. The hamlet lay just south-west of Ecclesfield village on a site now covered by modern housing, approached by Creswick Lane. It is marked on Thomas Jeffreys's map of Yorkshire (1772). Although the family must have taken their name from the place, no record connects them to it. They had left by the late thirteenth century, when Adam de Creswick took a lease of lands three miles to the west in Onesacre. In the sixteenth century they spread both in the town of Sheffield and in rural parts of Hallamshire. All the twenty-two Creswick households who were recorded in the hearth tax returns of 1672 for south Yorkshire[16] lived in Hallamshire. The place-name was obscure but the family were well-known locally. Six Creswicks served as Master Cutler between 1630 and 1667.

Crossley is a common place-name, meaning the clearing by the cross. The surname has been derived from various crosses in Yorkshire and perhaps elsewhere in England. The local Crossleys, however, took their name from the particular cross which gave rise to the place-name Burnt Cross, near Chapeltown. The first element of the place-name has nothing to do with burning but is probably derived from the same personal name as that in Barnes Green and Barnes Hall, nearby.[17] The connection between the surname and the place-name was made clear in 1323, when Richard, the son of Peter de Crosley, was admitted to a farm at Crossleys. The family remained there until at least 1565 and

J.R. Joɒɒms

The meaning of the place-name Whitley is contentious. The hall that William Parker built in 1584 was one of the first to be built in stone in South Yorkshire. It was greatly extended by the Shirecliffe family during the seventeenth century.

probably longer. No-one now speaks of Crossley as a local place-name, but Burnt Cross is well-known in its modern form of Burncross.

Whitley Hall lies about a mile to the south of Burnt Cross. The English Place-Name Society's first volume for the West Riding explains the name, which was first recorded in 1366, as 'bright forest clearing', but as the place was often recorded as Whaley the first element may have a different derivation. It is not clear which of the two forms is the earliest. The place-name volume also notes the lost name Launderhouse, first mentioned in 1407, and offers the explanation that it comes from the Middle English word, *lander*, meaning a launderer, possibly used as a surname. The place can be identified with confidence, for a document of 1587 speaks of 'Launderhouse alias Whitley Hall'. The old house had just been rebuilt as a gentry residence by William Parker and the name had been changed. The offered explanation of the name is incorrect, however. An earlier document of 1579 refers to 'Launderhouse sometyme Loundhouse nowe Whitley'. The earlier form, Loundhouse, is explained by a transfer in 1528 of a farm and four crofts in Whaley that had once been held by John Lound, and the inheritance in 1531 of 'a parcel of cultivated land in Whitley Carre called Loundhouse'.[18] It is clear that Launderhouse was a corruption of Loundhouse, which in turn came from the surname Lound. This surname was derived from a nearby hill formerly called The Lound, which is now known as Loundside.

Surnames from Lost Place-Names

Some place-names which have given rise to surnames are difficult to pinpoint. Have these places really disappeared from the landscape or have they been replaced by a different name? Hawley illustrates the problem. Both the place-name and the surname are found in different parts of the country, but the local surname is derived from a lost place-name which can be placed somewhere in the northern part of Sheffield parish, in the Shirecliffe – Norwood – Pitsmoor area. The English Place-Name Society note *Houlay juxta Schefeld* in 1385[19] and give the meaning as 'clearing near the [prehistoric burial] mound'. Although the Hawleys were never described as being 'of Hawley' in surviving records, they were settled there or close by in 1376. Not long afterwards, they moved to Fulwood, where they remained for several generations. Hollow Meadows, high in the Rivelin Valley, was known as Auley meadows in 1637, probably because of this family.[20] The examples of other changes of place-name upon the arrival of a new family (such as the Hatfields or the Machons) raises the possibility that Hawley has been replaced by a later name. Raisen Hall and Crabtree House are candidates in the appropriate district, for both took their names from families and both were first recorded in the seventeenth century. No evidence has been found to verify or disprove this speculation, however.

Ashurst is not only a lost place-name in the western half of the parish of Sheffield, but the source of a local surname which did not survive beyond the Middle Ages. Present-day Ashursts come from another place, near Wigan, known as Ashurst Beacon. The English Place-Name Society's volume notes *le Ashehurst*, in Ecclesall or Hallam (the rural western townships of Sheffield parish), with references dating from 1246 to 1593.[21] The earliest spelling is in the Old Norse form of Askehurst, meaning a small ash wood. The surname which was derived from this place was recorded between 1347 and 1441. So far, all attempts to identify this particular wood have proved elusive.

Morton is another minor place-name which has not been identified, though its general location is known. It too produced a local surname, which in this case ramified greatly. As the family were in the Westmondhalgh township in the chapelry of Bradfield in the fourteenth century the settlement is likely to have been on the moorland edge in that part of Hallamshire, between Ewden Beck and Bradfield. Westmondhalgh means 'Westmund's nook of land'.[22] It was probably a district name like Ecclesall rather than the name of a small settlement and it was often shortened to Westnall. No clues as to the precise whereabouts of Morton within the township of Westmondhalgh seem to survive. Morton is, of course, a common surname with many different origins, but the Hallamshire Mortons came from the edge of the Bradfield moors.

The lost place-name Moldicliff was once to be found in the same area. A likely meaning of the name is 'the cliff covered with earth'.[23] As Adam de Moldecliff was named in fourteenth-century deeds concerning nearby Broomhead and Dwarriden, and all other early references to the family were from the chapelry of Bradfield, it is likely that Moldicliff was the name given to the dramatic landslip that descends northwards from Bar Dike. This landscape feature is now named Canyard Hills, after the farm called Canyards, which was first recorded in 1592.[24] This later name puzzles the place-name experts, their only suggestion being that it comes from *coninger*, meaning a rabbit warren. Perhaps it replaced the older name Moldicliff? The surname Moldicliff died out in the late sixteenth or seventeenth century.

Another lost place-name from the same area which cannot be identified is Fearnley. In 1297 Robert de Fernileye was taxed in the chapelry of Bradfield. Other early deeds in and around the Ewden Valley were witnessed by members of the Fearnley family, but the evidence is too thin to pinpoint the site of the place-name. Present-day Fearnleys may be descended from this medieval family, but equally they might have come from immigrant stock, for the surname has more than one point of origin.

Ramsker is a lost place-name from a mile or two to the south in Bradfield Dale, near the Dale Dyke reservoir. The place-name was recorded in 1295, but the surname did not appear in local records until the poll tax return of 1379.[25] The family never became prolific. In 1672 John Ramsker, who paid tax on two hearths at Attercliffe, was the only person of that surname in south Yorkshire.

Meanwhile, however, his namesake had prospered as a cutlery dealer in London. The Hawkesworths who lived at the top end of Bradfield Dale became far more numerous than the Ramskers. The surname has different origins elsewhere in the West Riding, but the numerous Hawkesworths in Hallamshire came from Hawkesworth Head, whose site is now under or near Strines reservoir. At the time of John Harrison's survey of the manor of Sheffield (1637) the moorland area at the head of Bradfield Dale was known as Hawksworth Firth. The family was first recorded in the manor court rolls of 1283 when Adam Hawkesworth took half an acre of new land in Thornsett, further down the dale; the following year he took a small piece of new land in Hawkesworth. The senior branch of the family remained at Hawkesworth until at least the first half of the sixteenth century, but junior branches spread into other parts of Hallamshire.

Failed Surnames

In some other cases, the medieval place-name has survived but the surname which was derived from it has withered. Four families who took their surnames from place-names within the chapelry of Bradfield were amongst the better-off farmers who paid tax in 1297, but they did not last for much longer and may possibly have been wiped out (at least in the male line) by the Black Death. The family named Bradfield appear only twice in local records. A William de Bradfield paid tax in 1297, and in 1345 William, the son of William, the son of Matilda de Bradfield, was farming in Bradfield. We have a little more evidence for the Brightholmlees. Ralph de Brightomlee witnessed deeds at Westmondhalgh and Wigtwizzle in 1309 and 1314, and upon his death in 1335 his son, John, inherited lands in Westmondhalgh and Onesacre. After 1345 nothing more is heard of this family. The former Anglo-Saxon estates at Ughill and Holdworth also gave rise to surnames which did not last very long. In a deed dated before 1290 John, the son of John de Uggil, and Ralph de Uggil were recorded. In 1295 a deed of Adam de Ughill was witnessed by Roger de Ughil and John, the son of Robert de Ughil, so the surname had become hereditary. It did not survive. Finally, Thomas de Haldeworth was recorded on three occasions between 1270 and 1314 and a deed of 1326 refers to land that once belonged to William del Haldeworth Ynge, but the name continued no further. The present-day Holdsworths take their name from another place, further north in the West Riding, near Halifax.

Several surnames which were derived in a variety of other ways also failed to survive. Two personal names which became surnames were prominent in the earliest records of Hallamshire but neither lasted very long. In 1297 Henry Rosselin paid tax in the parish of Ecclesfield and in 1359 Roger Rosselyn of Mortomley granted lands there to John de Houselay. Nothing more is heard of the Rosselins. In 1297 Nicholas Knut paid tax in the parish of Sheffield and in 1345 Edmund Knout was said to have formerly held a smallholding at Wincobank. This family survived the Black Death, for in 1379 Robert Knotte paid poll tax in the parish of Sheffield and in 1410 Robert Knott and two others surrendered a farm in Bradfield, but that is the last record of them, unless the William Knott who was taxed on one hearth and a smithy in Greasborough in 1672 and the George Knott who paid on one hearth there were descended from this old Hallamshire family.

Some Hallamshire surnames which were old personal names in origin survived until the late Middle Ages. Harsand is an Old French and Old German personal name which became a surname both in and beyond Hallamshire. The local Harsands were long connected with Stannington but in the earliest record of the family, in 1288, William Hershand was admitted as tenant of $1\frac{1}{2}$ acres in Hawkesworth. In 1342 Rose, the widow of Thomas Harsand of Stannington, passed to Richard, her son, a piece of arable land lying in the open fields of Stannington at the townhead. In 1379 Henry and Richard Harsand each paid poll tax in the chapelry of Bradfield. In 1422 John Harsand took a twenty-year lease of Stannington Hall and in 1440–42 was the lessee of Owlerton mill. In 1493 his son, Henry, surrendered his Stannington property to Isabel, his daughter, the wife of Henry Greave. Another branch of the family survived in the male line for a further generation, for in 1527 William, the son

This aerial view of a natural land-slip in the Chapelry of Bradfield is now named Canyard Hills, but was probably once known as Moldicliff, 'the cliff covered with earth'.

and heir of John Harshand, inherited a small farm in Stannington. After 1550, when William surrendered this property to Roger Barber of Wadsley, the Harsands disappeared from local records. None was recorded in the hearth tax returns for south Yorkshire in 1672.

Another family that were prominent in their locality for a few generations before they disappeared in the male line were the Lynotts. Their surname was derived either from a pet form of a woman's name or as a nickname from the linnet (*linott* in Old French). In 1283 William, the son of Simon Lynott, was admitted to three acres of land in Fulwood, so the family were already in the district where they are known to have farmed a grange of Beauchief Abbey. In 1297 Robert Linot paid tax in Sheffield. There is then a gap in the records concerning this family until the poll tax returns of 1379, when Robert Lynot and Adam Lynot were both described as farmers of the grange and were each taxed at a shilling, three times the basic rate that was paid by most of their neighbours. Alice, Thomas, Beatrix and William Lynot paid fourpence tax in Sheffield. The Lynotts also held land in Fulwood of the Lord of Hallamshire from at least 1380 onwards. In 1428 Adam Lynot's daughter Agnes, the wife of John Fox of Fulwood, inherited a farm in Fulwood and some land in Hallam. John Lynot rented two pastures in Sheffield Park in 1442 and was recorded as a Sheffield's church burgess in 1430 and 1454. In the Hallamshire manor court rolls of 1440–41 Joan Lynot and John Lynot were living in the town of Sheffield, another John was recorded in the soke of Ecclesfield, a third John was at Fulwood, a fourth at Broom [Hall], and Alice, the widow of Thomas Lynot, was also a tenant of the lordship of Hallamshire. The 1451 Book of Feudal Aids named John Lynot in Sheffield and John Lynot in Fulwood. The family seemed well-established, but all their male lines came to an end soon afterwards. No further references to the surname occur in the later Hallamshire court rolls, no Lynots appear in the first Sheffield parish register and none was recorded in the south Yorkshire hearth tax returns of 1672.

One or two families with surnames derived from occupations did not last very long. The Washers, for instance, were recorded in 1297, when William le Wassar paid the lay subsidy in the chapelry of Bradfield and in 1379 when Roger Washar paid poll tax there, but no further references to the name are found in Hallamshire. The Stringers trace their ancestry back to iron-workers in charge of string hearths, but the family that were present in the Sheffield district in the Middle Ages failed to survive or perhaps moved elsewhere. In 1277 Henry Stringer farmed land at Hawkesworth and in 1379 William Stringer paid poll tax in the parish of Sheffield, but the name then disappeared from local records. In 1672 Stringers were taxed at Brinsworth, Whiston and Bentley, but not in Hallamshire.

A few surnames that were derived from occupations lasted much longer. The surname Bottery was given to men who were keepers of the buttery at a palace, castle, manor house or great religious establishment. In Hallamshire four generations – Robert, Geoffrey, Robert and Geoffrey Bottery – held official positions in the manor and the town, though there is some doubt about the first Robert, who appeared as Robert Butre, a witness to a deed at Sheffield in 1413. Six years later Geoffrey Butre was the town bailiff and in 1442 the parker of Sheffield Park. In the 1451 Book of Feudal Aids he held land in the Balne (now Balm Green) and elsewhere in Sheffield, and at Upperthorpe. Robert Botery, who was recorded at Sheffield in the same document, was the bailiff of Sheffield in 1489. Ten years later, Geoffrey Buttery was one of the 'Greve or Churche Maisters' of the parish church of Sheffield, a position that became known as church burgess. There are no further references in local records to this family.

The Wrastlers were descended from a wrestler. In 1270 Thomas de Furnival granted to Thomas, the son of William de Reyner of New Mill, Bradfield, a farm called Reyner House in Westmondhalgh and a farm called Case House near New Mill bridge, all of which were once held by Henry Wrastereler, then formerly of Stannington, deceased. In 1379 Alice and John Wresteler paid poll tax in the chapelry of Bradfield. In the early fifteenth century Thomas Wrastler farmed at Dwarriden and New Mill; in 1433 his son and heir, John Wrastler, inherited land in Westmondhalgh; in 1438 Henry Wrastler of Stannington took a farm in the town and territories of Bradfield; and in 1440–41 held the position of forester of Rivelin. In 1450 a farm in Stannington was said to have been formerly in the possession of Thomas, the son of Robert Wrastler, and in the following year the Book of Feudal Aids noted that Henry Wrastler held a farm in Bradfield, which he left fourteen years later. The forester's job passed to Henry's son and namesake, who in 1505 joined with the Vicar, Thomas Clark, in paying for a stained glass window in the north side of the north quire of Ecclesfield church. This second Henry seems to have been the last of the line No Wrastlers were recorded in the Bradfield chapelry register, nor in the 1672 hearth tax returns for south Yorkshire.

One might expect Cutler to be a common local surname, but despite the importance of the cutlery

Sheffield parish church. The 'Greve or Churche Maisters' were the fore-runners of the Church Burgesses, whose responsibilities included the maintenance of the parish church, seen here in an engraving of 1793 upon the completion of major new work.

trade in medieval Hallamshire only one local family took their name from this occupation and it is doubtful whether present-day Cutlers are descended from them. Did Robert le Coteler, who paid tax in the parish of Sheffield in 1297, and who is thus the earliest recorded cutler in Hallamshire, acquire his surname because he was the leading organiser of the trade? He may perhaps have lived at Attercliffe, where the family were settled in the fourteenth and the first half of the fifteenth century. John Cutler was living in Attercliffe in 1329 and he or his namesake witnessed deeds there in 1351 and 1369. Between 1333 and 1349 Adam Cotelar was a regular witness to deeds signed in Sheffield. In 1379 poll tax was paid by John Coteler (Sheffield parish) and by another John Coteler, who was a baker, together with his son and namesake (Handsworth parish). The description of the second John Coteler as baker shows that the surname had become hereditary and was uninfluenced by a change of occupation. Although he paid only the lowest rate of poll tax, the first John Cutler was a Sheffield burgess, who witnessed four deeds in Sheffield, Darnall and Bradfield between 1384 and 1397. Between 1399 and 1432 Richard Cuteler of Darnall witnessed three deeds in Darnall and Tinsley, in 1417 John Cutler relinquished a farm at Neepsend, and in 1440 Richard Cuteler was recorded in the manor court rolls under the soke of Bradfield and was a witness to a deed in Darnall. The following year, Joan, the widow of Richard Cutler of Darnall, surrendered a farm in Dungworth and in 1449 Ralph and Thomas Coteler were involved in a property transaction in Sheffield. In 1451 land at Upperthorpe was said to have formerly belonged to John Cuteler and a farm in Attercliffe was tenanted by Richard Cutler. The surname then disappeared from Hallamshire records, except that in 1542 James Coteler attended the Ecclesfield manor court and the 1614–15 list of cutlers that has survived

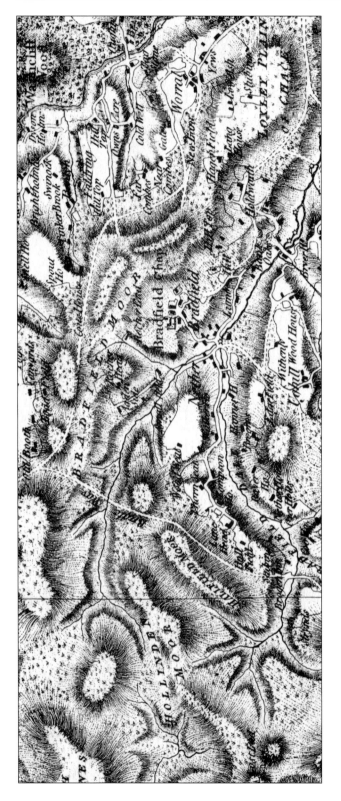

in the archives of the Cutlers' Company included Thomas Cutler. The south Yorkshire hearth tax returns of 1672 noted John, Robert and Rose (Kimberworth), William (Rawmarsh), Christopher (Rotherham), Roger (Sikehouse) and George (Thorne), but no-one of that surname in Hallamshire, which by then was the most famous centre of cutlery manufacture outside London.

Two of the most interesting surnames have been left till last. The surname Stickbuck is thought to be a nickname for a hunter. In 1377 Alice Agays surrendered three acres and three roods of land (which became known as Agascroft) in Hallam and Fulwood to John Stickbuck. In 1428 William, the son and heir of John Stikbuke, inherited a farm in Hallam, including Agascroft, which he surrendered eleven years later to Robert Stykbuke. A John Stickbuck, who was recorded in 1467 and 1495, was said in 1505 to have lately held the old farm in Hallam and Fulwood. In 1508–9 Richard and William Stickbuck were farming there and one of their fields retained the old name of Agascroft. The male line died out in 1522, when Richard Holland and Agnes, his wife, one of the daughters of William Stickbuck and of kin and heir to John Stickbuck, inherited half the farm in Hallam and Fulwood, as the share she had with Alice, another daughter of William. No further references to the Stickbucks appear in local records. They had lasted in the male line at the same farm for a century and a half.

Holdworth was recorded as a small estate in Domesday Book. The Smallbehinds of Holdworth eventually changed their name to Smallbent. The name died out early in the eighteenth century.

So far we have been dealing with nicknames of multiple origins, but one that was coined in Hallamshire was unique to that district. Smallbent was a corruption of Smallbehind. This nickname seems to have been applied to just one person who farmed at Holdworth during the period of surname formation. It had become hereditary by the late fourteenth century, for in 1379 William Smalbyhind paid poll tax in the chapelry of Bradfield and in 1393 John Smalbeehind acquired 11/2 acres of land in Holdworth. During the next few years this John gradually built up a holding, which was to remain in the family's hands until the middle of the sixteenth century, when it was split between daughters. In 1420 John surrendered the farm in Holdworth to Thomas Smallbeehind, who was probably his son. Meanwhile, in 1417 William Smalbeehind became tenant of another farm in Holdworth and in 1432 was said to have lately held land across the Rivelin valley in Upper Hallam. In the manor court rolls of 1440–41 the only person recorded with this surname was Thomas Smallbend, a shortened form of the name that eventually became Smallbent. He was succeeded by 1480 by John Smalbeehind of Holdworth Bank, who in 1500 surrendered the farm to his heir, Robert Smalbeehind. The property remained with the family until 1546, when 'Robert Smalbynd, otherwise called Smalbent', passed it on to his daughter Alice and her husband, Walter Hurt (the ancestor of the family that changed their name to Sitwell upon inheriting the Renishaw Hall estate). A few Smallbents were recorded in the early Bradfield and Sheffield registers and at Braithwell between 1563 and 1668, but the name disappeared soon afterwards; no Smallbents were recorded in the south Yorkshire hearth tax returns of 1672, nor in those of neighbouring counties. The Anna Smallbent who married at Tankersley in 1712 and the Sarah Smallbent who married at Penistone in 1718 seem to have been the last bearers of this name.

The lost place-names and failed surnames of Hallamshire make an interesting collection, but they are few in number when compared with those medieval place-names which are still in daily use and with those family names which originated in Hallamshire and which are still so well-known in the locality.

We saw in chapter three how several local families rose from modest beginnings in the Middle Ages to the ranks of the gentry by the seventeenth century. Here, we shall be concerned with the fortunes of the yeomen and husbandmen, those ordinary farmers whose families remained further down the social scale but who formed the majority of the English population. Their stories are of interest to all of us, for it is from such stock that most of the people of this country are descended. In Hallamshire many of these ordinary families possessed surnames that were formed locally in the thirteenth or fourteenth centuries. They stayed close to their original homes, often on the same farm, for generation after generation, pursuing a way of life that had long been familiar to their ancestors. Together, they were the stable core of local society. In the Tudor and Stuart period younger sons increasingly turned to the cutlery trades or to nailmaking for a living and so they too did not need to move far. Unless a young man fancied his chances in London, he tended to remain within a few miles of his birthplace. These then were the long-resident families which helped to form the distinctive character of Hallamshire. We shall start with those who possessed surnames that were derived from local place-names.[1]

Family Names from Hallamshire Places

Many of the best-known local surnames were derived from Hallamshire farms and hamlets. The Hartleys, for instance, took their surname from two hamlets in Ecclesfield parish, known as Over Hartley and Nether Hartley, otherwise Hartley Brook. Other place-name origins for this surname exist beyond Hallamshire, from further north in the West Riding and in Lancashire, but the local Hartleys came from Ecclesfield parish. The earliest reference to the family is in an undated thirteenth-century deed which named Henry de Hertelay as a witness concerning lands at Chapel, now known as Chapeltown. In 1287 Henry de Hertelay acquired a farm at Raynaldthorpe (alias Hatfield House), and three years later, William, the son of William de Hertelay, also acquired land there. Raynaldthorpe was just up the hill from Hartley and was one of the largest farms in the parish. Henry de Herteley was amongst the better-off farmers who had to pay the tax known as the lay subsidy in 1297 and whose namesake was one of the jurors for Ecclesfield parish in 1341 for another tax return known as the *Nonarum Inquisitiones*. John de Hertelay, who paid 12d poll tax as a mercer in 1379, was probably living at Raynaldthorpe. The other Hartleys of Ecclesfield parish – Richard, John, and two Williams – each paid the lowest rate of 4d. The family's connection with Raynaldthorpe came to an end in 1412 when John de Hertelay's son, Henry, sold the farm to William Robinson, but the Hartleys continued to live nearby. The manor court rolls of 1440–1 record Henry de Hertley and John Hertley in the soke of Southey and Thomas de Hertley in the soke of Ecclesfield. In 1477, at the court of the Rectory Manor of Ecclesfield, William Hartley surrendered a farm in Nether Hartley. Perhaps this was the end of the family's connection with their ancestral home? The Hartleys were named in sixteenth-century transactions in the Rectory Manor, though not specifically at the hamlet of Hartley.

Thomas Jeffreys's map of Yorkshire (1772) marks hamlets and farmsteads in the Chapelry of Bradfield that were the homes of distinctive local surnames, such as Combes, Dungworth, Holdworth and Worrall.

The family began to multiply at that time, with large numbers appearing in the parish registers of Sheffield and Ecclesfield during the second half of the sixteenth century. Several Hartleys found employment in the cutlery trades. Three were named in a 1614–15 list of Hallamshire cutlers and six joined the Cutlers' Company soon after its incorporation in 1624. The hearth tax returns for south Yorkshire in 1672 name twelve households of Hartleys, including three in Handsworth and one each in Brightside, Ecclesfield, Sheffield, Stannington and Wadsley. To this day, Hartleys are found close to their medieval point of origin in the parish of Ecclesfield. Their story is a typical one.

Another characteristic Hallamshire surname, that of Dungworth, is derived from a hamlet in the chapelry of Bradfield. In 1323 William, the son of Anne Dungworth, was admitted to a small farm at Storrs, half a mile from Dungworth. The surname seems to have had a single-family origin, for in the 1379 poll tax return John Dongword of Handsworth was the only bearer of this name. A generation or two later the manor court records name William Dungworth (1402) and John Dungworth (1436) at Dungworth, but by 1440 a junior branch of the family had moved a few miles to Carbrook on the eastern edge of Hallamshire. John Dungworth was there in 1451 and ten years later his son and namesake inherited the property. The senior branch of the family long remained at Dungworth, however. When Richard Dungworth died there in 1556 he was succeeded by his son and namesake. Four years later this younger Richard surrendered a cottage and lands in Dungworth (that were in the occupation of Elizabeth Dungworth) to Nicholas Dungworth. The line continued to flourish during the following century. A John Dungworth appeared in the 1624–30 list of cutlers and the 1672 hearth tax returns for south Yorkshire name William, Thomas and Francis at Stannington, George at Bradfield, and two more Williams in Attercliffe township (which included Carbrook). The link with the hamlet which had given rise to the surname had been broken, but the members of the Dungworth family had not moved very far. Eight years later, however, Richard Dungworth was one of a group of Yorkshire Quakers who emigrated to New Jersey, America!

Some families stayed at or close to their point of origin but if the elder branch eventually died out in the male line the surname became associated with a junior branch which had moved to another farm within Hallamshire. The Coombes family are a good example. Their surname has multiple origins and is found all over England and Wales, especially in south-west England, for coumb simply means 'short, broad valley'. Margaret Gelling notes that such valleys were usually bowl- or trough-shaped with three fairly steeply rising sides.[2] The source of the local surname is Coumbes Farm near Oughtibridge and Onesacre. The surname had become hereditary by 1277, the year that local manorial records began, when Peter de Coumbes became tenant of new land in Southey. In 1297 Robert de Cumbes was taxed in the parish of Ecclesfield, but not in the chapelry of Bradfield, so the Southey branch was doing better than those who stayed at their place of origin. A definite link with Coumbes Farm in the chapelry of Bradfield was made in 1339, when John del Coumb surrendered land in le Coumbes to Roger Palin. As we shall see, this transaction was not the end of the connection between the farm and the family. The surname was sometimes shortened to Coo (which can be derived separately as a nickname from the jackdaw). In 1341 William, the son of Henry Coo, was one of the jurors for the *Nonarum Inquisitiones* return in the parish of Ecclesfield and in 1376 William del Coumb witnessed a deed at Pitsmoor. In 1379 John Coombe paid poll tax in the parish of Ecclesfield and two John de Combes (listed together) and Richard Koo were taxed at the same basic rate in the chapelry of Bradfield. The family were involved in property transactions at Wincobank (1399), Over Hartley (1412) and Hawkesworth (1427), and in 1441 John de Coumb (Southey) and John Coo (Bradfield) were named in the manor court rolls. The two branches of the family were therefore still living at the same places where they were settled in the late thirteenth century. The chapelry of Bradfield family then disappeared from the records, but the branch at Wincobank in the soke of Southey can be traced over several generations. In 1444 John Coumb surrendered a farm at Wincobank to his son and heir, William. The 1451 Book of Feudal Aids noted William Coumbe at Wincobank and Hartley and John Coumbe at Staniforth, nearby. In 1460 John de Coumb surrendered his Staniforth property to his son, John Coumb, in 1476 another John Combe held two tenements and land in Wincobank and Shiregreen after the death of William Combe, his father, and in 1500 John Comb surrendered two farms in Wincobank and Shiregreen to Henry Comb, who in 1536 bequeathed them to his son and namesake. Robert Coumbe appeared in the 1614–15 list of cutlers and in 1672 Anthony Combe and Matthew Combe were living next door to each other in the Hartley-Shiregreen district. The family just managed to keep going in the male line. A few members of the Coombes family still live in the same part of Ecclesfield parish.

Some other long-established Hallamshire families who took their names from local farms and hamlets had already moved a short distance away from their original homes before written records began. Creswick is an example, which we noted in chapter four, of a surname which had been formed before the 1280s, for the family were then at Onesacre and were never recorded at Creswick in surviving documents. But after an early move families such as the Creswicks were often rooted in a particular place for centuries. Even those that spread a little further usually remained within Hallamshire, unless (like the Creswicks) a branch was tempted to go all the way to London.

Loxley is another surname that was long associated with the district whence it came but which cannot be linked to its precise point of origin. The name was not recorded until 1379, when Adam Lokeslay and Thomas de Lokeslay both paid poll tax in the chapelry of Bradfield. In 1396/97 this Thomas Loxley had a farm in Bradfield that had formerly belonged to William Joyes and another small farm in Dwarriden. In 1415-16 he passed the Bradfield farm to his son and heir, Richard, and the other farm to his second son, John. In 1428 John Loxley crossed the Rivelin Valley to take a farm in Upper Hallam, but he surrendered this four years later. In 1440–1 Richard de Lokesley was the reeve of the soke of Bradfield and in 1442 John was collector of the issues of the Bradfield court. The manor court rolls inform us that in 1447 William Locksley inherited the farm in Bradfield which his father, John, had inherited in 1416. A firm line of descent from this William cannot be established but the old farm at Bradfield continued in the possession of the Loxleys. William, the son and heir of Henry Lockesley, inherited it in 1532 and in 1559 bequeathed it to his son, John. During the following year it passed to Richard, the son and heir of Richard Loxley. The Loxleys had not yet spread into other parts of Hallamshire and none was included in the early lists of cutlers. By the time that Thomas Loxley was taxed in Bradfield in 1672, the senior branch had continued at the same farm for nearly three centuries. By then Henry Loxley was living at the other side of the Don in the Grenofirth quarter of Ecclesfield parish.

The Broomheads are another well-known Hallamshire family. Their surname is derived from a minor place-name high in the Ewden Valley, which in the seventeenth century became the site of a gentry hall belonging to the Wilson family (see chapter three). They were first recorded in 1290, when Henry del Bromhede witnessed grants at Waldershelf and White Lee Moor, and in 1311 at Wigtwizzle. We do not know whether the family had already moved a short distance from their original home. Perhaps this came about in 1326 when Thomas del Bromheade acquired a third of a farm in the village of Bradfield. The surname had become hereditary by then, for in 1336 Alice, Elena, Henry, Juliana, John and Thomas de Bromyheued were involved in property transactions at Wigtwizzle and Dwarriden. In 1379 William Bromhed was taxed in the chapelry of Bradfield, but at that time the Wilsons were living at Broomhead. In 1385 this William de Bromyhed leased some property in Bradfield and Ughill Wood and was fined at the manor court for cutting wood in Agden. In 1419 John de Bromehed of Bradfield held land in the townfields of Bradfield. The manor court rolls of 1440–41 contain references to John and William de Broomhead, and in 1442 to William Broomhead, senior, who inherited the Bradfield farm. In 1451 Richard Broomhead was at Bradfield and John Broomhead at Worrall and in 1484 Henry Broomhead granted the Worrall property to John Broomhead, his illegitimate brother. The Broomheads continued at their farm in Bradfield in the sixteenth and seventeenth centuries, with younger sons and cousins at other farms nearby. No Broomheads were included in the lists of early cutlers but some were involved in the trade later in the seventeenth century. In 1672 hearth tax was paid by Henry, Ralph, Reynold, Richard and Widow Broomhead at Bradfield, John at Waldershelf, John, the miller at Stannington, another John and two Henrys at the other side of the Rivelin valley in Upper Hallam, Mr John Bromhead at Laughton-en-le-Morthen and Robert Broomhead at Warmsworth. The Broomheads were by then also well established in various parts of Derbyshire and Nottinghamshire. They had become a prolific family, but most of them still lived in the chapelry of Bradfield close to their original home.

By the late thirteenth century a family of farmers had acquired their surname from a farm called Smallfield on the northern banks of the present Agden reservoir. They are first mentioned in 1290 when Thomas de Smalfeld witnessed a document at White Lee, a nearby farm which they eventually tenanted. Seven years later, Thomas was amongst those moderately-prosperous Bradfield farmers who paid the lay subsidy. A John de Smallfield was recorded on several occasions between 1326 and 1342 and a William Smallfield paid poll tax in the chapelry of Bradfield in 1379. The family were never numerous but they produced just enough male heirs to continue farming in the same district for centuries. When William de Smallfield died in 1434 he was succeeded at Smallfield, White Lee and Dungworth by Thomas Smallfield 'until such time as John son and heir of the said William who is in

The present Cowley Manor is an eighteenth-century successor to the moated house of the Mounteneys, one of the leading families in medieval Hallamshire.

parts foreign to England shall return'. Perhaps John had been obliged through his feudal tenure to accompany John Talbot, first Earl of Shrewsbury, as a soldier in France? We hear no more about him. Over two centuries later, in 1672, however, another John Smallfield paid tax on his hearth in the township of Bradfield and Jeremy Smallfield paid on two hearths across the valley in Upper Hallam. The family name disappeared through the lack of male heirs shortly afterwards.

Colly, or Cowley, is a common place-name, meaning 'charcoal clearing' and the surname has several different origins. Locally, it is probably derived from Cowley, near Chapeltown, but in what capacity is not clear, for the family seem to have had humble beginnings and to have had no connections with the Mounteneys, the Norman lords of Cowley. An undated, fourteenth-century deed signed at Onesacre named Bate de Colley. No Colleys were taxed locally in 1379, but in 1395 John Colley obtained a croft and garden in Norwood on the northern boundary of Sheffield parish. In 1402 a deed of the Wilkinsons of Crowder House, near Southey on the southern edge of Ecclesfield parish, noted that their property was adjacent to that of John Colley. The Colleys were therefore already at the farm where they were to remain for several generations. In 1412 John was a witness at Raynaldthorpe and in 1415 at Hartley. In 1413 Henry Cowley acquired two acres in Grenoside and in 1419 he surrendered a small farm in Woodside within the soke of Ecclesfield. This was probably the same place as the Woodhouse where later generations of the family were settled (Crowder House was also said to be in Woodhouse); the name eventually became Colly Elm or Elm Green and was commemorated by Colley School. In 1440–41 Edward Colly (Ecclesfield) and John Colly (Southey) were recorded in the manor court rolls. Late-fifteenth and sixteenth-century documents show that five generations of John Colleys lived at Woodhouse in the parish of Ecclesfield and soke of Southey. The family continued there until soon after 1592, when John Colly, yeoman, surrendered lands and tenements in Woodhousefields to himself for life, then to his daughter, Elizabeth, the wife of Edward Dickenson, with the remainder to his two other daughters. The male line had come to an end after several generations at the same farm, but junior branches of the family preserved the name elsewhere. Two Cowleys were included in the 1624–30 list of cutlers and in 1672 William Colley was taxed on a hearth and a smithy in Southey, four branches of Colleys were taxed in Sheffield (three with smithies) and one was taxed in Handsworth. The Colleys with one hearth in Wombwell and Kirk Sandall, well beyond Hallamshire, were probably unconnected.

Immigrant Families

Some of the families that were settled in Hallamshire by the late Middle Ages possessed surnames which were derived from places beyond the lordship. Most of these names came from neighbouring parishes. The surname Bullas, for example, is derived from Bullhouse, three miles west of Penistone, a place which is still pronounced Bullas locally. In the thirteenth century an undated deed at Penistone was witnessed by Robert and Thomas de Boleholis and in 1326 land in Bradfield was said to have been held formerly by Henry, the son of Richard Bullouce of Bradfield. In 1379 John Bolhes paid poll tax in the parish of Sheffield. Perhaps the Robert Bolous who took a farm at Neepsend in 1417 was his son? In 1428 this Robert Bullhouse took another farm in Skinnerthorpe, more than a mile away over the hill to the north, but in 1438 he was still described as 'Robert Bolous of Neepsend', with property abutting on Harvest Lane. In the manor court rolls of 1440–41 Robert de Bulhous was the only person recorded with this surname in Hallamshire, so it looks as if just one family had settled in north Sheffield, with land in both Neepsend and Skinnerthorpe. In 1478 Thomas Bulluse inherited a farm from his father, John, in 1502 William Bullos was farming at Skinnerthorpe, and in 1518 William, the son and heir of Thomas Bullhouse, inherited a farm in the soke of Southey (which included both Neepsend and Skinnerthorpe). The manor court rolls allow us to follow the family line during the sixteenth and early seventeenth centuries. In 1534 Robert, the son and heir of William Bulloes, inherited the properties that his father held in 1502, in 1558 these passed to Robert's son, William, and in 1560 to William's son, John. In 1587 George, the son and heir of John Bullous, inherited the farm at Neepsend. When George died in 1617, his son and namesake, inherited this property. Meanwhile, in 1608 the farm at Skinnerthorpe had passed to a younger son, William. These Bullases had by then long been involved in the manufacture of cutlery as well as farming. George, Hugh and Thomas Bullus were named in the 1614–15 list of cutlers and John Bullus of Darnall was soon added to their number. The hearth tax returns of 1672 record George Bullus (1 hearth and a smithy) and John (2 and a smithy) in Attercliffe, John (1 and smithy), Thomas (1), Nicholas (2) in Grenofirth, Robert (2) in Southey, William (1 and a smithy) at Handsworth, John (2), William (4), Richard (3 and a smithy), George (2) and Thomas (2 and a smithy) in Sheffield, and Richard (1) and Widow Bullus (1), next door to each other in Wentworth. The surname has remained a local one.

Oxspring is another surname from the parish of Penistone which had migrated to Sheffield by the late fourteenth century. In 1379 John Oxspryng paid poll tax in the parish of Sheffield and in 1389 Richard de Oxspring granted to Robert de Birlay all his lands and tenements in Birley, which he had inherited after the decease of Richard de Oxspring, his father. In 1433 Robert Oxspring acquired a share in a farm at Walkley. The line cannot be traced with certainty, but in the manor court rolls of 1440–41 John and Robert Oxspring were recorded under Sheffield soke, in 1442 William Oxspring was a witness to a deed at Barnes, and in 1453 Robert Oxspring was a witness at Stannington. In 1499 Robert Oxspring was a 'Greve or Church Maister' (i.e. a church burgess) and in the following year he was at Walkley. Upon the death of John Oxspring in 1515, the Walkley property went to his widow and then to his married daughter, but there are many other sixteenth-century references to different branches of the Oxsprings in the parishes of Sheffield and Ecclesfield. John and Thomas Oxspring

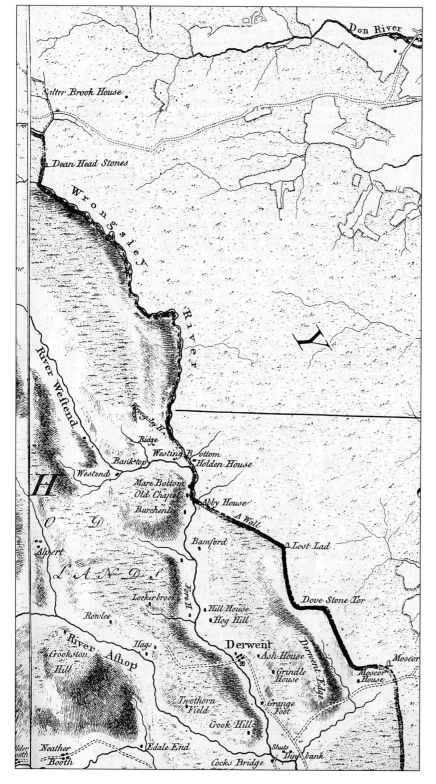

P. P. Burdett's map of Derbyshire (1767) marks Ronksley Farm as 'Wrongsley H.' on the Derbyshire bank of the River Derwent (whose upper reaches he names 'Wrongsley River'). The Ronksleys crossed into the Chapelry of Bradfield and became a long-established Hallamshire family.

appeared in the 1614–15 list of cutlers. In the hearth tax returns of 1672 for south Yorkshire George and James Oxspring were entered under Southey, Thomas under Nether Hallam, George and Thomas under Bramley, Robert under Greasborough, and Richard under Braithwell. The Derbyshire hearth tax returns recorded two Oxsprings at Ashford and one each at Darley and Wensley.

Ronksley was a farm at the foot of Linch Clough in Upper Derwent Dale, just across the Hallamshire border. It was demolished upon the construction of Howden reservoir, but the site can still be found and Ronksley Moor and Ronksley Wood retain their names. A John de Ronkeslai witnessed a deed at Upper Midhope in 1366 and thirteen years later Agnes, Thomas and John de Ronkeslay each paid poll tax in the chapelry of Bradfield, whose borders came close to Ronksley Farm, while John Ronksley was taxed nearby in Thurlstone township. In 1440 Bartholomew Ronkesley was recorded in a deed at Wigtwizzle. Four years earlier, as Barten de Ronkysley, he had taken 'the Mickle Holden and Holden Hedes pastures' that had lately been rented by Thomas de Ronksley in Howden, close to Ronksley Farm, and in 1445 he began to farm at Moorwood. A William Ronksley was recorded in 1478 and many other Ronksleys appear in the earliest Bradfield and Sheffield parish registers, though they had left their original farm by 1546. John and Peter Ronksley were included in the 1624–30 list of Hallamshire cutlers and in 1672 hearth tax was paid by Francis (Stannington), George (Upper Hallam), James (Bradfield) and William (Brightside); no Ronksleys appear in the Derbyshire and Nottinghamshire returns. The surname remains a rare one, with only thirty-five subscribers in the national telephone directories, most of them in and around Sheffield.

By the late thirteenth century the Beightons had travelled across Sheffield from the north Derbyshire village from which their surname was derived to settle high on the moorland fringe. In 1283 Adam de Beighton was admitted to half an acre of land in Ughill Wood and in the following year John de Beighton was admitted to a farm in Bradfield which he had by the gift of Adam Beighton, his brother. The surname was therefore already hereditary. In 1379 Thomas de Beghton (chapelry of Bradfield) and Richard de Beghton (Sheffield parish) paid poll tax and in the 1390s this Thomas Beighton held land in Holdworth. The Beightons moved from farm to farm within Hallamshire. In 1442 John Beighton held a parcel of land in Heeley, but two years later, his son and heir, Robert, inherited a farm in Fulwood, which had come to the family through his mother. Robert's son, John, inherited the Fulwood property and was one of the 'Greve or Churche Maisters' in 1499. In turn, he was succeeded at Fulwood by his sons, Robert and John. The Beightons began to multiply during the sixteenth century; numerous references to them occur from the 1540s onwards in the manor court records and in the Bradfield and Sheffield registers. Hugh and John Beighton were included in the 1614–15 list of cutlers and ten households of Beightons were recorded in the south Yorkshire hearth tax returns of 1672; John Beighton (1 hearth and a smithy), Widow Beighton (1 poor) and Robert Beighton (1 and a smithy) were taxed in Attercliffe, John (3) at Bradfield, John (3) in the Westnall quarter of the chapelry of Bradfield, two Widow Beightons (1 each) at Upper Hallam, Jonathan (4) at Handsworth, William (1 poor) at Rotherham and Nicholas (1) at Treeton. They were all living within or just beyond the borders of Hallamshire. The fourteen Beightons who were recorded in the Derbyshire hearth tax returns were mostly from the south of the county and were probably not related.

One of the longest distances travelled by immigrants into Hallamshire at the time when surnames were being formed was by the Scargills, who came from the place of that name in north Yorkshire. It is possible that they were a junior branch of the knightly family at Scargill Castle and Thorp Stapleton, but this claim can be settled only by DNA testing. A William de Scargill held important manorial offices under the Earl de Warenne at Wakefield and Conisbrough in the middle years of the fourteenth century and in 1379 Joan de Skargill (Ecclesfield parish) and Thomas Scargill (Sheffield parish) paid poll tax in Hallamshire. In 1411 Thomas de Skargyll was living in the town of Sheffield; in 1427 Thomas Skargill was described as 'of Little Sheffield'; in 1435 Thomas Scargel of Little Sheffield passed a small property to his son and heir, John; and in the previous year the manor court rolls name Matilda, the widow of Thomas Skargill, and Margery, the widow of John Skargill. In 1441 John and William Scarghull attended the Sheffield court and during the following two centuries the Scargills were recorded on numerous occasions in the Sheffield, Ecclesfield and Bradfield parish registers. A Thomas Skargell was one of the assistants of the Cutlers' Company in 1625–26 and Robert Skargell was Master Cutler in 1640. Thirteen Scargills were taxed in south Yorkshire in 1672 but none was recorded in Derbyshire or Nottinghamshire. Nine of these Scargills lived in Sheffield, two were in Stannington, and one each lived in Wath and Wentworth. The numbers of male Scargills began to fall soon afterwards, however, so that by 1841 Sheffield had only thirteen people with this name.

The Hattersleys, another family that became well-established in Hallamshire, had crossed the Pennines from Hattersley in Cheshire (probably by the old salt track over Woodhead) by 1367, when William de Hattersley witnessed a deed at Langsett in the neighbouring parish of Penistone. The poll tax returns of 1379 for the township of Langsett record William de Hatyrlay (mercer) and his wife, Helen, together with Amis Hattirslay (marshal) and Joan Hattirslay ('mayden'). The medieval manorial records of Hallamshire are silent about this family, except that in 1483 John Hattersley of Langsett and Robert Hattersley of Waldershelf witnessed a deed at Broomhead. By Elizabeth I's reign, however, some of the Hattersleys had moved further down the Don valley into Sheffield or had moved north into the West Riding textile district, but others remained close to their original settlement. Nine households were recorded in the hearth tax returns for south Yorkshire in 1672 and five had settled just over the border in Derbyshire. The south Yorkshire Hattersleys were settled at Bradfield (2), Wortley, Dodworth, Hoyland (2), Wentworth, Tinsley and Anston. Although they had lived on the borders of Hallamshire since the fourteenth century, the Hattersleys took no early interest in the cutlery industry.

Surnames from the Landscape

The families that took their names from local farmsteads and hamlets were the most numerous amongst the long-established farming dynasties of Hallamshire, but some families with surnames which were derived in other ways were just as tenacious as the ones that have already been described. As we have seen in chapter three, some families with common names like Wilson or Greaves continued over the generations in the same way as the Hartleys or the Broomheads. Medieval Hallamshire had a number of common surnames which were derived from features in the landscape, names such as Booth, Bridge, Cliff, Green, Hill, Lee, Marsh, Shaw, Stones and Wood. It is surprising that the surname Hall, which is encountered in great numbers in local records during the sixteenth and seventeenth centuries, should appear only once in the poll tax returns of 1379, namely Richard de Hall (chapelry of Bradfield). It is likely that other Halls came into Hallamshire during the fifteenth century and spread the name. It denoted someone who lived by a hall or who worked there as a servant. Two surnames that were derived from landscape features are particularly worthy of comment.

The surname Carr has multiple origins from farms situated in low-lying, marshy areas. The local Carrs were very numerous in the medieval records of Hallamshire. Adam del Ker was the only person of this surname in the 1297 tax return for Sheffield, but the Carrs can be traced in the manorial records from 1276, when Thomas del Ker was admitted to land in Wardsend. In 1379 poll tax was paid by John Care and by John and William del Kerre (Ecclesfield parish), Richard and Roger del Kerre (chapelry of Bradfield), and Thomas Carr, Peter in le Kare and William att Karr (Sheffield parish). The most prosperous of the local Carrs lived at Southey and at Birley. Eight Carrs were named in the 1614-15 list of cutlers and twelve in the 1624–30 list. Robert Carr was Master Cutler in 1639 and Stephen Carr in 1660. Forty-one Carrs were recorded in the south Yorkshire hearth tax returns of 1672.

Shaw, meaning a small wood, has given rise to surnames in many parts of England. The Shaws of Hallamshire may have had more than one origin, but in the poll tax returns of 1379 two Williams, and a John, Thomas, Richard, Margaret and Isabella de Shagh were all recorded in the chapelry of Bradfield. The Shaws had farmed at Storrs, near Dungworth, since 1288, when Ralph del Shagh became tenant. It is likely that the surname was already hereditary, for a family of that name continued at the same farm for at least four centuries. The surname had certainly become hereditary by 1341, when John, the son of Thomas Shagh, surrendered land in Storrs to John, the son of Roger Shaw. A junior branch of the Shaws had moved a short distance to Syke House Farm by the early fifteenth century, for in 1418 William Shagh surrendered it to his son, Thomas Shagh. John Shaw, a puritan preacher of national repute, was born at Syke House in 1608. The manor court rolls show that in the fifteenth century the Shaws were also to be found at Dungworth, Thornsett, Moorwood, Ughill, Onesacre, Bradfield, Midhope and across the river Don in Birley. They are too numerous to disentangle. Two Shaws were cutlers in 1614–15 but most lived just beyond the district in which the trade was practised at that time. No less than sixty-four Shaws paid the hearth tax in south Yorkshire in 1672. They included eleven in Dungworth, five in Westnall and one each in Bradfield, Stannington and Waldershelf. These local Shaws had continued in the same small district where they were first recorded in the thirteenth century. They were as rooted in their locality as were their neighbours who bore surnames derived from farms, hamlets or villages.

Nicknames as Surnames

Nearly all the nicknames which became Hallamshire surnames were ones that were used in other parts of the country. Nevertheless, several families bearing such names can be shown to have remained in the same district for hundreds of years. We cannot usually tell why a nickname was given to its original bearer. Grubb seems to have been a widespread nickname for a small person. The local Grubbs have been in Hallamshire since the fourteenth century, though they were never prolific. They were first recorded in 1374, when John Grubbe of the parish of Ecclesfield and Isabella, his wife, gave up their share of land in Micklebring, near Braithwell, which Isabella had inherited. In 1379 John Grubbe, senior and junior, paid poll tax in the parish of Ecclesfield and in 1440–42 John and Thomas Grub were recorded in the soke of Ecclesfield, where Thomas was the rent collector. The 1451 Book of Feudal Aids shows that John Grubb's farm was at Barnes. A firm line cannot be traced, but in 1510 Robert Grubbe appeared at the manor court and John Grubbe of Nether Hartley was mentioned in a will. Some Grubbs were named in the first Ecclesfield, Bradfield, Sheffield and Rotherham registers and Ralph Grubb appeared in the 1624–30 list of cutlers. In 1672 Thomas and Edmond Grubb of Sheffield were the only householders with this surname in south Yorkshire. In 1841 Sheffield had only thirteen Grubbs and in the 1980s the Sheffield telephone district had twenty-three telephone subscribers with this name. The family never became prolific but just managed to keep going in the male line over the generations.

The surname Kent is always said to indicate an origin from the county of Kent, but it seems unlikely that a family from so far away would have settled on the edge of the Pennines in the chapelry of Bradfield by the mid-fourteenth century. The widespread distribution of this surname in England by that period suggests that we ought to look for more than one etymology. For example, in the north of England a kent was a long pole for punting or leaping. Could the surname sometimes have been a nickname for a tall, thin man who resembled such a pole?[3] Whatever the origin of the name, the first local reference to the family is to John Kent, a witness at Onesacre in 1344. In 1379 Cecilia Kent and her children, Robert and Agnes Kent, each paid the poll tax in the parish of Ecclesfield and Joan Kent and three John Kents paid the tax in Sheffield parish, all at the basic rate of fourpence. The Kents were not, therefore, brought into Hallamshire as estate officers but were at the same social level as the majority of their neighbours.

In 1388 Robert Kent acquired an acre of land in Birley. In 1404 Cecily Kent (who was possibly Robert's widow) surrendered two buildings, two crofts and twelve acres of cultivated land in Birley to John Kent of Ecclesfield, her son and heir. In 1407 Robert Kent was in possession of these buildings and of crofts nearby at Birley Carr, Stubbing, and on the hill above Shirecliffe. In 1440–41 John Kent

This print of High Bradfield appears at the beginning of the chapter on Bradfield, which was written by the Revd Reginald A. Gatty for his father's *A Life at One Living* (1884).

was the constable of Ecclesfield and Robert Kent was a tenant at Osgathorpe. In 1442 Robert Kent, senior, added to his farm in Birley by taking in a piece of waste land. His son, Robert, junior, moved when he married to a small farm at Woodsetts, below Grenoside. This passed in 1447 to John, his son, who the following year inherited the old farm at Birley. The manor court records are then silent about the Kents until 1536, when Robert Kent surrendered a croft upon Shirecliffe Hill. Six years later, he surrendered all his property within Hallamshire to Ralph Kent, his son and heir. Cecily Kent had two sons: John and Robert. John's line failed, but Robert was succeeded by his son and namesake, followed by successive sons: John, Robert and Ralph. Since the late fourteenth century at least six generations of Kents had lived at Birley, but by the seventeenth century the male line had failed, perhaps with Ralph. However, the Kents had spread to other parts of Hallamshire and beyond. Their names appear on numerous occasions in the early Sheffield and Ecclesfield parish registers and Thomas Kent, shearsmith, was amongst the cutlers listed in 1624–30. The hearth tax returns of 1672 record Joseph in Attercliffe, Richard, Robert, and two Williams at Kimberworth, two Thomases at Rotherham, and Mr Kent at Ryhill, north of Barnsley. The Kents were also well-established in north Derbyshire, where another Mr Kent paid tax on seven hearths at Coal Aston, Henry Kent paid on five hearths at Kent House, Ridgeway (where the family's gabled hall survives), and others were taxed at Barlborough, Heath and Whitwell. It is not known whether the Derbyshire Kents stemmed from the family that had once lived at Birley.

The Revells were another long-established Hallamshire family. The surname, which had multiple origins, was usually derived from a nickname for a reveller, but some of the Revells in other parts of England may have come from Reville in La Manche, Normandy. The Revells of Stannington and other parts of the chapelry of Bradfield have lived in Hallamshire since at least the thirteenth century. In 1288 Adam Ryvell held land in Dungworth and William Ryvell was said to have formerly held land in Brightside. In 1297 Richard Rivel paid the lay subsidy in the chapelry of Bradfield, probably at Dungworth where the family continued to farm over the next few centuries. In 1379 poll tax was paid by Alice, John, Richard, Roger and three Thomas Revills in the chapelry of Bradfield and by Adam and John in Handsworth. The family had not yet acquired the status which they were to enjoy in later centuries, although the senior branch may already have settled at the farm that was known later as Revell Grange, to the west of Stannington. There they stayed until the middle of the eighteenth century, having risen from yeoman status to parish gentry. These Revells were Catholics who lost property during the Civil War. Although Mr Revill was taxed on six hearths in 1672, by the early nineteenth century Joseph Hunter observed that there was 'nothing of the least curiosity' about their farmhouse. Other branches of the family lived in north Derbyshire (Brampton, Coal Aston and Dronfield) and at Whiston, but they were not recorded in Sheffield before 1584, when a branch was living at Heeley. William Revell of Heeley was the only man with this surname in the list of cutlers of 1624–30. Thirty-four Revells were recorded in the south Yorkshire hearth tax returns of 1672, nine of them in Stannington, Dungworth and other parts of the chapelry of Bradfield. Another fourteen Revells were taxed in Derbyshire and eleven in Nottinghamshire. It is unlikely that they all shared a common descent.

Patronymic and Occupational Surnames

Surnames in the category known as patronymic include those where an old personal name or a pet form became adopted as a family name and those where -son was added to a father's name in the common fashion of northern England. Some families in this category died out after a few generations but others have flourished in the neighbourhood to this day. Three examples of long continuity require our attention.

The surname Bacon was probably derived from an Old German personal name, Bacco, though it is possible that in some instances it was an occupational name for a pork butcher. The name has multiple origins, but the local Bacons have lived in Hallamshire since the Middle Ages to the present day. The first reference to the local family is to Adam Bacun who paid poll tax in the chapelry of Bradfield in 1379. In 1402 his widow, Magote, passed to Agnes, their daughter, a farm in Bradfield, which had descended to her by inheritance after the death of the son of Robert Tynker of Bradfield. As 'Magot Tynker' she also surrendered another small farm in Bradfield to John Bacon, her son and heir. The family connection with the chapelry of Bradfield persisted; in 1439 William Tinker surrendered a croft in Hawkesworth to John Bacon, senior, in 1440–42 John Bacon, elder and younger, were recorded in the manor court rolls and in 1446 John Bacon held property in Dungworth after the death of John Bacon, his father. It seems likely that the earlier references to 'Bradfield' meant Dungworth, a hamlet within the chapelry. The descent of the property was therefore through Adam to John (his son) and John (his grandson) and on through several more generations. The Thomas Bacon who was recorded in 1483 and 1504 may have been the son of the younger John. In 1516 this Thomas surrendered the farm at Dungworth to his son, John, who in 1535 passed the property to his son, Richard Bacon, on condition that he paid all the rents for seven years to his brother, Robert, and his sister, Agnes. In 1571 this Richard Bacon and Ann, his wife, surrendered the old properties to his son Robert, with remainder to his second son, Richard. By 1592 Richard Bacon, the elder, and Robert had both died, so Richard Bacon of Woodsetts, aged fifteen, was admitted to the family farm in Dungworth, with his mother Ann as guardian. During the second half of the sixteenth century numerous Bacons were

Crowder House in 1884, shown in this print from Revd Alfred Gatty's *A Life at One Living*. The Wilkinson family farmed here from 1402 to 1859.

recorded in the Bradfield register and some were named in the Sheffield register, but none was included in the early lists of cutlers. In 1672 hearth tax was paid in Dungworth by two Johns and a William, in Ecclesall by Richard, and in Sheffield by Andrew and Daniel. No Bacons were taxed in other parts of south Yorkshire. By that time the family had remained in Dungworth and neighbouring parts of Hallamshire for at least three centuries.

The surname Drabble is probably derived from an Old English personal name, Drabba, though it might have been a nickname for an untidy woman. The surname is a local one that is concentrated in the chapelry of Bradfield and adjoining parts of the High Peak. Robert Drabill paid poll tax at Thurlstone in 1379 and William Drabul was taxed at Bakewell in the following year. The first appearances of the surname in Hallamshire records are in 1430, when William Drabull acted for another man at the manor court regarding property at Birley, and six years later when John Drabull of Ecclesfield, junior, took possession of a farm in Birley. The manor court rolls record John Drable, elder and younger (1440–41), John Drabill (1477), William Drabble (1500–6) and Henry Drabble (1517). In 1518 Richard Drable inherited the farm at Birley from his father, William Drable, but the family did not stay there much longer. Numerous Drabbles were recorded in the early Bradfield and Sheffield registers and in those of the parishes of Norton, Hathersage and Rotherham. Richard Drabble was included in the 1614–15 list of cutlers and many later Drabbles were apprenticed to the cutlery trades. In 1672 hearth tax was paid in the chapelry of Bradfield by Jonathan (Westnall) and John and Francis (Stannington), and further east by two Richards (Doncaster), Robert (Hickleton) and Widow Drabble

(Conisbrough). Twelve households of Drabbles were taxed in Derbyshire: four in Dronfield, two in Chelmorton, and one each at Abney, Brampton, Edensor, Eyam and in the south of the county at Holland and Shottle. No Drabbles were at that time living in Nottinghamshire. In the twentieth century the name is still concentrated near its medieval points of origin in the Peak District

Wilkinson is a common northern surname which is derived from a pet form of William. The first local reference is from 1385 when Richard Wilkynson was a witness at Greenhill, in Norton parish. Neither he nor the William Wilkinson who was a witness at Onesacre in 1409 can be linked to the main branch of the local Wilkinsons, who were settled at Crowder House, near Southey, for four and a half centuries. They were there before 1402, when Julyan Wilkinson of Crowder House, the widow of John Wilkinson, passed the property to her son, Henry. (The only local reference to the Crowders – whose surname is derived from the occupation of fiddler – is in 1377, when Alice, the wife of Thomas Crowder, surrendered property in Grenoside to Peter Adamson; the Crowders were not recorded in the 1379 poll tax return.) In the 1451 Book of Feudal Aids Henry Wilkinson held a farm called 'Crowderfeld in the Woodhouse'. Upon his death in 1470 the farm went to his son, John, and then through direct inheritance to Thomas, Robert, William, Robert, two Williams, Nathaniel, John, William and William, whose daughter sold Crowder House in 1859. The manor court rolls record the numerous transactions of this yeoman family, including those of junior branches at Woodseats, Wincobank, Bell House and other parts of Ecclesfield parish. Six Wilkinsons were named in the 1614–15 list of cutlers, and twenty-nine Wilkinsons were taxed in south Yorkshire in 1672, including six in Southey, three in Brightside, two in Sheffield and one each in Grenofirth and Waldershelf.

Hallamshire had numerous surnames that were derived from common occupations – Barker, Chaloner, Chapman, Cook, Farrier, Fisher, Horner, Milner, Shepherd, Smith, Tailor, Tinker, Turner, Wright, etc. – but few from rare ones. Several of these names were confined to the town of Sheffield and were not found in rural parts of Hallamshire. Some did not last very long. One that did was Crapper. The original bearers of this name may have been iron-workers, like the first Stringers, but it is equally likely that they cropped textiles. The name was recorded at Ecclesfield, Emley and Idle in 1379 and it remains heavily concentrated in the West Riding. The first local mention of the surname was in 1348 when John Crapper was a witness at Chapel. In 1379 Richard Crapper and Matilda Crapper paid poll tax in the parish of Ecclesfield and in 1393 Richard Crapper was farming land in Woodsetts. In 1415 Simon Crapper moved a short distance to a farm in the soke of Southey. The family name did not multiply, but the marriage of Agnes Crapper (1559) and the baptism of Roger, the son of Peter Crapper of Mortomley (1606) are recorded in the Ecclesfield parish register and in 1633 William, the son of Godfrey Crapper, was baptised at Sheffield. The three Crappers who were taxed in south Yorkshire in 1672 – Henry in Southey, Anthony in Sheffield, and William in Stannington – each had only one hearth. The Crappers had managed to survive, but their standard of living was not high.

The Shemelds

We end with a surname whose meaning is unknown but which is confined to a single family that originated in or near Hallamshire. Over time, Shemeld was spelt in a variety of ways and gradually became Shemmell, then Shimmell, then Shimwell (the spelling that is still favoured in Derbyshire). The family was first recorded at Handsworth in 1379, when Robert Schemyld (smith) and Adam Schemyld paid poll tax. Robert Shemyld witnessed deeds at Attercliffe and Darnall between 1380 and 1392, and from 1400 to 1418 William Shemyld was tenant of the manor house at Norton. Meanwhile, in 1407 Robert Shemeild moved across Hallamshire to take part of a farm in Dungworth, in 1410 John Shemeld became tenant of a small farm in the township of Bradfield, and five years later John Sheimeld, junior, took a small farm in Fulwood. The two branches of the Shemelds remained at Dungworth for the rest of the fifteenth century and at Fulwood for several generations. The descent of the Dungworth property can be traced to its dramatic end in 1499 when John Shemeld was convicted of murder and his farm went to his victim's son and namesake, John Thompson. The Fulwood farm descended peacefully through several generations of Shemelds. In 1442 John Shymelde of Broom took the farm, after it had been leased by Robert Shymelde for the past six years and in 1444 John Shemeild moved there from Little Sheffield. The farm then passed from father to son, to Richard (1464), John (1509), Richard (1544) and John (1560).

During the second half of the sixteenth century a few Shemelds were recorded in the Bradfield register, but by then most were living in Sheffield parish. Junior members of the family had moved into the town, where they worked as cutlers and tanners. Castle and Robert Shemeld were included in the 1624–30 list of cutlers and in 1672 John Shemeld was taxed at Brightside, Joseph at Ecclesall, Castle and two Josephs at Sheffield, and Francis and Richard much further east at Auckley, beyond Doncaster. The surname had therefore remained very local, except for the two households at Auckley and that of Thomas Shemilt at Ashover, in north Derbyshire. The Shemelds provide yet one more example of the long continuity of ordinary families within Hallamshire.

Farm Houses and Outbuildings

What survives of the oldest houses and other buildings of the farming families of Hallamshire? Like the great majority of English men and women in the medieval and Tudor periods, local people lived in timber-framed houses. In this district the change to stone occurred only slowly from the second quarter of the seventeenth century onwards. A wide number of types and styles of timber-framed

Rocher Farm, Chapelry of Bradfield. This farmhouse dates from 1663, by which time Hallamshire families built in stone instead of timber. The barn was attached in the late eighteenth or early nineteenth century, following the same roof line as the house in typical Pennine fashion.

Hawkesworth Cote cruck-framed barn. Most Hallamshire farmers used the cruck-frame method when building their barns. This Midhope barn was photographed during its demolition about 1903. The rafters were fastened to the ridge pole and were supported by purlins resting on the cruck frame.

Green Farm cruck barn. The stone walls of the barn are inscribed with the names of William and Sara Couldwell and dated 1688, but during this rebuilding the old cruck frame was retained intact.

buildings were erected in south Yorkshire, where highland traditions met those of the lowlands and northern traditions met those of the midlands. In Hallamshire, two traditions prevailed: king-post trusses were used for the better houses that consisted of a central hall and cross-wings, and cruck frames sufficed for ordinary farmhouses, cottages and outbuildings. Dendrochronology dates for superior houses in the king-post style, such as Broom Hall and Bishops' House, point to the end of the fifteenth century and the early years of the sixteenth century as the period of construction.[4] The simpler cruck frame was no earlier and continued in use well into the seventeenth century, in rare cases even later. Cruck frames within Hallamshire are dated by their tree rings to the sixteenth and seventeenth centuries. The cruck barn at Hall Broom Farm, Dungworth, was erected in 1495–96, that at Ughill Manor in 1504, a cruck blade at Hangram Lane Farm, Fulwood, was first used in 1541, a cruck barn at Hoyles Farm, Bradfield, was built in 1551–52 and that at Raynor House, Bradfield, in 1593. Other timbers elsewhere can be dated only to within plus or minus nine years. Thus, a purlin from Uppergate Road, Stannington dates from *c.* 1539, the tie-beam at Well House Farm cruck barn, Stannington, is from *c.*1591, and the purlins at Hallfield barn are from *c.*1620. Documentary evidence supports this range of dates. The inventory of William Barlow of Coal Aston (1610), for example, recorded 'two peeces of Wood for two payer of Crookes praised to 5s. 0d.'.[5]

Hallamshire has one of the largest collections of cruck-framed buildings in England, with seventy-eight surviving examples and thirty-one known demolished ones. It is not surprising that S O Addy and C F Innocent, the pioneer writers on the subject of vernacular architecture, came from this district.[6] These buildings are all hidden from view by later stone roofs and walls and therefore are not widely known. Occasionally, as at Concord Park, the bases of cruck blades protrude through a wall or a sagging, exposed roof provides a clue, but generally the timber-frame is not evident from outside. Surviving cruck-framed buildings are from one to six bays stretched out in a line. In some cases, domestic and agricultural accommodation were contained under one roof in the manner of the medieval long house. At Stumperlowe, for instance, a one-bay cottage was attached to a three-bay barn and at Hall Broom, Dungworth, the end bay of a barn contains evidence of former domestic use. More often, the position of a cruck-framed barn or cowshed in line with a house that was rebuilt in stone in the seventeenth or eighteenth centuries (e.g. Oaks Fold, Shiregreen and a farm on Ecclesfield High Street) suggests the adaptation of a former long house.

Less than a quarter of the surviving cruck frames surveyed by Peter Ryder are houses and cottages; most of the rest are barns. Only a few frames are of better than average quality and even they lack architectural detail. Pond Farmhouse, Stannington, is one of the exceptions in that it has a two-bay open hall with a decorative octagonal oak post rising from the tie-beam. The cruck-framed houses are probably earlier than most of the local cruck barns. Many of the barns appear to be contemporary with seventeenth-century stone-built houses, for the old method of construction was thought to be adequate for outbuildings even when newer methods were used for a house, though sometimes these later barns were given stone walls from the start. At Concord Park some of the original wattle-and-daub infilling survives. Many of the barns did not get new stone roofs and walls until the eighteenth or nineteenth centuries. It seems surprising now, but even in an area where stone was readily available timber was the preferred building material in the Middle Ages and during the reigns of the Tudors.

RIVELIN CHASE AND HALLAM MOORS

On the western edge of Sheffield lies a moorland landscape rich in archaeological evidence from prehistoric times to the twentieth century. The moors that stretch down the eastern side of the River Derwent to the southern edge of the Chatsworth Estate rank with Bodmin Moor, Dartmoor, Stanton Moor and the North York Moors in the extent and quality of their remains from the Bronze Age. On Hallam Moors, when the heather has been burnt by gamekeepers or in an accidental fire, the rambler near the Headstone stumbles across dozens of burial cairns and clearance cairns and occasionally reaches a larger monument such as the barrow at Crow Chin on the Stanage escarpment. The remains of three Bronze Age barrows near Lodge Moor Hospital have been excavated.[1] They date from a time when this moorland landscape was very different in character, with much more wood and far less peat, and with a milder climate. Bronze Age people shaped the local environment in a significant way, but the survival of so much evidence of their activities is due to deliberate decisions in later times to use the moors for particular activities. In the case of the Hallam or Stanage Moors the present character of the landscape was largely determined by the fashion for hunting deer in the Middle Ages and the enclosure of the moors for grouse shooting at the end of the eighteenth century.

The age and purpose of archaeological features on the moors are often difficult to determine. A deep trench might have been dug as an ancient boundary or simply to assist drainage. Some were cut through the peat in the nineteenth century to stop the spread of fire.[2] What appears to be a trench in dry weather is often more convincing as a natural watercourse in wet. Other trenches peter out because of the drift of silt and the deposit of sand and gravel in storms. A trench that descends northwards from Crow Chin Rocks and is well-marked in the peat as it heads towards Moscar disappears in this way. It is the most intriguing trench on the moor, for it appears to have served as a boundary between the lordship of Hallamshire and the manor of Hathersage and between the counties of Yorkshire and Derbyshire. The old county boundary had certain fixed points, such as Stanedge Pole and Moscar Cross, and it incorporated natural features such as Dovestone Tor on the skyline high above Derwent Edge, but before large-scale maps were available the exact line between these points was often disputed, even after a trench had been dug. The trench between Crow Chin Rocks and Moscar was not fully accepted as the boundary between the lordship of Hallamshire and the manor of Hathersage until 1724.[3]

In a confirmation charter of the late thirteenth century Thomas de Furnival, lord of Hallamshire, granted to Ellys of Ughill and all the men of Ughill, Nether Bradfield, Thornsett and Hawkesworth:

the Herbage as it lies in length and breadth between Ugghill Brook, Eventrevick, and the way leading from Hope to Sheffield, Bradrake, Seven Stones in Horderon, Weanston, to the Water of Agden, for the depasturing and agisting of their own proper Cattle, to be taken Yearly, without any hindrance of me or my Heirs, as they have held the same to Farm at the Will of my Ancestors

at a yearly rent of four marks of silver.[4] The area so defined is that which was known as Hawkesworth Firth within the chapelry of Bradfield. Eventrevick cannot be identified but the way from Hope to Sheffield came along the ridge via Crawshaw Head and is known now as Long Lane. The boundary then veered south up Oaking Brook and west across the moor to Crow Chin (on the same line as the

Stanedge Pole graffiti. The rocks that form the base for the Hallamshire boundary pole are carved with graffiti dating back to the seventeenth century.

present parliamentary constituency boundary marked on the Ordnance Survey map) before turning north along Broad Rake towards Moscar Cross. Our trench was not named but was on the line of this thirteenth-century boundary. The Seven Stones have gone but, as we shall see, 'Weanston' was an alternative name for the Wheelstones, the eye-catching rocks on the horizon.

Our trench may have been dug to mark the medieval boundary but we cannot be sure that it is as old as that. It was certainly in existence by 1559 when the manor court of Francis, fifth Earl of Shrewsbury, settled a dispute over grazing rights between the tenants of Rivelin and Hawkesworth Firths. Part of the agreed boundary followed 'the ditch that parteth Sheffield and Bradfield parish unto the north end of Stanage'.[5] The trench starts near Stanage End and runs parallel with the present county boundary, which is only a few yards away to the west, in a northerly direction. As we shall see, however, the inhabitants of Hathersage (rightly) denied that it parted Sheffield from Bradfield, claiming that their territory extended up to it and that the rights claimed by Bradfield men were fictitious.

A perambulation of the bounds of Hallamshire in 1574 went

from the Broad Rake straight downwards to a place where certaine stones are sett upon the ends and haveing markes upon them called the Seavenstones ... straight over the broke or sicke there, to a place called the Wainstones, being distant by estimation three quarters of a mile.[6]

Further perambulations of the boundary between Hallamshire and Hathersage in 1574 and 1656 also proceeded along Stanage and the Broad Rake to the Seven Stones, across the brook, and on to the 'Wayne Stones or Wheele Stones'. Coming the other way, a perambulation of the Hathersage boundary,

Right: Thomas Jeffreys's map of Yorkshire (1772) shows how the township of Stannington stretched over the moors to the Derbyshire border and included the northern part of Rivelin Chase.

This ancient boundary ditch at Moscar, which separates Hallamshire from the lordship of Hathersage, goes back to at least the Elizabethan period and was probably dug in the Middle Ages.

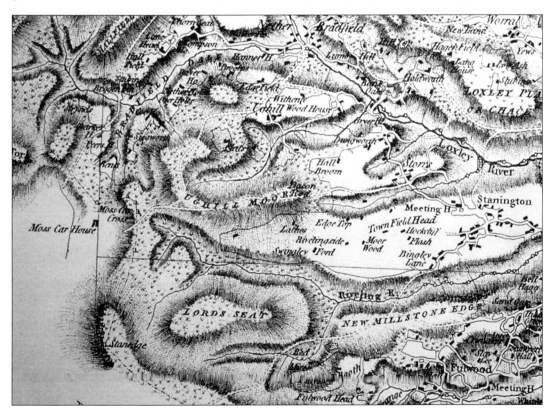

also taken in 1656, went via Moscar Cross (at that time called Humble Stone Cross or Hambleton Cross) 'following the Top of the Hill to a place called Broadrake, and so following the Torr top to a place called Crow Chin'. Broad Rake therefore appears to have been the name given to the broad path along the escarpment from Stanage End to Crow Chin. The dispute between Bradfield and Hathersage in 1724 was settled by an arbitrator, William Jessop of Broom Hall, who accepted the line followed by the Hathersage men, the same line as that of the present county boundary.[7] On the map attached to the Enclosure Award of 1805 for the Manor of Sheffield our trench was marked as 'Ancient Ditch'. It formed the north-western boundary of the 'Black Moors' that lay within Stannington township in the chapelry of Bradfield. The manor of Hathersage lay immediately beyond.[8] Just how ancient the ditch is we cannot say, but it has served as a boundary line for well over 400 hundred years and is possibly much older.

The Medieval Chase

The medieval lords of Hallamshire set aside huge tracts of land for the hunting of deer and the grazing of livestock. When the Crown enquired into his privileges in 1281 Thomas de Furnival claimed that he and his ancestors had enjoyed the right to hunt within his lordship since the Norman Conquest.[9] Across the River Sheaf from Sheffield Castle the lords of Hallamshire enclosed 2,461 acres of land into a park and built a hunting lodge on one of its most prominent ridges. In 1637 a thousand deer were said to roam in this park.[10] The favoured retainers of the lords enclosed smaller parks at their sub-manors of Ecclesall, Wadsley, Shirecliffe and Cowley or hunted on the moors around Midhope. The lords of Hallamshire also hunted over moorland in their chases at Loxley and in the Rivelin Valley. Chases were larger than parks but were not enclosed by palings. They were a lord's equivalent to a royal forest. Elsewhere in south Yorkshire Wharncliffe Chase and Hatfield Chase are two well-known place-names that survive from the Middle Ages. An alternate name for a chase was firth or frith, as in Chapel-en-le-Frith in the High Peak. Rivelin Chase was sometimes called Rivelin Firth and the adjacent moorland area at the top of Bradfield Dale was still known in 1637 as Hawkesworth Firth.[11]

The chase or firth in the Rivelin Valley covered thousands of acres on the moorland fringes of the parish of Sheffield and the chapelry of Bradfield. John Harrison's survey of the manor in 1637 measured that part of 'Rivelin Firth that lyeth in the parish of Sheffield' at $5,531\frac{1}{2}$ acres, Stannington woods within Rivelin Firth at 217 acres, and 'the other part of Rivelin Firth lying ... in the parish of Bradfield' at $1,114\frac{1}{2}$ acres, making 6,863 acres in all. Near the end of the thirteenth century, in a confirmation of the grazing rights of the inhabitants of Stannington, Moorwood, Hallam and Fulwood within the chase, the boundaries were said to extend from the confluence of the rivers Loxley and the Rivelin at Malin Bridge, towards Bell Hagg and Whiteley Wood, then up the Porter Brook and on to Stanage, and back along 'the common way which leads from Sheffield towards Darwent'.[12] In other words, it included most of the township of Upper Hallam (one of the six townships into which Sheffield parish was divided for purposes of local government) and a large part of the township of Stannington within the chapelry of Bradfield. The 'common way' seems to have headed back east towards Stannington via Moscar (whose name means the 'moss marsh') and Long Lane, the track already mentioned as being the southern boundary of Hawkesworth Firth. The hunting of deer and of hares was only an occasional pastime of the lords, so the right to graze livestock was allowed not only to freeholders and tenants within the bounds of the chase but was rented to other farmers from further afield. In the 1440s, for example, the accounts of Henry Wrasteler, the forester of Rivelin, included 'pasturing-rents for divers plough-cattle on the moor from strangers there'.[13]

The buildings within the chase were erected for special purposes, either by the officers of the lord or by the lay brothers of abbeys that had been granted special privileges. The most prominent building was the lord's hunting lodge, which stood high above the river valley on the edge of Lodge Moor, close to the track known as the Long Causeway, which crossed the moors from Sheffield to Hathersage, following in part the line of an old Roman road heading for Brough (Navio). The site is now occupied by a house known as 'Rivelin Lodge'.

Fulwood means 'dirty wood' and was the name given to the south-eastern end of the chase. A mid-thirteenth century charter in the Beauchief Abbey Cartulary refers to the canons' grange there, probably on the site of the present Fulwood Grange Farm.[14] Moorland granges such as this were geared to the rearing of cattle. The medieval lords of Hallamshire had their own specialist cattle farms or vaccaries nearby at Fulwood Booth and at Old Booth, Bradfield. (Booth was an Old Danish word for such a farm; most of the old farms in Edale have the name Booth attached to them for this reason.) In 1184 these two Hallamshire booths were restocked with forty cows, four bulls and eight oxen. The nineteenth-century Fulwood Booth Farm stands a few hundred yards west of the Beauchief Abbey grange, right on the edge of the moor. It is the first building to come into view when travelling from Stanedge Pole towards Redmires. In 1637 John Harrison's survey of the manor measured 123 acres at:

A Piece of Pasture Called fulwood booth lying Betweene Rivelin firth North and South and abutteth upon Roper hill East and Red myers West (this part hath a house on it Belonging to one of the keepers).[15]

In Elizabethan times the lord's young beasts were still being raised there and wool was carded and spun into coverlet yarn for local weavers. The servants' quarterly wages which were due at Michaelmas in 1574 included those of 'William Brodhead at Fulwood bowth', 'the shepperd at Fulwood bowthe', and 'Jennet Smith the servant mayde at Fulwood bowthe'.[16] This record provides the first definite reference to the keeping of sheep within the chase. Other parts of the Hallamshire moors, such as at Agden, were set aside as sheep pastures, but Rivelin Chase was originally used for deer and cattle, with seasonal grazing by pigs in the woods.

Parts of Rivelin Chase were wooded in the Middle Ages and haggs of holly were planted for the deer. Later, the woods were turned into coppices.

By the seventeenth century (and possibly from long before) part of the chase on the northern bank of the upper reaches of the River Rivelin was enclosed by a stone wall and used for grazing. In 1637 John Harrison described the enclosure as 429 acres of pasture, though he named it Auley Meadows. It seems to have acquired its name from the Hawley family who lived in Fulwood in the later Middle Ages and who were probably tenants. The name had taken its modern form of Hollow Meadows by 1724. Harrison also noted a pasture at Redmires, immediately west of Fulwood Booth, that was 'reserved for the Red deare except eight Cow gates and A horse gate which two of the Keepers hath in regard of their office, 73a.2r.27p.'.[17] On the Stannington side of the Rivelin 'the Old Laund' was 'reserved for the Deare being Invironed with Rivelin Firth ... 62a.0r.28p.'.[18] The chase was still being used for the rearing and occasional hunting of deer in 1637 but its days were numbered. The Dukes of Norfolk, who had acquired the lordship of Hallamshire through marriage, did not live at Sheffield and during the later seventeenth century the deer were removed from both Sheffield Park and Rivelin Chase. The 'Old Laund' became 'The Lawns' farm and the Duke's officers cut down the great trees which for centuries had adorned the park and chase. A survey of 1624[19] spoke of the 'great store of timber' in the Rivelin Valley and in 1662 John Evelyn included eulogies of these trees in his book about English woods.[20] He wrote, 'In the upper end of Rivelin stood a tree, called the Lord's Oak, of twelve yards about, and the top yielded twenty-one cord; cut down about thirteen years since'. Mr. Halton, the auditor to the Duke of Norfolk, told him that 'Rivelin itself is [now] totally destitute of that issue she once might have gloried in of Oaks, there being only the Hall Park adjoining, which keeps up with its number of Oaks'. Hall Park, which stretched up the present Liberty Hill towards Stannington, still contained trees of enormous girth. Harrison observed that travellers had 'not seen such Timber in Cristendome'. By the early eighteenth century, however, all these woods had been felled and the timber sold. Neither Hall Park nor Rivelin appeared in a list of the Duke's woods in 1720.[21] Much of the old character of the Rivelin Valley had disappeared. John Wilson, the antiquary of Broomhead Hall, noted in his journal later in the century, 'This Riveling was formerly full of wood and a chace of Red Deer therein'.[22] The only wood to survive was The Coppice, which stretched down from Rivelin Lodge and up the opposite bank of the river. Part of it remains to this day, though it has not been coppiced for a century or so.

The removal of the deer brought another, more subtle, change to the Rivelin Valley woods. For centuries, holly trees had been specially nurtured as winter fodder for the deer and in other moorland areas for sheep. The accounts of the forester of Bradfield in 1441#42 note 'holly sold there for the fodder of the animals in winter'. As late as 1712 the Duke of Norfolk's woodward paid four shillings to Henry Broomhead for going on horseback for two days 'in the Great Snow to see if anyone Cropped Holling'. Small woods known as 'hollin haggs' were carefully managed and some leased to tenants. In 1574, for instance, 'one hage of hollen at Bell hagg' was let to 'Phillipe Morton of the Cloughe feilde' for five shillings a year. In 1637 John Harrison recorded several 'Hollin Rents', including 'Thomas Revell for a Hagge in Rivelin, £1.2s.2½d.'. After the removal of the deer, sheep continued to be fed in this way during winter time. Near the end of the century Abraham de la Pryme, the minister of Thorne, near Doncaster, noted in his journal that:

In the south west of Yorkshire, at and about Bradfield, and in Darbyshire, they feed all their sheep in winter with holly leaves and bark, which they eat more greedily than any grass. To every farm there is so many holly trees; and the more there is the farm is dearer; but care is taken to plant great numbers of them in all farms thereabouts.

In 1725 a member of the Earl of Oxford's party passing through Sheffield Park observed:

the greatest number of wild stunted holly trees that I ever saw together. They extend themselves on the common, on each side of the brook ... for a considerable way. This tract of ground they grow upon is called the Burley Hollyngs ... having their branches lopped off every winter for the support of the sheep which browse upon them, and at the same time are sheltered by the stunted part that is left remaining.

By that time new fodder crops were making the old practice redundant. In 1710 the Duke of

This nineteenth-century farmhouse at Fulwood Booth occupies the site of the medieval *booth* or cattle-rearing farm of the lords of Hallamshire.

Norfolk's bailiff recorded several holly haggs 'unlett but most of them destroyed'. The final reference to this use of holly in the manorial records came in 1737, when a Bradfield man agreed 'to take all that hag of Hollin called Ugghill Wood'.[23]

In the summary of his survey of 1637, John Harrison commented:

This Mannor is not only profitable, but for pleasure alsoe, being furnished with red Deare and Fallow, with hares and some Rowes, with Phesants and great store of Partridges, and moore Game in abundance both black and red, as moore Cockes, moore Hens and young pootes upon the moores, as also Mallard, Teale, Hearnshewes [heron] and Plover, the chiefest fishing within this Mannor is in the River that passeth through the same, wherein are great store of Salmon, Trouts, Chevens [chub], Eles and other small fish.

Much of this pleasure was obtained in Rivelin Chase, where deer and hares could be hunted and birds trapped in nets or brought down by falcons. The 'moor game' included black and red grouse (male, female and young) and golden plover. The absentee Dukes of Norfolk took little interest in the sporting opportunities on their manor, however. The deer were withdrawn and the craze for grouse shooting had not yet begun. During the eighteenth century Hallam Moors were largely given over to the grazing of sheep and cattle by tenant farmers. Evidence presented in the boundary dispute of 1724 included that of George Brownehill, who twenty years previously had lived in 'a Cabbin at the End of Broadrake' while he looked after cattle that Hathersage farmers grazed on Moscar. Others spoke of burning bracken and digging turf there. Signs of industrial activity, from the seventeenth to the nineteenth centuries, can also be found on Hallam Moors. Millstone Hole survives as a place-name near Wyming Brook and dozens of abandoned millstones lie below Stanage. More surprisingly shallow coal pits are dotted about the moorland landscape.[24]

Parliamentary Enclosure

Millions of acres of commons, wastes and open fields in England and Wales were enclosed by thousands of private Acts of Parliament during the second half of the eighteenth century and the first half of the nineteenth. The first local Act allowed the enclosure of the Ecclesall commons between 1779 and 1788, including 268 acres of 'High Moors' beyond Ringinglow. Then between 1791 and 1805 the moors of Upper Hallam, Nether Hallam, Stannington, Storrs and Dungworth were enclosed. The proposal for enclosure, which was put forward by the Duke of Norfolk and other landowners in 1787, met with opposition from 'several of the freeholders and inhabitants', but these opponents owned insufficient land to defy those who wished to enclose.[25] The enclosure of the 'Black Moors' of the former Rivelin Chase was not contentious but the loss of Crookesmoor, on the edge of Sheffield, aroused deep feelings of resentment. When the Act was passed in 1791, the enclosure of Crookesmoor was resisted by a large crowd and the authorities called for armed forces to restore order. The *Sheffield Register* of 29 July 1791 reported that:

> *On Wednesday at noon there arrived here from Nottingham a detachment of Light Dragoons in consequence of application to Government for them. The grounds which gave occasion for the application were, we believe, a violent repulse given to the Commissioners of Enclosure for Stannington and Hallam in this neighbourhood some days ago, on their attending to mark boundaries.*

The enclosure went ahead, but the surveying, settling of claims and marking out of boundaries took fourteen years before an award was made.[26]

It is a popular, though mistaken, view that everyone had rights on the commons. In fact, common rights belonged only to that minority of the inhabitants who were landowners and their rights varied in proportion to the size of their farms. Common rights to graze animals, collect fuel, and so on were carefully regulated through the manor courts. Only those people who possessed common rights received 'allotments' in lieu upon the publication of an enclosure award. A first problem for the commissioners therefore was to listen to claims and to establish just who were legally entitled to recompense. The inhabitants of Hallam, Fulwood, Stannington and Moorwood were allotted land in lieu of their ancient right to herbage in Rivelin and the lord of the manor no longer asked them for the token fee which they had paid from time immemorial. Seventy other men had their claims for compensation dismissed. A Mr Gibson, acting on their behalf, claimed that 1,000 acres on the Black Moors were 'Rocks where the Poor burn Fearne and raise £120 by the Ashes'. He also claimed that the poor kept flocks of geese and 'many Galloways for Grinders to carry goods'. The claimants – including thirty-five cutlers, eighteen grinders, seven husbandmen, two shoemakers, a gentleman, a schoolmaster, a tailor and a wheelwright – were dismissed by Mr Wood, whose legal opinion was sought by the enclosure commissioners, as being 'most of them Wheelfellows – probably many not Inhabitants'. He judged (correctly) that the late-thirteenth century charter which we have quoted did not include the poor but allowed grazing rights only to the inhabitants who were freeholders.[27] The grazing of geese and galloways and the burning of ashes were not customary rights but were practices that had arisen with laxer manorial control after the removal of the deer and because of the spread of cutlers' grinding wheels up the Rivelin Valley as trade and population increased.

The Duke of Norfolk received large 'allotments' not only in recognition of his previous ownership of the chase but in lieu of the great and small tithes, which Francis, fifth Earl of Shrewsbury, had acquired at the dissolution of the priories at Coventry and Worksop. (A system which had been designed to provide revenue for religious institutions had been corrupted for the benefit of the Crown and rich landowners when the monasteries had been dissolved by Henry VIII.) The enclosure surveyors measured a total of 7,232 acres of moorland and commons, including 3,935 acres in Upper Hallam and 2,004 acres in Stannington. The Duke of Norfolk got the lion's share.

William Fairbank's map of the parish of Sheffield (1795)[28] marks some of the new enclosures, long before the publication of the Enclosure Award. Parts of Hallam Moors and Lodge Moor were already divided into the large, rectangular fields which can still be recognised on the map and on the ground today. Four large fields, starting in the east with Ash Cabin Flat, were set out in line, with another to the north west, they have since been sub-divided but their original shape can still be recognised immediately north of Redmires Reservoirs. Some have reverted to moorland but others are green pastures. One of these fields (which occupied the site of the former 'Lord's Seat') took the name of Rape Piece because rape was the first crop to be grown there, followed by black oats, turnips and potatoes.[29] Fairbank also marked two routes across the moors: the ancient track of the Long Causeway, and a new road that a generation later would form part of the Snake Pass from Sheffield to Glossop.

The former Auley Meadows, which had long since become Hollow Meadows, assumed its present character in the mid-nineteenth century. In 1844 the Duke of Norfolk let much of his land there on long leases to small occupiers. For the first ten years the rents were nominal and afterwards never exceeded five shillings per acre. Houses were built and small enclosures were brought 'into a good state of cultivation'.[30] For instance, three small cottages nicknamed 'Sparrow Barracks' were erected by a blade and scissor forger and a file forger; they were occupied until the end of the century, when they were demolished by Mr William Wilson of Beauchief Hall, who (as we shall see) had bought Hallam Moors from the duke. A 'Truant School', which was used from *c*.1871 to 1922, was built by able-bodied paupers, who walked three to five miles from Sheffield each morning to be there by eight o'clock. A Jews' Burial Ground was constructed nearby and Mark Firth, the Sheffield steelmaster, built a tiny Methodist chapel at Moscar. The area acquired the sarcastic nickname of 'New England'.

A more dramatic change to the moorland landscape came with the construction of reservoirs by the Sheffield Waterworks Company to supply the needs of the rapidly-expanding town. Between 1830 and 1854 three reservoirs were constructed at Redmires and two were built in the Rivelin Valley. The water flowed by gravity along conduits to Crookes and thence by pipes into the town.[31]

The conduit across Hallam Moors brings water to Redmires Reservoirs and on to Crookes, to supply Sheffield. The whole system was built by the Sheffield Waterworks Company between 1830 and 1854.

Grouse shooting

In 1637 John Harrison had included the hunting of moor fowl, both black and red, amongst the pleasures of the manor of Sheffield. At that time, red grouse (*Lagopus lagopus*) were commonly known as moor fowl or moor game.[32] Black grouse have since declined so sharply in the Peak District that they are now almost extinct; just a few pairs survive on the Staffordshire Moorlands. The right to hunt all forms of game had been severely restricted since the Middle Ages but the two dozen Acts which Parliament passed between 1671 and 1831 made hunting the sport of a rich minority. In 1671 the medieval laws were strengthened to prevent the hunting of hares, pheasants, partridges and moor fowl by those who did not own freehold land worth at least £100 a year or leaseholds worth £150. The Act also authorized lords of manors whose rank was at least that of a gentleman with a coat-of-arms to appoint gamekeepers, who had the right to seize guns and dogs from suspected poachers.[33] In 1762 Parliament began to regulate the seasons in which game could be legally killed and by 1773 the present dates were agreed. The grouse-shooting season was established as 12 August to 10 December and anyone caught shooting outside that season was fined heavily.[34]

Until the late seventeenth century the usual methods of taking grouse, partridges or pheasants were the inexpensive ones of hawking and netting. Hawking had largely disappeared by the beginning of the eighteenth century but netting survived a little longer. The royalist gentry who returned from exile on the Continent in 1660 had learned to use the flintlock – a shorter, safer and more accurate gun than its predecessor, the matchlock.[35] John Wilson, the eighteenth-century antiquary of Broomhead Hall, claimed that a member of his own family, who died in 1687, had been the first person who had shot grouse on the wing on the local moors.[36] George Walker, *The Costume of Yorkshire* (1814), contains scenes depicting a moor guide and a dog-breaker, who led small groups of shooters with guns and dogs on to the moors, and who carried the game bag and ammunition.[37] At that time, grouse-shooting still involved vigorous physical exercise.

These grouse shooting butts on Bradfield Moors are amongst many local ones that were first constructed during the 1860s.

During the second half of the eighteenth century the way that grouse-shooting was organized began to change. By the end of the century some 'sportsmen' were keeping game books to record the kill. They began to boast of the huge numbers of partridges, pheasants and grouse that they had shot. As early as 1773 'vast wastes' in Yorkshire were rented 'for the purpose of shooting Moor Game' and by the early nineteenth century some moors had been taken over by grouse-hunting clubs, whose members paid for 'tickets'.[38] During the 1790s a new method of shooting – the *battue* – was imported from the Continent on to the Holkham estate in Norfolk. Pheasants and partridges (though not at first grouse) were driven into the line of fire by beaters, servants were at hand to re-load the guns, and gamekeepers offered advice and support. Gun technology improved enormously during the nineteenth century; in 1815 the percussion cap replaced the flintlock, by the 1860s the breech loader was replacing the muzzle loader.[39] During the 1860s the grouse-shooting butt, from which the 'sportsman' aimed his rapid-firing gun at the birds which had been driven over the horizon by beaters, was introduced on many of the local moors.[40] The annual slaughter of grouse rose to almost unbelievable heights. In August 1913 a record 'bag' of 2,843 birds was shot by nine guns on a single day on Broomhead Moors.[41]

Hallam Moors

The enclosure of Hallam Moors and of the 'Black Moors' on the Stannington part of the former Rivelin Chase allowed the Duke of Norfolk to set aside huge tracts of moorland for grouse-shooting. All the local moors to the east of Sheffield and Chesterfield were converted into exclusive grouse-shooting tracts by the major landowners at this time, either for their own use or to rent to others. In his new edition of Hunter's *Hallamshire* (1869) the Revd Alfred Gatty wrote:

Prior to the year 1821, the game on the Bradfield Moors had for a long while been preserved by the Duke of Norfolk, and a man named Bamford was the keeper. A lodge was built for him between Moscar and Hollow-meadows, tower-shaped in form, very conspicuous in situation, and overlooking the moors far and wide. It was called "Bamford Lodge", and as a ruin - the outer walls alone remaining - it still bears the name. So much did Bamford neglect his duty to preserve the game, that the grouse became very scarce; and in 1819 several sporting gentlemen of Sheffield conceived that, by a little exercise of trouble and perseverance, the game might yet be restored. A game association was therefore formed.[42]

This Bradfield Game Association continued into the twentieth century.

At first the 'bags' were modest. Gatty thought that:

a good shot on the 12th of August may kill forty or fifty brace of red grouse. This wonderful improvement of the sport is greatly attributable to the alteration of the game laws, which in 1832 conferred the power over game upon the owners of the land, instead of its being vested in the lord of the manor. This change at once raised the rent payable per acre to about four times its previous value; the Duke of Norfolk, in his capacity as lord of the manor, having hitherto owned the game.

The first day of shooting attracted widespread interest. Gatty enthused:

On the 12th of August the moors attract crowds from Sheffield as spectators, who come by thousands, and but for the wild space over which they are distributed, they would mar the sport. But there is a good-humoured view to be taken of this motley invasion; and as all vehicles, varying from the costermonger's donkey-cart to the four-horsed omnibus, are strictly kept on the roads, those who have the enjoyment of shooting need not grudge or resent, which they do not, the universal interest felt in this locality in all which concerns the sportsman's recreations.

The Hallam or Stanage Moors were leased not to the game association but to private individuals. B P Broomhead, a lawyer who lived at Wales Lodge, Kiveton Park (and previously in Broomhall Park, Sheffield), built Stanedge Lodge about 1869, in the early years of his lease. He used it as his shooting box and summer house.[43] Stanage Moors (725a.1r.5p.), Stanedge Lodge and Lord's Seat, with farm lands (98a.0r.36p.), the Grouse and Trout Inn at Redmires (since demolished), a homestead and farm (66a.0r.10p.), and Perkin's Farm (74a.3r.19p.) were purchased by Mr Broomhead Cotton Fox in

Grouse moors are carefully managed by the regular burning of sections in rotation to encourage the growth of fresh green heather. The rotation is evident from the patterns on Moscar Moor, seen from Stanage.

1881 for £14,250. Fox spent many thousands of pounds in improving the estate, which was sold by his representatives upon his death in 1893 back to the Duke of Norfolk for £26,600. On 11 May 1897 the Duke of Norfolk sold 3,672 acres of 'Grand Grouse Moors ... White Path Moss, Stanedge, and Hallam Moors' for £63,000. The bill of sale listed the game as grouse, snipe, curlew, golden plover, black cock and rabbits. Stanage Moors, the Lodge and part of Hallam Moors were sold to William Wilson of Beauchief Hall for £40,000, at £19 per acre. Wilson also bought the Grouse and Trout Inn for £3,000. 'The Old Hallam Shooting and Farm Lands' (648 acres) were sold to Mr Alderman Gamble of Sheffield for £11,000. 'White Path Moss Grouse Moor', (c. 900 acres) was sold to Mr Wilson Mappin for £9,000. This sale of the duke's was described as 'The Finest Sporting Estate ever offered in Sheffield or District'. Meanwhile, the adjacent Moscar Moor (1,172a) had been sold in 1895 to Mr Wilson Mappin for £24,000.[44] A series of eleven identical stones, inscribed WW on their eastern sides and WM on the west, mark the boundary of Wilson's and Mappin's moors between the quarry at Stanage End and Moscar, close to the ancient boundary trench.[45]

William Wilson (1850–1927) was the head of the family that had made its fortune from the Sharrow Snuff Mill. He was a Justice of the Peace for Derbyshire and Master of the Barlow Hounds from 1878 to 1900 until a spinal injury caused by a hunting accident forced him to turn to the less strenuous activity of shooting grouse.[46] Wilson Mappin was the younger son of Sir Frederick Mappin, Sheffield cutler and benefactor; his first name came from links to another Wilson family in Sheffield. Wilson and Mappin immediately ensured that their moorland estates were used only for the rearing and shooting of grouse and to a lesser extent rabbits. In 1897 the 250 sheep that had grazed on White Path Moor were driven off on Mappin's orders. Wilson soon took similar steps. A touch of variety was provided by a herd of Highland longhorns, but sheep were banned so that grouse could graze unimpeded.[47] And, as on all the local moors, gamekeepers were instructed to stop anyone who tried to ramble across what was now very private property.

In 1907 William Wilson began an extraordinary project to assist the rearing of grouse and to encourage his game not to fly off on to someone else's moor. He or his gamekeepers had probably noticed that natural basins in rocks collected rainwater, which the grouse drank.[48] Wilson therefore decided to employ his masons to create artificial troughs in the natural boulders that were littered around his moorland estate. A typical basin is about eighteen inches long and twelve inches wide but some are much larger. Number 19 on Stanage Edge – the largest of all – has a trough that is five feet long by two feet wide. Rainwater is fed into the basins by long runnels, which were cut to fit the shape of the rock. Each stone is numbered in sequence. Such 'grouse-drinking troughs' or 'rock basins' are a familiar sight to walkers along Stanage Edge and they have become a subject of much discussion.[49] In what we regard as a healthy 'fun-project' in our retirement, but which others think is a decidedly cranky pastime, my next-door neighbour, Barrie Blanksby, and I are attempting to locate and map all the 108 troughs that exist in three different sequences on the moor. So far, with the help of Alan Yates, Mike Hayes and Peter Hayes, we have found 103. Number 1 in the Stanage Edge sequence is on the path at OS reference 237848, some 400 yards away from number 2, which lies twenty yards into the moor, only fifteen yards away from number 3, which takes the form of a unique double-trough. It is clear from the start that the troughs were not arranged in a systematic manner and that the basic design of a basin fed by two runnels was adapted in numerous, idiosyncratic ways. William Wilson is reputed to have chosen the stones himself, tapping them with his stick. The availability of suitable stones was obviously a prime consideration. The chosen ones come in a wide variety of shapes and sizes. They lie close together on the approach to High Neb but are set far apart as the escarpment swings round to Crow Chin. Some look almost as fresh as when they were first cut but others are obscured by heather, bilberries or grass, some totally so. The basin and runnels of number 21 on the Stanage Edge sequence are now completely covered; only the number

One of eleven identical stones that mark the boundary between the grouse moors of William Wilson (within Hallamshire) and Wilson Mappin (within Hathersage).

The following photographs are troughs carved by George Broomhead for William Wilson from 1907. Wilson ordered the carving of 108 troughs in three groups on Hallam Moor.

catches the eye. Number 37 is easy to miss, even though a path goes over it. In other cases, troughs are visible only after a stretch of heather has been burnt. Number 61 is hard to find in normal years. The few that have not yet been found may well come to light when the next controlled burnings take place.

The Stanage Edge troughs are found along the escarpment as far north as the quarry at Stanage End, where they veer to the northeast along Crow Chin Rocks and continue in an erratic line in and out of the moor and then down the slope as far as number 75 at OS reference 235874, near the start of Black Clough. Another line of twenty-seven troughs, running from near the start of the Conduit at the top of Oaking Clough past the Headstone to Mare Folds, Wyming Brook, is less well known. These are mostly cut to a standard design of a basin fed by two runnels but no two are exactly alike. Numbers 13 and 14 are the most unusual of all the 108 troughs on the moor, for the basins on the ground are filled by channels which descend almost vertically from an upright rock. The numbers on the first few stones in this sequence (especially 2, 3 and 5) are cut in an unusually

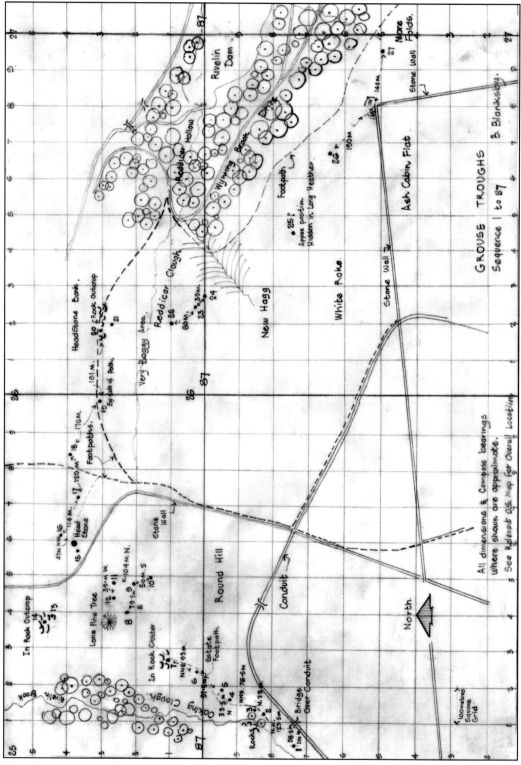

Map of Oaking Clough - Wyming Brook sequence of troughs

ornate manner. Number 21 was exceptionally difficult to find as all the evidence was hidden under a mass of bilberries and heather that had spread across the rock. The line of troughs zig-zags across the moor in an unpredictable manner. The first fourteen are separated from the rest by a high stone wall to the west of the prominent natural rock known as the Headstone. In the eastern section the gaps between the stones lengthen considerably. Number 27, the last one, is a quarter-of-a-mile beyond number 26 and is half-hidden in heather 150 yards past the north-east corner of Ash Cabin Flat. It may well have been the final trough to have been cut out of the rocks on William Wilson's moor.

Ramblers are familiar with some of these troughs but few people are aware of the existence of another group of six near (though not accessible from) Stanedge Pole, which were in fact the first to be constructed. Alan Yates, the discoverer of this group, has solved the mystery of when the project began.[50] On a south-facing boulder, about a quarter-of-a-mile from Stanedge Lodge, at OS grid reference 245846, is a basin fed by two long channels on which is carved 'W. Wilson / 1907 / No 1.' The style of carving is identical to those of the other two sequences. Accounts in the possession of Jeremy Archdale of Moscar Lodge, the owner of the moor, show that this was indeed the first of the 108 basins and that all the rest were carved in the next few years, well before the outbreak of the World War I. The

accounts refer to 'Broomhead's drinking troughs' and show that William Wilson paid 7s $3\frac{1}{2}$d per trough. The memory amongst present members of the Broomhead family is that George Broomhead (born 1893) learned his trade with an experienced mason and that carving the basins was his first job. The second drinking trough in this short sequence, forty yards to the east of the first, has an ingenious arrangement whereby the basin was carved at the lower end of the stone and was fed by just one channel, which cleverly uses the natural slope of the rock. The other four troughs have simpler designs, which soon became standard ones. Some are now partly hidden amongst the heather, bilberries, grass and bracken. The number 6 on the last stone looks like the letter b. George Broomhead had acquired greater skill by the time that he carved the ornate letters on the troughs near Oaking Clough.

Wilson's idea was not taken up by any other owner of a grouse moor. The troughs are unique testimony to his passion for the shooting of game. Grouse are still shot from butts on Hallam Moors but on a much reduced scale. Stanedge Lodge is no longer used as a base for the pursuit of grouse but is now devoted to clay-pigeon shooting. In their present neglected condition the troughs have become a fascinating archaeological record. Although gamekeepers still manage much of the moor for grouse and fight a running battle with foxes, crows and other predators, sheep have been allowed back. Neil Taylor at Wethercote Farm keeps about 1,000 Swaledales and Woodlands sheep on Hallam Moors, Bamford Moor and Derwent Edge. In 1988 these moors were designated an Environmentally Sensitive Area, one of whose objectives is to conserve and improve moorland vegetation. In the breeding season the haunting notes of the curlew and the mournful call of the golden plover can be heard amongst the harsher cries of grouse and at twilight nightjar and woodcock can be seen flying low, uttering their distinctive sounds. This is a precious landscape, so close to Sheffield and yet so remote, a particular part of the south Pennine moors, with its own distinctive history and a lasting appeal to all who know it.

MILLSTONES ON THE MOORS

The modern visitor to the Peak District is welcomed to the first of Britain's National Parks by a distinctive symbol formed by a millstone perched on top of a rectangular stone base. It is an appropriate emblem for it conveys something of the rough character of the Dark Peak while at the same time commemorating a former rural industry whose products were known throughout the land. So characteristic of the south Pennine escarpments was this particular trade that when geologists classified the different strata of rocks that form the backbone of England they named the underlying hard beds of sandstone the Millstone Grit series. Long before the invention of the water mill these rocks had been fashioned by men into rotary querns. Stones shaped into querns during the Roman period lie abandoned in various stages of manufacture on Wharncliffe Edge, whose very name is a corruption of 'Quern-cliff'; others are on display at Weston Park Museum, Sheffield.[1] This centuries-old industry came to an end between the first and second world wars when markets could no longer be found for its products.

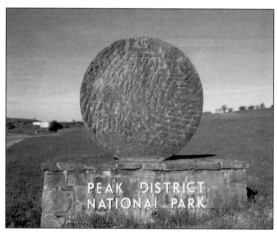

Old millstones have be re-used as signs to mark entrances to the Peak District National Park. This one stands at Owler Bar.

Abandoned millstones litter the countryside around the prominent gritstone edges that dominate the skyline east of the river Derwent, on or near the western borders of Hallamshire.[2] They are found in profusion on the Chatsworth and Rivelin grits which form one of the middle layers of the Millstone Grit series, ranging in depth from 60 to 150 feet, and they can be seen in ones or twos in many a small delph on the surrounding moors. Those which are stacked together by the loading-bays look remarkably crisp as if they had been freshly cut. Others protrude from the undergrowth at odd angles or are sunk into the ground, cracked and therefore rejected at an early stage of manufacture. From time to time a stone had to be discarded almost as soon as the hewers had begun to fashion it out of the rocks.

The ones that look new are usually smaller and thicker than the older millstones and they have sharp, right-angled edges. The traditional stones used by the corn miller have a distinctive shape, with a flat side for grinding, a convex top, and narrow, rounded edges. They lie alone, wherever they have been cast aside after an edge had been damaged or a flaw had rendered them useless. Now they are often covered in moss or lichen and are partly hidden by vegetation. A survey has shown that these older stones commonly had a diameter of 60, 64–66, or 70 inches, but that they varied in size from as little as 30 to as much as 80 inches; the crown had a maximum depth of fourteen inches and the rounded edges were from six to nine inches thick.[3] Most of these older stones are propped up on a smaller stone so as to allow the hewer to work the uppermost side with his tools and occasionally to inscribe it with his personal mark.

The Early History of the Trade

Evidence for the development of the trade in the Middle Ages is scrappy, but enough survives from the fifteenth century to show that by then it was organised on similar lines to later enterprises. We find, for instance, that millstones were being quarried at Baslow in 1427–28 and in 1500 the local manorial court ordered that anyone who transported a pair of millstones over the bridge at Baslow would be fined 6s 8d.[4] In 1479 a man was paid fourteen shillings to carry a pair of millstones from Nicholas Eyre's quarry in the manor of Hathersage to Whiston Mill, sixteen miles away.[5] The Eyres

also had a millstone quarry at 'Ernclyf', the 'eagle-cliff' now known as Yarncliff, in their manor of Padley within the parish of Hathersage, probably in that part of Yarncliff Wood that lies to the west of the present B6521 road, where huge boulders are strewn all over the hillsides under mature oaks and amongst bracken. Searchers after millstones have to be particularly diligent here. Documentary evidence from this period survives in the form of some small cash books, possibly written by Ralph Eyre of Offerton, which include accounts of millstone making at Yarncliffe in 1466.[6] Could some of the abandoned millstones in Yarncliff Wood possibly be as old as that?

At Yarncliff, as at other quarries for which we have early records, a gentry family owned or leased the quarry; they employed hewers on a piece-rate basis to make millstones to the satisfaction of an overseer; and their chapmen distributed the stones to customers. The organisation of the trade does not seem to have altered in its main outlines from the Middle Ages to the twentieth century. Thus one item reads:

> *Jankyn Stonhewer shall wyrke with us in Ernclyfe to make mylnstones and he mon haffe iiis. for a draughte be foure to make a draughte and thay mon be schapmons ware after xv hond and xvi be the schyght of Richard Paton.*
> *Jankyn Stonhewer had iiis. be fowr of me for my parte.*

Wages were therefore partly paid in advance to guarantee a contract. The hewers seem to have bargained with their employers but not always successfully; for example, a later entry reads: 'Richard

Wright had iis.vid. not quit. He sayd hit was vd. more'. The three shillings paid in advance to Jankyn Stonhewer appear to have amounted to half the wage for a pair of finished millstones of fifteen or sixteen hands diameter. A hand is a precise measurement of four inches, so these accounts tally well with the eleven millstones of 60 inches diameter and the four larger stones of 64 inches diameter that have been found in Yarncliff Wood. The smaller stones were the uppermost of each pair, the 64-inch stones were the lower ones.

In the fifteenth century millstone making was a

This stone trough at Burbage Edge was abandoned almost when finished when a crack allowed water to seep away.

seasonal occupation undertaken during the summer months. The accounts note that William Wethyngton had agreed to work in Yarncliff until Martinmas and that John Barker had contracted to make three pair of millstones by the same date. The Eyres employed eight hewers at Yarncliff and supplied mills as far away as Loughborough, which is some forty-five miles distant. The scale of operations was probably as large as any in Derbyshire during the Middle Ages, but we have no way of telling how many quarries were being worked at any one time.

The parish of Hathersage, Hallamshire's western neighbour, was the main centre of production in later times. A tithe dispute in 1590 reveals that thirteen hewers were then at work, each of them making twelve pairs a year, or one a fortnight.[7] Many of the hewers also farmed a smallholding, so the work would not have been continuous. Their income from millstone-getting was around 10d a week, which is comparable with the wages earned by other craftsmen at the time. It is clear from this tithe dispute that over three hundred millstones a year were being made in the parish of Hathersage alone in the late sixteenth century. We have no way of judging how many stones were being manufactured throughout the whole of the Peak District, but clearly the industry was an important one. The gritstone edges that are such a distinctive feature of the Dark Peak owe much of their present appearance to the activities of millstone hewers over the centuries.

Our information is just as fragmentary for later periods, but by the second half of the seventeenth century the Peak District millstone trade was attracting the attention of commentators of national repute. In 1673 Richard Blome wrote that Derbyshire had 'great quarries, out of which Mill-stones are got, also Grindstones, and Scyth-stones, which imploy many hands in working up, and are dispersed over great part of the Nation'. Nearly twenty years later John Houghton informed his readers that Derbyshire had 'rich Quarries of Mill-stones and they served most part of the Kingdom, and they are worth 8, 9 or 10 Pounds the Pair, and Grindstones of all sorts, from 5 or 6 Foot Diameter and under, and Scythe-stones in abundance, which serve all parts of the Kingdom'. Blome also noted that Bawtry, the nearest inland port on a tributary of the Trent, had a 'great trade for Millstones and Grindstones'. Millstones had been exported this way in the late-Elizabethan period, by which time Bawtry had recovered from the late-medieval recession that had affected so many towns. As this was the shortest and most convenient route no doubt millstones had been taken in this direction in earlier times.[8]

Most of the grindstones mentioned by Blome and Houghton were obtained from quarries on the softer sandstones further east, particularly at Brincliffe Edge (Sheffield) and at Wickersley. Millstone grit was too hard for grinding the cutting edges of Hallamshire knives. The most important millstone quarries overlooked Hathersage at Millstone Edge and Stanage but several other escarpments, notably those at Reeve Edge (Burbage) and in the Rivelin valley, were major sites and numerous small delves were worked for a time in many parts of the Dark Peak. For example, a small quarry at the top of Padley Gorge and a larger one near Mother Cap are littered with abandoned millstones and discarded pieces of rock and Beeley Moor is pitted with shallow depressions which are only two feet deep and from twelve to twenty feet in diameter; querns and scythe-stones lie scattered all around.[9] Some quarries also provided huge stones for crushing lead or for making into gateposts, lintels or drinking troughs. A trough that was almost finished before a large crack appeared in it stands abandoned below Reeve Edge. Later, the millstone quarries at Hathersage and Darley Dale became famous for the quality of their building stones.

The small, ephemeral quarries are not well-documented. John Wilson, the eighteenth-century antiquary of Broomhead Hall, tells us that 'Mill stones were formerly (time out of mind) got in some closes adjoining to Whitwell Moor called the Millstones, one or two yet remain' and that 'Grindle stones were got in ... at Hartcliffe Rocher but the sale not answering was discontinued'. Even the large quarries were not worked continuously. Wilson went on to say that, 'In Riveling has been got great quantitys of mill stones and many still remain. About the year 1710 the work was discontinued since when the Mill Stone Edge near Hathersedge, has been in vogue. Mr. Rotherham has taken this in Riveling and will not let it be worked least it should damage the sale of the other'.[10]

Millstone Hewing

'Peak' or 'Grey' millstones were used for grinding the inferior grains: oats, barley, peas and beans. From at least the seventeenth century onwards English millers ground their wheat with either Rhenish stones, known as 'Cullin stones' or 'Dutch blues', or by 'French burrs' from the Paris basin. The blue stones were really black until they were powdered with flour. They were volcanic in origin, lined with quartz, and quarried in the Andernach district. 'Cullin' was a corruption of Cologne; they were perhaps called Dutch from 'Deutsch' or because they were shipped down the Rhine through Holland. Even Derbyshire millers used these superior stones for grinding wheat; in 1745, for example, the Holymoorside mill had 'A Pair of Blackstones'.[11]

'French burrs' or 'Buhr stones' were made from crystallized flints dug out of the chalk rocks in the eastern part of the Paris basin and western Belgium. These flints were neither large enough nor strong enough to form a millstone by themselves and so they had to be cemented together and bound with an iron ring. In that form they were extremely hard and were the best stones available for making wheat flour. They had probably been introduced into south-east England by the mid-seventeenth century. In 1693 Henry May, a miller in the Essex parish of Writtle, had a pair of Cullen stones, a French stone and a Peak stone amongst his possessions.[12] The Peak millstones could not compete when it came to fine grinding but they were perfectly adequate for the rougher work that sufficed for other grains. A pair of Derbyshire stones ran efficiently for about 100 tons of grain. If a mill was constantly at work, then the stones would have had to be dressed once every three weeks or so, but most country mills managed with dressing only twice a year.[13]

In the parish of Hathersage millstones were made at Booth Edge (which had acquired its present name of Millstone Edge by 1625), Stanage, Yarncliff and Reeve Edge overlooking Burbage, as well as on the open moors. During the later seventeenth century many of these quarries came under the control of the Rotherhams, a gentry family of Dronfield. In 1684 John Rotherham leased all the millstone quarries that belonged to the manor of Hathersage. Several generations of Johns and Samuels prospered as lead merchants and the owners of millstone quarries. Eventually, they moved into the Manor House at the top of Dronfield High Street (the building that is now the Library) and the line was continued into the nineteenth century, after the marriage of an heiress, as the Rotherham-Cecils Leasing a millstone quarry was of secondary interest to the Rotherham family, for their capital was invested principally in the lead smelting trade. When John Rotherham died in 1696 the neighbours who appraised his probate inventory described him as a lead merchant and noted a number of items at his smelting mill. His son, John Rotherham II, was also described as a lead merchant upon his death in 1707, when his personal estate was valued at just over £600. The family were still leasing the major quarries of the area in the middle years of the eighteenth century.[14] Many of the fine seventeenth- and eighteenth-century halls in north Derbyshire were financed not just from agricultural profits but from investments in industrial enterprises. For example, the Ashtons of Hathersage Hall were lead smelters and millstone quarry owners at Stanage and the possessors of large flocks of sheep and herds of cattle.

Other families further down the social scale were able to live in modest comfort because of their dual occupations, but 109 of the 131 householders recorded in the hearth tax returns for Hathersage in 1670 had houses heated by only a single hearth.[15] In addition to lead-smelting and millstone-getting Hathersage families had opportunities of employment as carriers, button makers and wiredrawers. Wiredrawing began in Hathersage in 1565 when Christopher Schütz came from Saxony, armed with a patent, to set up a works for drawing wire that was suitable for knitting needles and for use in making sieves for washing lead ore.[16] One local man who was employed in this way was Anthony Wilcockson, a 'wayrdraer' who died in 1611 possessed of '3 half stones of waire, xs., toiles to draw waire, iis.vjd.'. Millstone-getting was not the only trade to offer welcome extra income.

The experienced eye of the millstone hewer sought a suitably-shaped rock that was protruding from the earth. In 1795 Erasmus Darwin wrote that:

> It is usual in separating large millstones from the silicious sand rocks in some parts of Derbyshire, to bore horizontal holes under them in a circle, and fill these with pegs made from dry wood which gradually swell by the moisture of the earth, and, in a day or two, lift up the millstone without breaking it.

A similar method was used in France, where in 1825 William Bingley noted that:

> wedges of willow, that have been dried in an oven, are then driven into the indentations with a mallet. When these have been sunk to a proper depth, they are moistened with water; and, after a few hours, the several stones that have been marked out are found to be perfectly separated.[17]

However, grooves and holes drilled into the quarry face at Millstone Edge show that in the later days of the trade gunpowder was used.

Oral memory relating to the Stanage quarries states that a block of gritstone was first hewn into a hexagonal shape, then placed on a rough pedestal so that it could be trimmed on both sides. Surviving unfinished millstones include some that have been worked on one side (sometimes with the central hole half done), then turned over and propped up so that work can take place on the other side, but then abandoned when a fault appeared. The tools used by millstone hewers in the early twentieth century included a pick, a heavy hammer or mall, a hammer called a kevel that was used for breaking stones and rough hewing, a reamer for drilling, a punch, wedge, pitcher, hammer, adze, and a 'plug and feather' which was a combination of conical and flat wedges. Smithies for sharpening tools were erected in shelters on the most exposed sites.[18]

Transporting Millstones

How were the millstones moved from the quarry to the customer's mill? The evidence is tantalisingly elusive. When Daniel Defoe visited Chatsworth early in the eighteenth century he observed that:

> on the East Side rises a very high Mountain, on the top of which they dig Mill-stones, and it begins so close to, and so overlooks the House, being prodigiously high that, should they roll down a pair of those Stones coupled with a wooden Axis, as is the way of drawing them, they would infallibly give a Shock to the Building.[19]

Defoe appears to have been the only visitor to the Peak who commented on the movement of millstones and so his observation has been accepted as a colourful but accurate description. It is supported by the oral tradition in the Hathersage district that three men could man-handle a millstone by putting a tree trunk through the central hole and trundling it along to the loading bay.[20] This tradition seems to be confirmed by a notice in the *Derby Mercury* on 24 January 1734 which refers to:

> 7 pairs of Millstones, sent to the Wharf at Derby many years since, and by reason of decay of Axle-Trees, they are fallen down and 2 or 3 Stones broke, and they have been and are a great incumbrance on the said Wharf.[21]

Were the axletrees used to couple the stones so that they could be moved along in the manner that Defoe had suggested was used in Derbyshire? The inventory of the possessions of William Barlowe of Coal Aston, taken on 4 June 1610, included 'Thirtie Axeltries for Mylnestones' at his windmill. Were these used in his mill or for shifting millstones? When Francis Curtis of Summerley, in the parish of Dronfield, made his will on 22 May 1647, he bequeathed to John Shelborne, his son-in-law, 'four paire milnestones now being at Reevedge all of them marked with the letters F and D, three paire of them are axled and the other paire is not yet bored'.[22] This evidence makes it perfectly clear that man-handling over short distances at the wharf or mill, or from the quarry face, was acceptable in the absence of a reasonable alternative, but it seems unlikely that millstones were moved very far by this rough-and-ready method, for they were too valuable to risk damage in an accident. Loading bays were positioned as near to the quarries as possible, so that millstones could be lowered on to wheeled vehicles or sledges. Many of the millstones that are still stacked by former loading bays could not have been moved by the method reported by Defoe, for they have no central hole into which an axle could be inserted.

In the late 1690s Celia Fiennes was surprised to see horse-drawn sledges commonly used in the streets of Derby, Bristol and Southampton.[23] Local tradition has it that quarry roads on the moors were laid out for sledges, but it is hard to find firm information. Some of the deepest and most artificial of the Peak District holloways were certainly dug out to facilitate the movement of millstones, whatever the form of transport that was used. The most striking one leads directly out of Millstone Edge and down the slope to Burbage Brook before joining the turnpike road system at Longshaw and continuing across the Big (or East) Moor. It was in existence by 1714, for on the 10th August of that year Ralph Burton of Dronfield, esquire, was 'killed at 10 o'clock at night in or near the Milne Stone gate on the East Moor, between Holmesfield & Grindleford bridge after falling from his horse'.[24] This track goes across the Big Moor in the direction of Bawtry, the river port on the Idle. After the opening of the Chesterfield Canal in 1777 millstones and lead were taken instead via Chesterfield wharf.

It is possible, however, that quarry-roads were given their regular inclines not for sledges but for carts and waggons. John Wilson, the eighteenth-century antiquary, observed that close to where he lived at Broomhead Hall:

> *The road to the new blew slate delf at Cartledge was begun by Mr. George Smilter of Sheffield on Monday 28th May 1750 & cut thro: the moss in many places three yards deep in twelve weeks time, seldom having under twelve & never more than twenty six men employed. The cut is about a mile & half long the deepest place about a yard and a half deep, the deepest places about 100 yards long each. The first waggon that came for slate was Richard Wilson's of Castle Fould, Sheffield. A good deal of the slate was sent to London & other places, was very fine and light but would not stand the weather. There has been none got many years.[25]*

It is noteworthy that waggons were used along this particular quarry road, albeit to transport stone slates rather than millstones. A lease from the Duke of Norfolk to George Smilter of Sheffield, wheelwright, dated 27 March 1750, confirms Wilson's account in some respects, for it gave Smilter the right to get slate-stones and 'paviors' in and around a place called Howden Chest or Cartledge 'with liberty to take and carry away the same through all convenient ways and passages to be made upon the Moors'.[26] The route is in one of the loneliest parts of the Dark Peak, high above Abbey Clough at the beginning of the Duke of Norfolk's road to Bar Dike. It is badly weathered and, because of the nature of the terrain, much less well-defined now than when it was freshly cut.

Edale people remember two of their local holloways being used to transport slate and peat on

sledges that were dragged either by ponies or by the combined human effort of a family. Stones were quarried near the prominent hill known as Ringing Roger and brought down to the village by a wide and deep track known as the Dry Gully, which may originally have been a stream that was diverted. The Peat Lane came down from the turbaries just below Grindslow Knoll, near the start of the Pennine Way; it is still known as the Sled Road by some old Edale farmers. Horse-drawn sledges were used for carrying hay and other loads on the hills, so it is possible that millstones were also moved in this manner.[27] Solid evidence is hard to come by, however.

The tolls charged by the various turnpike trusts are an ambiguous source on the particular form of transport that was used to convey millstones. In 1759 the tolls charged on the Sheffield-Wakefield road included 2s 6d 'for every pair of millstones, if drawn in pairs, and for every single millstone or block of stone or piece of timber, drawn by 5 or more horses or beasts

Peat Way to Grindslow Knoll.
The holloway by which the men of Edale brought down peat for winter fuel from their common turbary.

William Ibbitt's view of Sheffield from the South-east, 1854. Ibbitt depicts a simple wheeled vehicle loaded with grindstones. Millstones were probably moved in a similar manner for part of their journey from the moorland quarries to the inland port of Bawtry.

of burden'. The following year, on the Sheffield–Bawtry road, tolls seem to indicate wheeled vehicles rather than sledges, for they charged every 'Waggon, Wain, Cart or Carriage laden with a Block or Blocks of Stones or Marble, or with Timber, or drawing any Mill-Stone or Millstones, the Sum of Six Pence'. Grindstones for the Hallamshire cutlers were free of toll on that particular road, but the authorising Act stipulated that the wheels of carriages, etc., that were used to move grinding stones, had to be at least nine inches wide to avoid undue damage to the surface of the highways.

Other evidence points to the use of wheeled vehicles for the movement of cutlers' grindstones. In the second half of the eighteenth century William Simpson of Whiteley Wood, a 51-year old Sheffield labourer, stated in a deposition that he remembered how John Fox of the Hills in the parish of Hathersage brought small grinding stones in carriages to Sheffield for forty years before that particular highway was turnpiked.[28] And in the foreground of William Ibbitt's *South-east View of Sheffield* (1854) a horse stands between a pair of shafts linked to a primitive wain or cart on which rest a number of grindstones of varying sizes. Local artists, unfortunately, do not seem to have depicted the movement of millstones. We shall probably be correct in assuming that millstones were man-handled short distances and sometimes taken off the moors on sledges, but that for most of the way to the navigable river they went by cart, wain or waggon.

Who were the men who moved the millstones from the quarries to the river ports thirty miles or so away? Like most of the other carriers in the area they seem to have been small farmers who were prepared to use their animals and vehicles in this way whenever they had time and the opportunity presented itself to earn a little extra income. Perhaps the millstones were sometimes moved in stages so that each farmer did not have to travel very far? This might explain why Thomas Sutton of Oakerthorpe, who died in 1618, had a half share of a pair of millstones standing at Handley, four miles from his home, and a half share of two other pairs of millstones. They could have been on their way from the gritstone edges further west to the navigable river. Sutton's inventory shows that he was a farmer with ten kine, fifteen oxen, twelve young cows and calves, thirty sheep, some swine, bees, corn and hay, and three colts, two mares and one old lame nag. When Simon Dakin of the Booths, Hathersage (just below Millstone Edge), died in 1663, he owned two millstones worth £1.10s.0d. and nine picks, twenty-five wedges and other quarrying tools, but his neighbours described him as a husbandman, for his farm stock included three cows, a calf, four heifers, a bullock, a mare, an old horse, a foal, some swine and poultry, corn on the ground, hay, manure, and equipment which included two cheese presses. The Dakin family had long been supplying King's Lynn merchants with millstones via Bawtry.

Heavy goods such as millstones were normally moved in the summer months when the roads were relatively firm. Fitzherbert's advice in *The Book of Husbandry* (1534) was that:

> in May, when thou hast falowed thy grounde, and set oute thy shepefoulde, and caryed oute thy dounge or mucke, if thou have any wodde, cole, or tymbre to cary, or suche other

> busyness, that muste nedes be doone, with thy charte or wayne, than is it tyme to do it. For than the ways is lyke to be fayre and drye, and the days longe, and that tyme the husbande hath leeste to doo in husbandry.[29]

When Francis Sykes of Dronfield Woodhouse died in 1677 the neighbours who drew up his probate inventory that March described him as husbandman, but when making his will he himself had preferred the description of 'millstone carrier', which suggests a regular involvement in carrying. Sykes lived in a two-up, two-down house with a kitchen (possibly a lean-to). He paid tax on two hearths in 1670. His farm stock consisted of:

> the quick goods two Cows one calfe foure oxen, £32, two piggs 8s.0d., one horse three pack sadls and gears three hackney sadls, £4.6s.8d.
> the husbandry gears one corn wean body two cort bodys one paire of wheels one oxe harrow one horse harrow one plow with iorns one oxe sled, £4.15s.0d., seaven teames three paire of Cliviss three Lanyard pins, £1.3s.0d.
> goods in the barn sertin hay, £1.6s.8d., and sertin yocke, £1.6s.8d., the horse gears and weanrope, 8s.0d., sertin meaner in the fold, £2.1s.0d.
> sertin peas and oats sowne upon the ground, £2.13s.4d.

The farm was obviously a small one and Sykes's own assessment of the relative importance of the two sides of his dual occupation was probably realistic. The inventory goes on to record:

> millnstones standing at Bawtrey seaven pair, £35.
> millnstones in the edge sixteen pair and one stone, £30.

Francis Sykes was clearly taking the millstones all the way from the quarry to the river port. The millstones 'in the edge' were valued at less than £2 a pair, whereas those at Bawtry were worth £5 a pair, but as the measurements of the two sets of stones were not given we can obtain only a rough idea of Sykes's profit. Unfortunately, the inventory does not indicate how he set about moving the stones. One horse would not be enough, so probably the four oxen were used. Oxen certainly had the strength and stamina to move stones over long distances. Was Sykes's ox sled used for the first part of the journey, linked to the animals by the 'teams' (harness chains), cleavies (strong hooks) and lanyard pins? And were either the wain body or the 'cort body' fitted up with the pair of wheels to carry the millstones along the highways from his home in Dronfield Woodhouse once he had got off the moors?

The opportunity for part time employment as a carrier was an important asset for people living in those parts of north Derbyshire and south Yorkshire that lay between the millstone quarries and the inland port of Bawtry. A 'Particular of certaine tenurments in Killamarshe' (1632) stressed the value of the rents 'in regarde it lyeth in the best place for letteing grounds in all this parte of the Cuntrye, the place consisting most of Lead carriers'. Killamarsh inventories drawn up between 1612 and 1671 include eight references to lead wains (six belonging to yeomen and two to husbandmen) and at least fourteen references to packhorses, lead-horses, work-horses, and 'horses with their furniture'.[30] In her will of 1703 Mary Atkin, widow, left to her son-in-law 'all my part of the horses, geldings and mares which wee two use in carrying lead with the pack saddles and furniture belonging to them'. The debts for carriage listed in the inventory of Ralph Dobbe, husbandman, in 1582, included 'one payre of mylnestones that one Foster hath to sell a lytle beyond'. A petition opposing the proposed River Derwent navigation in 1720 was signed by many inhabitants of Tickhill, Firbeck and Letwell in south Yorkshire and Harworth, Styrrup and Oldcotes in north Nottinghamshire, most of whom were 'maintained by the Land-carriage of Lead, Millstones, and several other commodities to Bawtry ... bringing back Raff [timber], foreign Iron, Groceries and several other Sorts of Goods, to supply themselves and the Towns adjacent'.[31]

Bawtry lay about thirty miles away from the millstone quarries and lead smelting houses, but despite the difficult nature of the terrain transport costs could still be absorbed in the selling prices. Daniel Defoe described Bawtry as 'the center of all the exportation of this part of the country, especially for heavy goods ... such as lead, from the lead mines and smelting-houses of Derbyshire, wrought iron and edge tools, of all sorts, from the forges at Sheffield ... Also millstones and grindstones, in very great quantities, are brought down and shipped off here, and so carry'd by sea to Hull, and to London, and even to Holland also'.[32]

The Offerton Moor Millstone Quarry

The traveller from Hathersage to Hope who casts his eye up to the western skyline will see a well-defined group of holloways descending the steep slopes of Offerton Moor. The rambler who climbs up these tracks will come to a few shallow delves near the top of the moor, and in one of them close inspection will reveal the outline of an unfinished millstone. This is all the physical evidence that remains of a business venture of the 1720s, but a series of letters about the enterprise illuminates many aspects of the Derbyshire millstone trade.[33] The letters were written by Thomas Eyre of Thorpe (a farmstead situated in Outseats within the parish of Hathersage) to his third cousin, William Archer of Highlow Hall, a sixteenth- and seventeenth-century structure which still stands on the opposite side of the valley. Archer had changed his name from Eyre upon inheriting an estate in southern England, where he normally resided. Thomas Eyre frequently made journeys on his behalf and saw to his affairs in north Derbyshire.

Thomas Eyre was optimistic when he wrote on 4 October 1720 that millstones from Offerton Edge were extraordinary good ones. The biggest problem was getting hewers:

> *I have inquired privately amongst Mr. Rotherham men and they are all bound in fivfty pound bond not to make any when they have left him, notwithstanding I think som insite may be gote amongst som old workmen that has left him but it must be a great secrett.*

An old hewer had been to view the place and had said that the cutters were wasting the stone: 'Cutting to the best husbandrie is the greatest peice of inginnety in that buseynes'. His initial confidence had gone by 19 December, when he wrote:

> *I have inquired about workmen for the Edgge but can get none for the same rate that Mr. Rotheram has them att now because att present it is an uncertainty so they are not willing to leave a certainty without a little more advantage.*

The workmen were prepared to use their bargaining power. On 13 June 1721 Eyre reported:

> *Ther has been a difference with Mr. Rotheram and his men and is yett. They are now in sute about ther artickles so I have imployed three of them in Offerton Edge and ther is another which was overseier has a mind to come in to work and he says that he will inform me of the chapman. He has been to veiw the Edge and says if Bamford Edge and it were joined it would be a means to spoyle the other trade, for Mr. Rotheram has but six men left, ther is fivetoon gono of.*

Bamford Edge lay three miles away and was owned by a Mr Guisborn who had lost money in the South Sea Bubble, hence the possibility of its coming up for sale.

Finding customers in competition was an equally tricky business. On 7 February 1722 Eyre wrote to say that the bottom layers at Offerton had proved too fine for millstones but that sufficient stone was available to make hundreds of pairs.

> *Ther is about 8 pair made of severall sisces and very hopefull they are. The workmen like them very well. Now we must harken out for sale of them ... We have three men at work every day which is [enough] to fitt this place att present. We think it be proper to thro' up a parcell of stone att Derby now the river is made navigable. One of your mother's tennents which hold Shaw Croft, the Cunnery and North feild has warning to remove this Lady day ... It will be a proper place for sombody that will mannage a millston draught.*

On 4 April Eyre was able to report that:

> *I have lattly meett with an old millston carrior whom Mr. Rotheram has not dealt fairly with so he has left him somtime agoe and says now he will assist us and I think him a very proper man. He has the carrecter of a substantiall and honest man, he knows the countreys and chapmen so can putt us best into a way of selling them but he says Derby will be the only way to take them and he will carry them for five pound a pair, the largest stons, and stand att the loss of any stone.*

The largest stones could be sold at a profit of £1.10s.0d. or £2.10s.0d. a pair.

In the summer of 1722, Offerton Moor Holloway was constructed 'so as the milne stones might pass'. It is exceptional for holloways to be dated so precisely.

The following autumn Eyre wrote to say that eight pair of millstones had been sent to the navigable river at Derby, one pair to Bobbors Mill near Nottingham, one pair to Uttoxeter, and another pair to Poynton (Cheshire). Mr Elliott's bill for carriage came to £4 10s 0d a pair for stones of eighteen hands (72 inches) to Derby and £3 10s 0d for stones one hand smaller. An eighteen-hands pair of stones to Uttoxeter cost £4 10s 0d to carry, the eighteen-hands pair for Nottingham £5, and the seventeen-hands pair for Poynton £5 15s 0d.

The journey to Poynton was twenty-seven miles each way across the Pennines. That summer Eyre spent 15s 6d 'For making out of the Edge so as the milne stones might pass', presumably digging out those distinctive holloways that lead out of the delves on Offerton Moor.

The hewers had to find alternative employment when trade was slack. Eyre's letter of 17 September 1722 concludes:

> These that are gon to-day are the last that must goe out this winter so I disire you to give your orders about making of more this wintter. If you think convinent I would have noe more made yett but see som of these goe of first and not turn the men quit off neither but lett them cutt white coale in the woods or anything else which others dose, for it is but reason they should be imployed before others.

Archer apparently agreed to stop production during the winter, for on 4 February 1723 Eyre wrote to say that the millstone men 'disire to know wether they must gett any more, for Mr. Rotheram is for agreeing with his men again'.

Competition between the various owners of millstone quarries was keen and, as we have seen, sometimes rather underhand. A letter from John Eyre to his brother, William Archer, dated 22 December 1724, claimed that Elliott the chapman should never have been employed:

> Elliot that has the sale of your millstones is the most improper person to disspose of them. I know him, he married Joseph Rotheram's daughter of Bubnil or rather stole her, and is constantly employed by Sam. Rotherham of Draunfield and was all this last summer in his service, has not other way to live but by the Rotherams; he carried yours 20p more than what Rotherham gave. It is very strange that Mr. Ashton should sell his and you can't and yours rather the better.

Mr. Ashton was the squire of Hathersage Hall and the owner of Stanage quarry.

John Eyre wrote again on 2 March 1725 to say that:

> I hear Mr. Ashton has 80 pair of millstones upon sale and that he strives to put down Rotheram and undersells him. Rotheram pays a great rent and the other none for his Edge, that he will make it not worth R's while to follow that trade long. Suppose you joyn with Mr. Ashton you might have all the trade to yourselves.

Soon, however, it was William Archer who pulled out of the millstone trade. On 2 November 1725 Thomas Eyre reported that John Hawksworth, a merchant of Stumperlow Hall near Sheffield, had failed to sell any millstones for him and that he thought that Joseph Rogers, the Cowley lead merchant, might take the edge at £30 per annum. Rogers made no mention of millstones in his will ten years later, however, and the Offerton venture seems to have come to an end.

The Later History of the Trade

The seventeenth century was the most prosperous era for the Peak District millstone trade. Large stocks of millstones were sent via the coast to King's Lynn and London, especially when war prevented the importation of French and German stones. The return of peace and the growing fashion for wheaten bread meant less demand for Peak stones. The rents paid by the men who leased the quarries were progressively reduced.[34] The trade revived during the Napoleonic wars, but then faded again. John Farey wrote in his *General View of the Agriculture of Derbyshire* (1811) that, 'At Old Booth Edge the Peak Millstones now usually made are from 2ft 3in diameter and 8in thick to 5ft 7 in diameter and 17in thick. The prices are a pair of 5ft stones 10 guineas, 5ft 4in at 12 guineas, 5ft 8in at 14 guineas', and so on rising proportionately. Stephen Glover's *Directory of the County of Derbyshire* (1827–29) reported that Derbyshire had fifteen millstone quarries at that time, employing about 100 hewers; some of the stones were used not for face grinding but were turned on their edge to crush rape seed. A few years later, in 1833, William White's *Sheffield Directory* observed that Hathersage was still 'celebrated for excellent millstones'.[35]

Nineteenth-century census returns show that in Hathersage and surrounding townships such as Eyam Woodland, Stoke, Curbar and Nether Padley only small numbers of getters were then employed and that they usually worked in family teams.[36] In 1851 Hathersage had eight millstone makers (including a boy aged ten), three stone masons, two stone getters (including another boy aged ten) and a stone cutter. Ten years later Hathersage had seven millstone makers aged between 23 and 69,

three quarry men, two stone masons and ten stone cutters (including John Frost who was aged 79). At that time the local quarries were obviously being worked for building stone as well as for millstones. In 1871 Hathersage had fifteen millstone makers and a millstone merchant (John Cooper of The Dale), as well as three quarry men, six stone masons, a stone cutter and a stone merchant. Other elderly millstone getters included Joseph Vernon, who was described in the 1861 census return for Eyam Woodland as a 72-year old millstone maker journeyman, and Jonathan Hall of Hathersage, who was described in 1871 as a 60-year old farmer and millstone maker.

New technology dealt a fierce blow to the old industry at this time. Composite millstones, such as those made of carborundum grit, proved more efficient than Peak stones and roller milling made most of the older rural windmills and water mills redundant. The Derbyshire millstone quarries were turned increasingly to the manufacture of stones for grinding paint, pulping wood, crushing rape seed or grinding animal feedstuffs. At the beginning of the twentieth century the Millstone Edge quarry was extended southwards to Bole Hill and exploited on a vast scale for stones to build the huge reservoirs in the Upper Derwent valley. The first task was to remove the heaps of debris left by the millstone makers. Then, railways, loading bays, workshops and sheds were constructed, during each working day of ten hours a hydraulic ram pumped 12,000 gallons of water from a stream below, steam-powered travelling cranes were used to place the newly-cut stones into trucks, and cables connected to a self-acting winding drum lowered the stones by cables down a steep incline to the railway at Grindleford. The weight of each full truck pulled an empty truck back up the incline (which can still be climbed, with difficulty, in its present form of a wide grassy slope, much overgrown with bushes and trees). Huts, messrooms and a

recreation room were built for the workmen. In a working life of seven-and-a-half years over 1.2 million tons of stone were sent from Bole Hill Quarry to the construction sites in the Derwent valley.[37]

Just below the Surprise View, a graded green track runs from the Bole Hill Quarry to the main road from Sheffield to Hathersage (A625). It is earlier in date than the activities just described, for it was made to help the carriers to move millstones. A holloway that heads down the valley towards Hathersage from a huge amount of debris that was discarded as the millstones were cut is even older, for the green track goes over it. Scores of millstones of various sizes are stacked together at the side of the track, waiting for a delivery order that never came. Many others are scattered profusely down the hillside. These stones were not made for corn milling. Some were exported to Scandinavia and other parts of Europe, some to Canada and the United States, to pulp wood in the paper mills. The industry collapsed in the 1920s, but a few stones made at Millstone Edge were sold to a Swedish paper mill as late as 1939, just as war broke out.[38] The surviving stones date from the last days of the industry.

The area that is now encompassed within the Peak District National Park has never been a purely agricultural district. Industrial activities such as the getting of millstones and the mining and smelting of lead were carried on from time immemorial. Both of these trades have now disappeared but they have left permanent marks on the landscape, which have mellowed in time. The scene below the Surprise View now resembles a vast and peaceful millstone graveyard. The quarries have acquired a sublime quality and a silence that is almost eerie. The most important ones now come under the special protection of The Peak Park Planning Board and the National Trust. The millstone industry was always small-scale. It never disfigured the countryside of the Dark Peak in the way that the massive limestone quarries of recent years have spoiled so much of the White Peak

BEAUCHIEF ABBEY

The journey out of Sheffield towards Totley, Owler Bar and the Derbyshire moors takes us along Abbeydale Road, past Millhouses Park and the suburb of Beauchief, names that are all connected with a small Premonstratensian abbey that was founded on the southern border of Hallamshire over eight hundred years ago. Beauchief was a Norman French name for the 'beautiful headland' above the River Sheaf. Over time, the pronunciation of the name changed to 'Beechif', just as in other parts of the country Beauchamp became 'Beecham' and Belvoir was turned into 'Beever'. It is surprising how many of our great abbeys have retained the names that were given to them by the Normans. In Yorkshire they include Rievaulx, Jervaulx, Roche and the deserted site at Meaux. The Latin versions of Beauchief's name, which appear in medieval documents, were *Bellum Caput* or *Abbatia De Bello Capite*.[1] The abbey was dedicated to St Mary and St Thomas the Martyr (otherwise known as Thomas Becket and now more commonly as St Thomas of Canterbury). This dedication has given rise to the erroneous belief that the founder of Beauchief abbey was one of the four knights who brutally murdered Thomas in Canterbury cathedral. There is no truth in this old story, but such tales linger on without the burden of proof.

Beauchief abbey was founded sometime between 1173 and 1176 by Robert FitzRanulf, the former sheriff of both Derbyshire and Nottinghamshire and Lord of Alfreton and Norton in Derbyshire, Edwalton in Nottinghamshire and Wymeswold in Leicestershire. His father, Ranulf, had held these offices and manors before him and the family were probably Norman in origin. The Beauchief estate was created in a remote part of FitzRanulf's manor of Norton, right on the Yorkshire border, just the sort of place that was considered a suitable site for a monastery. The first canons came from Welbeck Abbey in Nottinghamshire, which had been founded in 1153, ten years after the first Premonstratensian abbey in England had been founded at Newhouse (Lincolnshire). The order had begun at Prémontré, in a secluded and marshy valley near Laon in northern France, to provide a communal life modelled on that of the Cistercians for canons who preached in local churches and chapels. The White Canons, as they were popularly known, lived under a rule that was less strict than that of the monks, but they attended regular services in the abbey church, ate a vegetarian diet in the refectory, slept in the common dormitory and accepted the strict discipline of their order. More than fifty successful Premonstratensian communities were founded in Britain, especially between 1150 and 1210. The order failed to expand subsequently, but survived until the dissolution of the smaller monasteries in 1537.[2]

Derbyshire had only three abbeys, the other two being in the south of the county at Darley (Augustinian) and Dale (Premonstratensian).[3] They were all of modest size compared with the great monasteries of Yorkshire. We do not know how many men and boys were at Beauchief in its hey-day during the twelfth and thirteenth centuries, but by the fifteenth century the abbot ruled twelve to fifteen canons. Their surnames suggest that most of them came from the neighbourhood. An unknown number of lay brothers and other assistants were also attached to the community and as the abbey church was 200 feet long they had once probably far outnumbered the canons. After the Black Death it was the common experience of monasteries that the number of men who were available for work as lay brothers fell dramatically and the outlying farms, or granges, had to be leased to tenants. When

The border position of Beauchief is shown in this detail of P. P. Burdett's map of Derbyshire (1767).

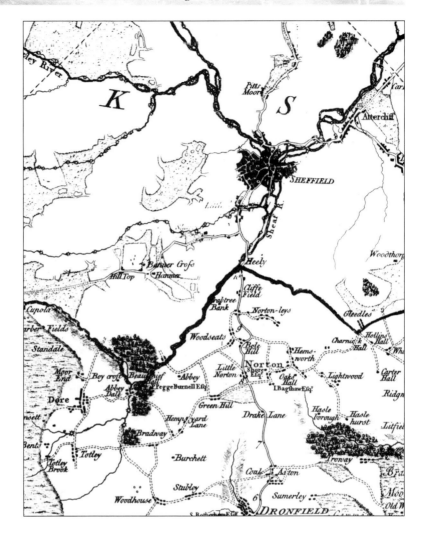

Beauchief Abbey was dissolved with the other minor religious houses on 4 February 1537, ten months after the death of the last abbot, John Greenwood, alias Sheffield, it was surrendered 'without giving any trouble or opposition'. Thomas Cromwell's commissioners had found no scandal to justify their seizure of the abbey but still forced the canons to accept pensions and leave. Beauchief was valued at only £126 3s 4d, which was well below the threshold value of £200 under which the smaller religious establishments were dissolved according to the Act of 1536.[4]

The abbey and all the surrounding land in that part of Norton parish which had become detached under the name of the Liberty of Beauchief was bought by Sir Nicholas Strelley, who at the time was Lord of Ecclesall on the opposite bank of the River Sheaf. The property remained with the Strelleys until the failure of the male line, when it passed in 1648 through the marriage of Gertrude Strelley to Edward Pegge of Ashbourne. Pegge used much of the stone of the abbey to build a suitable gentry residence which he called Beauchief Hall.[5] It stands seven bays wide and three storeys high on a high point of the estate, perhaps on the site of the home farm or grange. The lintel of the main door is carved with the date 1671 and a Latin inscription. The rest of the abbey's estate was split up and sold to local landowners.

Pegge was unhappy with the re-establishment of the Church of England upon the restoration of Charles II in 1660 and so adapted the ruins of the abbey church into a private chapel, with Nathaniel Baxter, an ejected non-conformist minister, as his chaplain. Beauchief Abbey thus took on a new lease of life as a religious building which continues in use to this day. The interior is still arranged as it was in Pegge's time, for it is one of a relatively small number of churches that were not transformed by the Victorians. (The church of St James at Midhope, within Hallamshire, is another.) The only substantial part of the abbey church still remaining by the 1660s was the great fourteenth-century tower, so Pegge built his chapel up to the tower's east wall and incorporated most of the space under the tower arch. To the west is a small vestibule which also serves as a baptistry. The roof of Pegge's chapel is unceiled and so gives a surprising impression of spaciousness. The original furnishings include box pews, some of which are carved with heraldic devices, a three-decker pulpit with reading desk and clerk's pew, a communion table, a little psalm board, and Strelley and Pegge monuments. The chapel is a remarkable period-piece in its own right, quite independently of its association with the ruined abbey. To use Mark Chatfield's memorable phrase, it is one of the 'Churches the Victorians Forgot'.[6]

The present appearance of the abbey grounds owes much to the excavations that were carried out over four successive summers between 1923 and 1926 by W H Elgar, a master at King Edward VII Grammar School, Sheffield, and his pupils.[7] Frank Crawford of Beauchief Hall, a local businessman and councillor, had encouraged these excavations and in March 1931 he gave the site of the abbey to Sheffield City Council. The excavators uncovered the remains of the rest of the church and the foundations of the chapter house, cloister, refectory, parlour and store-rooms. These were readily identified as the Premonstratensians built to a common plan and were judged to date from several periods between the late twelfth century and the fifteenth century. The large west window of the church tower (with nearly all its tracery missing and now re-glazed) is early fourteenth-century work. It had not lost its top storey when Samuel Buck drew it in 1727. The east end of the abbey church is believed to have contained an alabaster altar-piece of the martyrdom of St Thomas of Canterbury, which is now in the possession of the Foljambe family. Close by, in a recess in the wall to the north of the altar, is thought to have stood the tomb of the founder, Robert FitzRanulf. Other benefactors who were buried in the church before the main altar included three of the Chaworth family, later lords of Norton and Alfreton.[8] The excavators also discovered several, well-preserved floor tiles from the two chapels to the east of the south transept and the remains of a small chantry chapel and of a newel stair to the dormitory. Further digging around the south transept of the church in 1953–54 by Mr Peter Stiles revealed a fine carved head of a mid-fifteenth century canon and pieces of a Dutch majolica altar vessel of about 1500.[9]

As with all Premonstratensian and Cistercian abbeys, the cloisters were sited to the south of the church, the chapter house (where the formal business of the abbey was discussed) stood on the east side of the cloister and the refectory was to the south. The two columns which supported the ribs of the vaulting of the chapter house contained faint evidence of painted decorations. The excavations in the 1920s also produced two stone coffins containing human bones outside the chapter house doorway, which they thought were probably those of abbots.

The present appearance of the walled enclosure around the abbey is deceptive. New investigations in the 1990s showed that the abbey was larger than the walls suggest and that much more remains to be discovered by modern archaeological techniques of resistivity, surveying and excavation and from documentary research.[10] Some of the boundaries of the grounds surrounding the abbey can still be traced on the ground, but on the hills to the south twentieth-century housing at Greenhill and Bradway has encroached on parts of the original estate and similar housing to the north covers the land between Abbey Lane and Hutcliffe Wood. It is not clear from the documentary evidence how far the canons' property extended to the north. A map of the Liberty of Beauchief, which William Fairbank drew for Strelley Pegge in 1762,[11] shows Abbey Lane descending the hill from Woodseats to just beyond the abbey but it did not continue north of the river through Ecclesall Woods, as it does today. Nor was there a route along the river valley through Abbeydale to Totley before the turnpike road was

Norton Church. Robert FitzRanulf, the lord of Norton and founder of Beauchief Abbey, included the medieval church of St James amongst his gifts to the canons.

constructed in the early nineteenth century. These busy roads and the Sheffield-Manchester railway line along the Sheaf valley have destroyed much of the former sense of isolation and peace.

The history of Beauchief Abbey is reasonably well-documented for a small monastery, though we know little about the abbots, canons and lay brothers who shared the communal life. A rare survival amongst the usual range of monastic archives is the Beauchief Obituary, which was begun in the thirteenth century and continued to the Dissolution.[12] This recorded the names of departed abbots, canons and benefactors, whose souls were prayed for on fixed days each year, and their donations to the abbey. This record has been printed in S O Addy, *Historical Memorials of Beauchief Abbey* (1878), together with the surviving documents from the second half of the fifteenth century of the visitations that were conducted by senior members of the Premonstratensian order.[13] Now we can add the Beauchief Cartulary, which dates from the early fifteenth century and which contains transcripts of the abbey's 224 charters. The Cartulary is kept at Sheffield Archives and has recently been prepared for publication by the Derbyshire Record Society.[14] It contains a great deal of information on how the abbey gradually acquired substantial gifts of property in Derbyshire, Yorkshire, Nottinghamshire and Leicestershire.

Robert FitzRanulf's original grant of an estate on the edge of the manor and parish of Norton extended from the river Sheaf in the north west as far as Abbey Brook and Chancet Wood in the north and to the spring and stream by the present Twentywell Lane in the south west. Twentywell is a corruption of St Quentin well, the spring which was named after the abbey of St Quentin, not far from Prémontré in northern France. The charters show that FitzRanulf soon extended his original

In 1671 Edward Pegge used much of the stone of the abbey to build Beauchief Hall on a high point of the estate, perhaps on the site of the home farm or grange of the former abbey.

grant of land in the south as far as the Norton border, which lay between the hamlet of Greenhill and Birchitt in the parish of Dronfield. Other grants eventually enlarged the canons' estate on the northern side of Abbey Brook, until it stretched as far as the River Sheaf beyond Hutcliffe Wood and towards Woodseats and Norton Hammer. After the dissolution of the abbey in 1537 the compact estate around the abbey was known as the extra-parochial Liberty of Beauchief. The parish of Norton and the adjacent chapelry of Dore (which included Totley and formed part of the parish of Dronfield) lay just within Derbyshire and the diocese of Lichfield and Coventry. The earliest charters also record the gifts of Norton mill, some small properties in Norton Lees and Meersbrook, and all the rights of the churches of Norton, Alfreton, Wymeswold and Edwalton, such as the tithes and the right to present rectors or vicars. The abbey soon began to attract grants of land from the lords of other manors in Derbyshire, Yorkshire and Nottinghamshire and eventually received substantial donations from the Ranulfs' successors.

The FitzRanulf line ended in 1269 with two daughters, the elder of whom married Sir William Chaworth, Lord of Marnham (Nottinghamshire), whose ancestors had come from Chaurces (now Sources), near Le Mans. Their son, Thomas Chaworth, became regarded as the co-founder of Beauchief Abbey because of the generosity of his donations. His descendants were patrons of the abbey until well into the fifteenth century.[15] The Lords Furnival of Hallamshire were also benefactors and patrons. Those who were buried in the choir of the abbey church included Sir Gerard de Furnival, who gave valuable pasture rights at Fulwood for the canons' cattle and twenty shillings rent each year from his corn mill at Sheffield, in order to 'sustain the lamp of our church'. His descendant, Sir Thomas de Furnival, gave further land at Fulwood, confirmed all the donations of his ancestors in Hallamshire, and chose the abbey church as his final resting place. The goodwill of the Furnivals' successors, the Talbots, Earls of Shrewsbury, was essential to the canons because the lords of Hallamshire were their most powerful neighbour. In 1466 the abbot thought it well worth his while to grant the earl an annual fee of five marks for life in return for his 'very potent counsel, support, protection and aid'.[16]

The minor lords of south Yorkshire and north Derbyshire, many of them retainers and kinsmen of the FitzRanulfs, Chaworths and Furnivals, also appear in the Cartulary as benefactors. The De Ecclesalls, lords of a sub-manor within Hallamshire that lay on the opposite bank of the River Sheaf to the abbey, made substantial gifts and built a chapel near the top of Carter Knowle Lane where the canons held public services. Other residents of the manor, such as Hugh Hauselin of Little Sheffield, Adam the carter of Brincliffe, and William of Hollins, followed his example with smaller gifts. Meanwhile, the lords of Hathersage and Padley gave moorland grazing rights for livestock based at the canons' granges at Fulwood and Strawberry Lee and the lords of Beeley and Ashover and others generously donated moorland which the canons' livestock grazed from the grange at Harewood.

As we have seen, the White Canons were a preaching order. Canons from Beauchief Abbey served as vicars at the parish churches of Norton, Alfreton, Edwalton and Wymeswold, whose tithes and other dues had formed part of Robert FitzRanulf's grants. FitzRanulf may have been responsible for the Norman south doorway and the arches of the north side of the nave at St James, Norton, and the carved heads that frame the great Perpendicular east window seem to represent an abbot and a canon. The Beauchief canons also provided the chaplain for the chantry chapel that the Blythe family erected at Norton church. The chaplain lived in a house that was erected in 1523 on the west side of Norton Green.[17] In 1399 the right to present vicars at St John the Baptist's church, Dronfield was given to the canons by Ralph Barker of Dore and Dronfield Woodhouse. They built a vicarage in Dronfield in 1403 and continued to serve the church until the Dissolution.[18]

The lands which were granted by benefactors in Derbyshire, Yorkshire, Nottinghamshire and Leicestershire and which were the major source of income for the abbey were farmed by lay brothers. In this, the Premonstratensians had again followed Cistercian practice.[19] The lay brothers' farms were known as granges and their buildings were distinguished from contemporary farmhouses only by the addition of a chapel. After the dramatic fall in the national population caused by the Black Death the abbey, in common with other monastic institutions, was unable to recruit lay brothers and so leased its lands to secular farmers. Seven granges can be identified, but it is possible that one or two more existed. The nineteenth-century fashion for calling houses 'grange', with no historical justification, causes some confusion; neither Bradway Grange Farm nor Norton Grange seem to be medieval in origin or to have had any connection with Beauchief Abbey.

It is likely that a home grange was built close to the abbey, perhaps on the site of the later Beauchief Hall. An inventory of 1393 records the contents of 'the manor and storehouse at Beauchief Grange' and lists forty-one cows, bullocks and heifers, 172 wethers, ewes and lambs, eight horses, mares and foals, and seventeen pigs. At the Dissolution the grange had a similar amount of livestock and two corn wains, three dung carts, three ploughs, a sled and some yokes.[20] The grange was in effect the home farm of the abbey.

At Strawberry Lee, just in view three miles up the valley from the abbey, the canons built a grange in a moorland clearing.[21] A farm house occupied this site until 1936, seven hundred years or more after the land had been laboriously brought into cultivation, but now only some ruined walls mark the foundations. The clearing was extended in later centuries but is still surrounded by moorland on all sides. To the south a deep gulley provides a natural boundary with the moorland of Brown Edge. Blacka Hill rises to the northern horizon and the featureless Totley Moss stretches away to the west. The charter by which William of Dronfield and Agnes his wife granted the canons common of pasture for chickens and other animals at Strawberry Lee is undated. The first mention of the grange dates from the middle decades of the thirteenth century, when Matthew, lord of Hathersage, granted common pasture on Hathersage Moor for the livestock at the canons' granges of Fulwood and Strawberry Lee. In 1285 Richard of Bernak gave the canons similar grazing rights for their livestock at Strawberry Lee

Only the foundations of a later farmhouse and outbuildings can now be seen at Strawberry Lee, the abbey's grange on the edge of the moors beyond Totley.

Lady's Cross. The stump of the cross that marked the boundary of the abbey's moorland grazing rights on the Big Moor. The cross also divided Totley from the manor of Baslow.

on the adjoining moor in his manor of Padley. The stump of the Lady Cross, mentioned as a boundary point in Matthew of Hathersage's charter, survives in its original position on the moors, over a mile away from the grange.[22] In later centuries, the inhabitants of Totley and Baslow visited it during their Rogationtide perambulations of their boundaries and it marked an old route out of the Hope valley towards Sheffield. During the later Middle Ages the grange at Strawberry Lee was leased by the canons; in 1461 John Faunchall (or Fanshawe) took a lease for sixty years and in 1530 Thomas North obtained one for seventy years. Upon the Dissolution Strawberry Lee was sold to Sir Nicholas Strelley, who also acquired the main estate at Beauchief.

The present Fulwood Grange Farm, $3\frac{1}{2}$ miles north of Strawberry Lee, is the successor to the medieval grange which is first recorded in Matthew of Hathersage's charter, but which obviously had an earlier origin, close to the Lord of Hallamshire's cattle-rearing farm at Fulwood Booth.[23] The Beauchief Obituary informs us that Sir Gerard de Furnival, Lord of Hallamshire, was the man who gave 'sufficient pasture in his forest of Fulwode for 30 cows, with young under three years old, and one acre of land to build our cottages upon', but we do not know which Gerard this was. His descendant, Sir Thomas de Furnival, 'gave land to enlarge our grange in Fulwode', but there were as many Thomases as Gerards. In 1514 William Holland took a forty-year lease of Fulwood Grange and upon the Dissolution it was acquired by Francis, Earl of Shrewsbury, and so once more became part of the lordship of Hallamshire.

The Cartulary and the Obituary, together with place-name and map evidence, enable us to identify the sites of four more Beauchief granges in Derbyshire, though no medieval work survives. The abbey's largest grange stood on the eastern edge of Beeley Moor, where a nineteenth-century farm house bears the name of Harewood Grange.[24] The other three can be identified with Birley Farm, near Beighton, with Cotespark Farm, Alfreton, and with Stanley Grange Farm, to the south of Hardwick Hall.[25]

The canons derived most of their income from farming the lands that had been given to them. The ridge-and-furrow patterns on the present Beauchief golf course were formed by the annual ploughing of the corn fields, but the charters and inventories of the abbey's possessions make it clear that the granges specialised in rearing livestock. The charters contain many references to the services that had to be performed by neighbouring small farmers, to the clearing of new land, and to the importance of grazing rights on the moors. The canons had a deer park and fish ponds on their home farm. William Fairbank's map of 1762 marks 'Beauchief Old Park' as a wood (which is now called Old Park Wood) high on the southern boundary of the estate and fish ponds with a field called 'The Damm'. The successors to these ponds can be seen to the east of the abbey. The fine woods which enclosed the Beauchief estate provided both timber and coppiced underwood. One of the best-known woods in the Sheffield district is Ladies Spring Wood, which probably took its name (like Lady Cross on the moorland boundary of the grange at Strawberry Lee) from the abbey's dedication to St Mary and St Thomas. Coppice woods were commonly called springwoods (because fresh shoots soon sprang up after the felling at stool level) and the name was spelt Lady's Spring on the 1762 map. Much of the underwood that was cut was burned to make charcoal for the iron industry. A lease to Roger Eyre in 1496 allowed him to make charcoal in the abbey's woods at Hutcliffe and by the broad meadow and to work a bloom hearth by the smithy dam on the River Sheaf.[26] The Cartulary has little to say about the working of minerals on the abbey's estates, but three charters show that tenants mined coal, especially at Swanwick, near Alfreton. Lead smelting is not mentioned in any documentary source for the abbey, but the presence of bole hills in areas where the canons had pastures, near to their granges at Strawberry Lee and Fulwood and at the northern edge of Norton Park, suggests that they may have benefited from this lucrative activity. Bole hills were smelting sites on windy hill-tops before water-power was applied to smelting in the Elizabethan period. They are commemorated on maps by their names and at the Totley Bole Hill by extensive mounds of slag.

In common with other monasteries, the abbey probably had a tannery, but the site has not been identified. We are better informed about the mill sites along the banks of the River Sheaf, which in the later Middle Ages were leased to tenants.[27] Nothing can now be found on the ground of the Bradway corn mill, the furthest mill upstream, which Sir Nicholas Strelley acquired upon the Dissolution.[28] Nor can anything be seen of the nearby Walk Mill, for the site is occupied by Dore railway station.[29] This was the Ecclesall fulling mill that was erected about 1280 by the canons on land that had been granted by Sir Ralph de Ecclesall, with leave to turn the course of the river towards the mill. Such mills were known as walk mills because the original process involved the trampling of fullers' earth into the cloth by human feet. After the Dissolution this mill was converted into a cutlers' grinding wheel. Further downstream at Millhouses,[30] the manorial corn mill of the lord of Ecclesall was already in existence when it was granted to the abbey in the mid-thirteenth century by Sir Ralph de Ecclesall in return for the offering of daily prayers for his father's soul. After the Dissolution it remained part of the Beauchief estate and the site is now occupied by a building that was erected as a steam mill in

The sturdy church tower of Beauchief Abbey is the most substantial remaining part of the medieval abbey. Its lower part was converted into a chapel in 1662.

the nineteenth century. A large weir survives by the children's playground in Millhouses park and the site of the pond can be traced on the ground. Another corn mill, known as the New Mill, was erected downstream on an unknown site that was granted to the abbey by Hugh Hauselin of Little Sheffield. This mill may have occupied one or other of the sites that were known later as Norton Hammer, Smithy Wood or Little London. The Norton mill that was granted by Robert FitzRanulf, the founder of the abbey, may have occupied another of these sites. The canons had other mills on their distant estates, including a windmill at Coal Aston.

The Cartulary provides a record of the abbey's property but we have much less information on the communal life at Beauchief. The Obituary sheds occasional light, such as informing us that a canon who came from Sheffield gave a vestment valued at twenty shillings and that Robert of Edensor, a former prior, bought the great bell and paid for the erection of the belfry.[31] Otherwise, we have to depend on the reports of the regular inspections by official visitors, who ensured common standards of liturgy, accommodation, dress and conduct throughout the Premonstratensian order. These reports survive only from the second half of the fifteenth century, when the community was much smaller than in its hey-day. They mention the abbot, sub-prior, circator (who was responsible for discipline), deacon, cellarer, sacristan, novices, acolytes and licentiates. Twenty-one abbots are known by name.[32] The 1472 visitation mentioned chantry of eight priests within the abbey and that of 1490 noted that Christopher Haslam had been appointed as a secular chaplain to instruct boys and novices in singing and grammar at a stipend of 26s 8d a year, with board and lodging in the abbey. The visitors usually reported that all was well, but at the 20 October 1472 visitation a complaint was made that 'in the evening, after complines [the last service of the day at 7pm], the brethren go outside the cloister, stay up so long, and get so much to drink that at midnight, when matins should be said, they cannot keep awake'. Some canons were censured for leaving the abbey alone, instead of going in small groups and in 1500 the visitors ordered that the canons should not be allowed out to 'see common shows' or to visit any inhabited place. The most sensational event occurred in 1461, when Abbot John Downham was found guilty of 'solemn perjuries'. He and seven canons 'rose in insurrection with armed men and defensive arms, with swords and with staves and departed the monastery'. We know little more about this mysterious incident, but the canons eventually returned and Downham retired to Wymeswold.[33] The normal communal life was orderly and uneventful. In 1488 the visitation reported that 'in this monastery they consume every week 10 bushels of wheat, 16 bushels of oats, and four bushels of barley.' Like the Cistercians, their diet was strictly vegetarian.

In 1789, long after the Dissolution, the Hon. John Byng, soon to be Viscount Torrington, found 'a most happy situation for beauty and retirement' when he travelled through the district on horseback.[34]The medieval abbey had, of course, been a far busier place, even a noisy one at times, during the three-and-a-half centuries of its existence, but it had remained remote from normal life, enclosed by woods and reached only by winding cart tracks and footpaths. This isolation can still be experienced in part as soon as the visitor turns off Abbey Lane and enters a landscape that would still be recognisable to the medieval canons.

THE DRAGON OF WANTLEY 9

Everyone with an interest in the history of the countryside around Sheffield has heard of The Dragon of Wantley. The legend is easily the best-known of all the traditional stories of the locality and one that was once famous throughout the land. To this day, it features prominently in writings about folklore and in collections of old ballads. The story has, of course, been embellished over time and the facts upon which it is based are now only half-remembered. Nevertheless, everyone knows that the setting for this amusing and preposterous tale is Wharncliffe Crags, on the northern border of Hallamshire, and many recall that in the ballad the dragon was thinly disguised as one of the ancient lords of Wortley.

An old hand bill in my possession advertises a railway outing from Birstall, Batley and Dewsbury, on Saturday, 15 August 1885, to Wortley Hall and Wharncliffe Crags. The venue is described as:

situated in that pleasant district of merry England which is watered by the Don. The remains of the extensive Forest which in ancient times covered the hills and valleys are still to be seen here. Here haunted of yore the fabulous Dragon of Wantley; here also were fought the most desperate Battles in the Wars of the Roses; here also flourished in ancient times those gallant Outlaws, Robin Hood, Little John and others, whose deeds are so famous. It is believed that the Deer Park at Wharncliffe was once strewn with innumerable bodies of persons who had perished in some great pestilence. In Wortley Churchyard is to be seen the tomb of Nevison, the noted highway robber who is said to have murdered Fletcher near the farm at Howley Hills, Batley.

What an enticing prospect! And all for a third-class rail fare of 1s 6d, with the chance of tea at the Wortley Arms, or the opportunity for those taking their own provisions to obtain hot water and milk at 'Mr Webster's, near the Church gates, at 3d each'.

Needless to say, there is little or no evidence for most of the attractions advertised in the hand bill printed by the committee of the St John Ambulance Association of The Heavy Woollen District Centre. The ballad of The Dragon of Wantley, however, does deal with real historical events. Though the story is treated humorously, it is founded on fact. The truth is worth investigating in some detail, for it turns out to be as amazing as the bizarre verses of the old ballad.

The Ballad

A True Relation of the Dreadful Combat between More of More Hall and The Dragon of Wantley was first published as a broadside ballad by 'Randal Taylor, near Stationers Hall', London, in 1685.[1] The same ballad appeared, with only minor textual variations, in the major collections that were published during the following century. Tom D'Urfey included it in his *Wit and Mirth: Or, Pills to Purge Melancholy* (London, 1699), Ambrose Phillips published it in his *A Collection of Old Ballads, corrected from the best and most ancient copies extant with Introductions, historical, critical, or humorous* (3 volumes, London, 1723–5), and Bishop Percy printed it in his *Reliques of Ancient English Poetry* (3 volumes, London, 1765).

Wharncliffe Crags. Wharncliffe was the 'quern cliff', where querns for hand-milling corn were quarried and shaped in the Roman period.

The crags form a prominent escarpment high above the Don valley, by Hallamshire's northern border.

The Dragon of Wantley was one of only twenty-three ballads to appear in the large collections of both Phillips and Percy. It was so well known in Hanoverian London that in 1737 it was turned into a burlesque opera by Henry Carey, set to music by John Frederick Lampe, and performed at the Theatre Royal in Covent Garden. A printed version of Carey's opera (which quickly ran into at least fifteen editions) noted that it was 'Moderniz'd from the old ballad after the Italian manner by Sig. Carin', i.e. Carey. Sixty-three performances were given during the season, thus encouraging Carey and Lampe to write *Margery: or, A Worse Plague than the Dragon*, which was performed at the Theatre Royal during the following year.[2]

Carey moved in the circle of Ambrose Phillips[3] and of John Gay, whose *Beggar's Opera* (1728) had been the first to satirise the prevailing fashion for Italian opera. Carey's first attempt at this genre had been the very successful *Chrononhotonthologos* (1734), 'the Most Tragical Tragedy that ever was Tragediz'd by any Company of Tragedians'; another success was *The Honest Yorkshire-Man* (1736), in which 'Squire Sapscull, a Yorkshire Gentleman, of very great estate' was lampooned as 'a great Loobily Yorkshire Tike'. Such successes encouraged Carey to turn to Phillips's collection of old ballads to find another Yorkshire setting. In *The Dramatick Works of Henry Carey* (published by public subscription in London in 1743), the outline of the plot of *The Dragon of Wantley* was followed by a note advising that. 'For further Particulars, the Reader is refer'd to the Old Ballad, from whence this Opera was taken.'

The literary standard of the opera may be judged by such lines as:

> *Zeno, Plato, Aristotle*
> *All were lovers of the Bottle*

and the love duet:

> *Pigs shall not be*
> *So fond as we.*

It was all meant to be good fun, sending up Handel with the final chorus:

> *Sing, sing, and rorio*
> *An Oratorio*
> *To gallant Morio*
>   *of Moore-Hall*
> *To Margereenia*
> *Of Roth'ram Greenia*
> *Beauty's bright Queenia*
> Bellow and bawl.

To his credit, Handel apparently enjoyed this slapstick comedy.[4] For our present purposes, it is sufficient to note that the ballad was well-known in London and that Carey's burlesque opera gave it a rich new lease of life. When the Revd Joseph Hunter wrote about the area in which the ballad was set, in his *Hallamshire* (1819), he observed: 'Few of my readers are, it is probable, familiar with the name of Bolsterstone [which he had just been describing], but who has not heard of More of More Hall?'[5]

The ballad was published as follows in Percy's *Reliques*:

Old stories tell how Hercules
A dragon slew at Lerna,
With seven heads, and fourteen eyes,
To see, and well discern-a:
But he had a club, this dragon to drub,
Or he had ne'er done it, I warrant ye:
But More of More-Hall, with nothing at all,
He slew the dragon of Wantley.

The dragon had two furious wings,
Each one upon each shoulder;
With a sting in his tayl as long as a flayl,
Which made him bolder and bolder.
He had long claws, and in his jaws
Four and forty teeth of iron;
With a hide as tough, as any buff,
Which did him round environ.

In Yorkshire, near fair Rotheram,
The place I know it well;
Some two or three miles, or thereabouts,
I vow I cannot tell.
But there is a hedge, just on the hill edge,
And Matthew's house hard by it;
O there and then was this dragon's den,
You could not chuse but spy it.

Some say this dragon was a witch;
Some say, he was a devil,
For from his nose a smoke arose,
And with it burning snivel;
Which he cast off, when he did cough,
In a well that he did stand by;
Which made it look, just like a brook
Running with burning brandy.

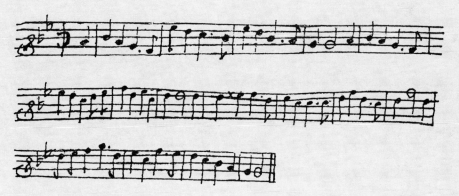

Have you not heard how the Trojan horse
Held seventy men in his belly?
This dragon was not quite so big,
But very near, I'll tell ye.
Devoured he poor children three,
That could not with him grapple;
And at one sup he eat them up,
As one would eat an apple.

All sorts of cattle this dragon did eat,
Some say he ate up trees,
And that the forests sure he would
Devour up by degrees:
For houses and churches were to him geese
   and turkies;
He ate all, and left none behind,
But some stones, dear Jack, that he could
   not crack,
Which on the hills you will find.

Hard by a furious knight there dwelt,
Of whom all towns did ring;
For he could wrestle, play at quarter-staff,
   kick, cuff, and huff,
Call son of a whore, do any kind of thing:
By the tail and the main, with his hands twain
He swung a horse till he was dead;
And that which is stranger, he for very anger
Eat him all up but his head.

These children, I am told, being eat;
Men, women, girls and boys,
Sighing and sobbing, came to his lodging,
And made a hideous noise:
O save us all, More of More Hall,
Thou peerless knight of these woods:
Do but slay this dragon, who won't
   leave us a rag on,
We'll give thee all our goods.

Tut, tut, quoth he, no goods I want;
But I want, I want, in sooth,
A fair maid of sixteen, that's brisk and keen,
With smiles about the mouth;
Hair black as sloe, skin white as snow,
With blushes her cheeks adorning;
To annoynt me oe'r night, ere I go to fight,
And to dress me in the morning.

This being done, he did engage
To hew the dragon down;
But first he went, new armour to
Bespeak at Sheffield town;
With spikes all about, not within but without,
Of steel so sharp and strong;
Both behind and before, arms, legs, and all o'er
Some five or six inches long.

Had you but seen him in this dress,
How fierce he look'd and how big,
You would have thought him for to be
Some Egyptian porcupig:
He frighted all, cats, dogs, and all,
Each cow, each horse, and each hog:
For fear they did flee, for they took him to be
Some strange outlandish hedge-hog.

To see this fight, all people then
Got up on trees and houses,
On churches some, and chimneys too;
But these put on their trowses,
Not to spoil their hose. As soon as he rose,
To make him strong and mighty,
He drank by the tale, six pots of ale,
And a quart of aqua-vitae.

It is not strength that always wins,
For wit doth strength excell;
Which made our cunning champion
Creep down into a well;
Where he did think, this dragon would drink,
And so he did in truth;
And as he stoop'd low, he rose up and cry'd, boh!
And hit him in the mouth.

O quoth the dragon, pox take thee, come out,
Thou disturb'st me in my drink:
And then he turn'd, and s... at him;
Good lack how he did stink!
Beshrew thy soul, thy body's foul,

Thy dung smells not like balsam;
Thou son of a whore, thou stink'st so sore,
Sure thy diet is unwholesome.

Our politick knight, on the other side,
Crept out upon the brink,
And gave the dragon such a douse,
He knew not what to think:
By cock, quoth he, say you so: do you see?
And then at him he let fly
With hand and foot, and so they went to't;
And the word it was, Hey boys, hey!

Your words, quoth the dragon, I don't understand:
Then to it they fell at all.
Like two wild boars so fierce, if I may,
Compare great things with small.
Two days and a night, with this dragon did fight
Our champion on the ground;
Tho' their strength it was great, their skill it
    was neat,
They never had one wound.

At length the hard earth began to quake,
The dragon gave him a knock,
Which made him reel, and straitway he thought,
To lift him as high as a rock,
And thence let him fall. But More of More-Hall,
Like a valiant son of Mars,
As he came like a lout, so he turn'd him about,
And hit him a kick on the a...

Oh, quoth the dragon, with a deep sigh,
And turn'd six times together,
Sobbing and tearing, cursing and swearing
Out of his throat of leather;
More of More-Hall! O thou rascal!
Would I had seen thee never;
With a thing at thy foot, thou hast prick'd
    my a... gut,
And I am quite undone for ever.

Murder, murder, the dragon cry'd,
Alack, alack, for grief;
Had you but mist that place, you could
Have done me no mischief.
Then his head he shaked, trembled and quaked,
And down he laid and cryd;
First on one knee, then on back tumbled he,
So groaned, kickt, s..., and dy'd.

The Background to the Ballad

Local legends that centre upon some specific place, person or object and which are a focus for local pride, have often been handed down in the form of well-known tales that have been adapted, frequently in a humorous way, to local circumstances. Thus the seventy-odd stories of dragon-slaying that have been collected in Britain usually depict a local figure, not St George or a knight errant, as the hero.[6] It is normally difficult, if not impossible, to explain how these tales began. *The Dragon of Wantley*, however, offers some unusual opportunities for delving into the historical context of a ballad that achieved national fame.

It has been argued that a very large proportion of the surviving ballads can be dated, on internal evidence, to the second half of the sixteenth century and the first decades of the seventeenth century. Once the custom of printing broadsides arose, the oral tradition was eroded and the printed text became accepted as the sole authentic version.[7] Thousands of ballads were enrolled by the Company of Stationers at their hall, just inside the City of London wall, during this period, but the index to their register contains no references to *The Dragon of Wantley* before Randal Taylor's publication of 1685. In fact, the only ballad about a dragon is one published in 1614 about the killing of a serpent in Sussex.[8]

Surviving versions of *The Dragon of Wantley* differ little from each other. The style is of the seventeenth century but of course the ballad might have been changed before then by successive singers. On the other hand, the farcical way that the ballad is treated, parodying earlier ballads, perhaps suggests a later rather than an earlier composition. Ambrose Phillips made the shrewd observation that the humorous treatment of *The Dragon of Wantley* is 'to old metrical romances and ballads of chivalry, what *Don Quixote* is to prose narratives of that kind; – a lively satire on their extravagant features'.[9]

Bishop Percy introduced the ballad by remarking that: 'The description of the dragon – his outrages – the people flying to the knight for succour – his care in chusing his armour – his being drest for fight by a young damsel – and most of the circumstances of the battle and victory (allowing for the burlesque turn given to them) are what occur in every book of chivalry, whether in prose or verse'. He noted, in particular, how the author drew upon the famous tale of Sir Bevis's battle with a dragon at a well and he suggested that the description of the dragon and the two-day fight in Spencer's *Faery Queen* might have been another source of inspiration. Jacqueline Simpson, the modern authority on dragon stories, has remarked that whoever wrote *The Dragon of Wantley* had 'a sound knowledge of dragon legends and did not invent his plot out of the blue'.[10] Such stories, she notes, have served three functions: to provide the hero with a worthy opponent; to explain a coat of arms or crest with a dramatic story; to offer explanations of material objects, place names, and topographical features.

The ballad is set in south-west Yorkshire, 'near fair Rotheram town' and not far from 'Sheffield town'. Wantley can be identified as Wharncliffe, the gritstone escarpment that rises high above the River Don and which is generally known as Wharncliffe Crags. As we shall see, an inscription that was cut into the rock in Henry VIII's reign, and which still survives, names the place as Wancliffe. More Hall lies in the valley bottom, half a mile from Wharncliffe, on the opposite bank of the river, in a different lordship and parish. Several generations of men bore the name More of More Hall in the Middle Ages, until the family moved away in 1547. The coat-of-arms of the Mores was shown in 1634 surmounted with a cockatrice or heraldic dragon. Hunter noted that 'The crest was formerly to be seen, carved in stone, about five feet long, at the north-east corner of Bradfield Church'.[11] More Hall lay within the chapelry of Bradfield.

The Dragon of Wantley therefore seems to fit the second of Jacqueline Simpson's functions for dragon stories, that it explained a coat of arms or crest with a dramatic story. Perhaps there was an

Left: Tune to the ballad. Ballads were sung to different tunes. This one is the only known survival for *The Dragon of Wantley*.

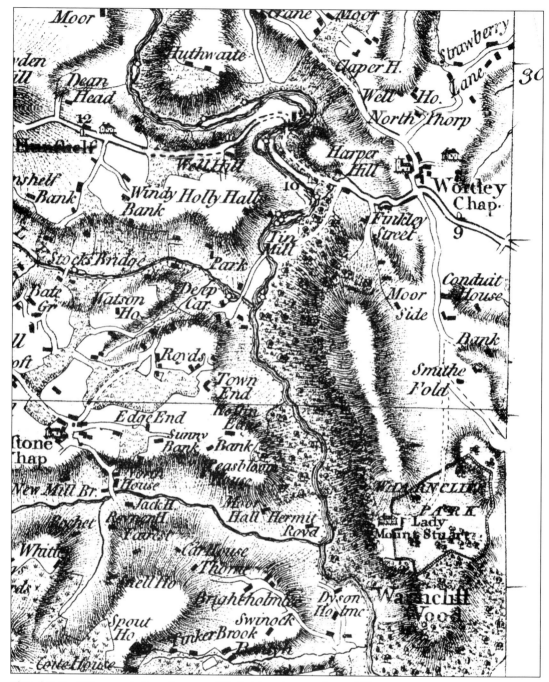

This detail of Thomas Jeffreys's map of Yorkshire shows Wharncliffe Chase in 1772 on the southern edge of the lordship of Wortley, Hallamshire's northern neighbour.

older version of the ballad (not necessarily in verse) which had one of the Mores as its hero? However, the possibility remains that the dragon crest dates from the early seventeenth century, after the ballad had become popular. We have no evidence for earlier Mores having a coat-of-arms and as the carving in Bradfield Church does not survive we have no means of knowing whether it was connected to the Mores or whether it was a piece of ecclesiastical sculpture of the type commonly produced in the Norman period. If the heraldic dragon on the Mores' crest was indeed a recent addition in 1634 this would give us a date by which the ballad was in circulation, long before it was printed.

On the crags high above More Hall stands Wharncliffe Lodge, the nineteenth-century successor to two previous buildings. The inscription of Henry VIII's reign is preserved on the floor of one of the rooms. A natural cave in the rocks close by was known by Hunter's time as The Dragon's Den. John Taylor, the London water poet, who visited the cave in 1639, made no mention of this romantic name, but as he was the guest of the Wortley family (who, as we shall see, were the villains in this story) perhaps he was not told about the ballad. Taylor's silence does suggest, however, that the fame of *The Dragon of Wantley* had not yet reached London. His account of the visit is as follows:

A natural cleft in the crags was adapted by the Wortleys as a place for picnics. It is close to Wharncliffe Lodge and when the ballad became well known it got the nickname of the Dragon's Den.

> *Sir Francis [Wortley] brought me to a lodge; the place is called Wharncliffe, where the keeper dwells, who is his man, and keeps all this woody, rocky, stony, vast wilderness under him, for there are many deere there ... Close to the said lodge is a stone, in burthen at least a hundred cart-loads; the top of it is four square by nature, and about twelve yards compasse. It hath three seats in the fourme of chaires, made by art as it were in the front of the rocke, wherein three persons may easily sit, and have a view and godly prospect over large woods, towns, cornfields, fruitfull and pleasant pastures, valleyes, deare, neat [i.e. cattle], sheep, and all things needfull for the life of man, contayned in thousands of acres, and all, for the better part, belonging to that noble knight's ancestors and himself. Behind the stone is a large inscription engraven, where in an old character is described the ancient memory of the Wortleys ... And about a bow-shoot from thence, by the descent of as many rings of the ladder, his worship brought mee to a cave or vault in a rocke, wherein was a table, with seats and turfe cushions around, and in a hole in the same rock was three barrels of nappy liquor. Hither the keeper brought a good red deere pye, cold roast mutton, and an excellent shooing-horn of hanged Martinmas biefe, which cheer no man living would think such a place could afford.[12]*

A correspondent told Bishop Percy that in the 1720s this cave had been pointed out to him as the dragon's den and that 'the stones we came over on the hill are those he could not crack'.[13] When Lady

Strafford of nearby Wentworth Castle went to see Carey's burlesque opera at Covent Garden in 1738 she misquoted the title as 'The Dragon of Wantcliff'; she must have known that Wharncliffe was the setting of the ballad.

In later editions of his *Reliques* Percy quoted a letter that he had received from Godfrey Bosville, Esq. of Thorpe, near Malton, whose ancestors had lived at Gunthwaite Hall in the parish of Penistone. In the 1590s the Bosvilles had been in dispute with the Wortleys over the tithes of Penistone. These had once belonged to the college of St Stephen, Westminster, but upon the dissolution of the college they had been purchased by the Earl of Shrewsbury, whose principal residence was at Sheffield Manor Lodge. The Wortleys had leased the right to collect the tithes but were prevented from making a substantial profit by an old agreement that allowed the parishioners to pay a modus, or fixed sum, instead of in kind. In an inflationary age this arrangement had worked to the disadvantage of the tithe owners. The Wortleys therefore attempted to break the agreement but were opposed by Bosville and others. A legal decision of the 37th year of the reign of Elizabeth (1595) favoured the parishioners.

Godfrey Bosville's memory was at fault on the details but clear on the essential facts. He knew that the Wortleys renewed the battle in 1603 and that 'the parishioners subscribed an agreement to defend their Modus'. He had this agreement in his possession. It was written on a large sheet of parchment, dated the first year of the reign of James I, and was full of names and seals. He was certain that the ballad related to the law suit. More of More Hall was not distinctly remembered but he was 'either the attorney, or counsellor, who conducted the suit'. Bosville identified Wantley as Wharncliffe and thought that the keepers at the lodge were named Matthew Northall over many generations, hence the reference in the ballad to 'Matthew's house nearby'. This cannot be substantiated; no Northalls were recorded in Wortley township (which included Wharncliffe) in the hearth tax returns of 1672.[14] Bosville let his imagination run riot in his explanation of the ballad, suggesting, for instance, that the seals on the document of 1603 were the inspiration for the description of the hero's armour being covered 'With spikes all about'. This provoked 'Fitzhopkins' to write to *Notes and Queries* from the Garrick Club in 1866 to ask 'Can anything be done for the Dragon of Wantley, who now lies smothered under a heap of Euhemerian rubbish?'[15] Fitzhopkins was content to rank the dragon of Wantley with the dragon of St George. The Wortley family preferred to believe that the dragon was 'a formidable drinker, drunk dead by the chieftain of the opposite moors'.[16]

Between the publication of his *Hallamshire* (1819) and of the second volume of his *South Yorkshire* (1831) Joseph Hunter came to the conclusion that Godfrey Bosville was right. He found the ruling of the Court of Exchequer in 1595 in favour of the parishioners of Penistone who had opposed Sir Richard Wortley's attempt to collect tithes in kind. He also saw a transcription (in the antiquarian collection of John Wilson of Broomhead Hall) of the indenture of the first year of the reign of James I, signed by ninety-eight parishioners pledging their mutual support in the renewed fight against the Wortleys. He also noted that Francis Bosville of Gunthwaite had taken the case to the Ecclesiastical Court at York and to the Court of Common Pleas at Westminster.[17]

Hunter had previously thought that the ballad must have originated in the first half of the sixteenth century, when the Mores still lived at More Hall, but now he concluded that, 'It is not necessary to interpret literally "More of More Hall", but that under the phrase some later owner of that house may be represented'. He observed that one of the leading signatories to the agreement of 1603 was George Blount, who at that time was living at More Hall. Blount was the son of a Shropshire gentleman; he had married a daughter of Sir Peter Freschvile of Staveley in north Derbyshire and sometimes resided nearby in Eckington. The similarity between the coat-of-arms that he claimed at the heraldic visitation in 1611 and those of the Blounts of Barton Blount in south Derbyshire suggests that he was a cadet of this ancient family. This was Bosville's half-remembered attorney or counsellor. Hunter also noted that Blount was active in another battle with the Wortleys that Bosville was unaware of, but which is central to our concerns.[18]

The Wortleys

The medieval lords of Wortley took their surname from their place of residence, though like other local lords they were probably of Norman or Breton origin. Nicholas, son of Alan of Wortley, who witnessed a deed in the twelfth century was the first of several generations bearing that name. Most of these Nicholases were knights. They acquired additional estates through marriages and for a time lived further north at Hemsworth, where some of them were buried. They improved their property at Wortley in the recognised ways of the age: by erecting a chapel-of-ease near their manor house, by acquiring a charter of free warren in 1252 to allow them to hunt throughout their lordship, and by obtaining a charter in 1307 which permitted a weekly market on Thursdays and a three-day fair at Pentecost.[19] The market and fair suffered the fate of numerous similar ventures in the later Middle Ages, when the national population declined and the economy went into recession; we hear no more about them. We hear a great deal about hunting, however.

The most illustrious member of the family during the Middle Ages was Sir Thomas Wortley (*c*.1440–1514), who was a trusted 'knight of the king's body' during the reigns of Edward IV, Richard III, Henry VII and Henry VIII. Sir Thomas was Sheriff of Yorkshire on five separate occasions and steward not only to the Lord of Hallamshire but to Fountains Abbey and the priories of Monk Bretton and Nostell. Two of his three wives were members of the prominent Fitzwilliam family. He entertained on a lavish scale at Wortley and at the lodge that he built upon the crags at Wharncliffe.[20] He was one of those rich and powerful men who were used to getting their own way, even if this meant ruthlessly disregarding the interests of their less-powerful neighbours.

This Sir Thomas Wortley was very fond of hunting and kept a famous pack of hounds. He created a deer park (which later came to be known as the Old Park) by his manor house in Wortley and in 1510 erected a hunting lodge on the summit of Wharncliffe Crags. An inscription which was cut into the rock at Wharncliffe, and which is now incorporated within the lodge, was read by Hunter as:

Pray for the saule of
THOMAS WRYTTELAY, knyght
for the kyngys bode to Edward
the forthe, Rychard therd, Hare the VII, and Hare VIII,
hows saules God perdon, Wyche
Thomas cawsyd a loge to be made
hon this crag ne mydys of
Wanclife, for his plesor to her the
hartes bel, in the yere of owr
Lord a thousand CCCCC.X[21]

The 'hartes bel' refers to the sound made by the deer.

Confused traditions speak of the ejection of some small freeholders on Wharncliffe so that Sir Thomas Wortley could hunt his deer. Hunter recorded one memory which claimed that Wortley 'allowed nothing to stand in the way between him and his fondness for the chase. He is supposed not only to have built the Lodge, but to have much enlarged the limits of the chase itself; and in order to do so, to have violently disenfranchised some ancient freeholders who were seated on its borders'. The Revd Oliver Heywood recorded a moral tale that was current in the late seventeenth century:

> *Sir Francis Wortley's great-grandfather, being a man of great estate, was owner of a town near unto him, only there were some freeholders in it, with whom he wrangled and sued until he had beggared them and cast out their inheritance, and so the town was wholly his, which he pulled quite down, and laid the buildings and town fields even as a common, wherein his main design was to keep deer, and make a lodge to which he came at the time of the year and lay there, taking great delight to hear the deer bell, but it came to pass that, before he died, he belled like a deer, and was distracted.*

But Hunter also mentioned another tradition, that the 'Deer park at Wharncliffe was once strewed with innumerable bodies of persons who perished in some great pestilence'.[22] Sir Thomas Wortley died four years after building the lodge; the construction of his will suggests that he was still of sound mind.

Hunter located the sites that were said to have been destroyed by Sir Thomas Wortley:

> A town to which tradition gives the name of Stanfield, is said to have stood on the top of Wharnclif moor, near the pond. Some small remains of a building on the moor, near the road from the Hay-stack-coppice to the Lodge, are said to have been Whitley-church. Some years ago, the foundations of some edifices were distinctly visible on this spot, Mr. Wilson measured them, and found that they inclosed a longitudinal area of nineteen yards by eight. Some unevenness in the ground, not far from the site of the supposed church, is said to indicate where the town of Whitley stood.

A field survey in 1949 confirmed the existence of these settlements.[23] A modern dwelling that bears the name of Stanfield Ash stands alongside the road that crosses Wharncliffe Chase from Grenoside

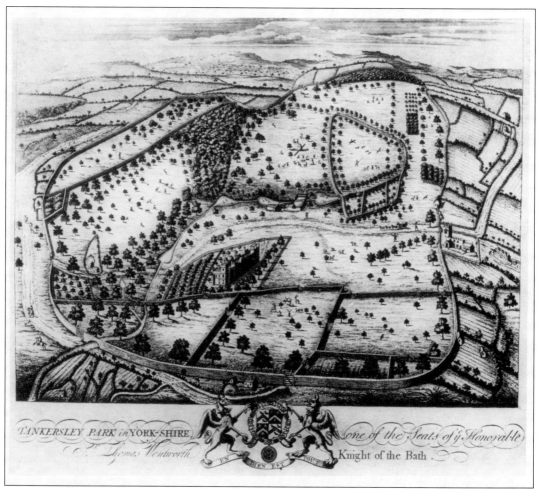

An engraving of 1725-28 of the park created at Tankersley in the early fourteenth century. The Elizabethan hall in the centre of the park was largely demolished shortly afterwards. The park was famous for its herd of large, red deer. The lords of Tankersley frequently clashed with the Wortleys.

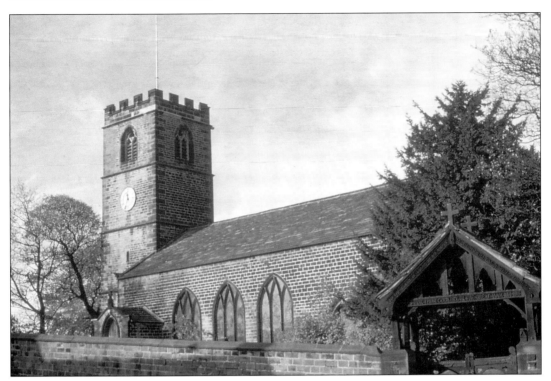

Wortley Church. The mid-eighteenth century successor to the medieval chapel, which was one of the focal points of the troubles in the 1580s and 1590s.

to Wortley. The deserted sites were only small, however; they certainly did not resemble villages, let alone the towns of tradition. Nevertheless, the local people who spoke to Heywood could still remember them 160 years after their desertion. The ballad writer may have drawn on these traditions when he wrote that the dragon devoured houses and churches.

Sir Thomas Wortley's son and namesake married a daughter of Sir John Savile of Tankersley and Thornhill, a member of a leading West Riding family with whom later Wortleys were to wrangle. Thus in 1527 Henry Savile and some of his men were charged in the Court of Star Chamber with breaking into Wortley (Old) Park at night time to hunt deer, armed with bows, arrows, bills, swords and bucklers, and accompanied with a pack of hounds. On one occasion they broke into the alehouse in Wortley and emptied barrels of ale in the street; on another they assaulted the park keeper.[24] Wortley lay within the parish of Tankersley and the Old Park included some land that stretched beyond the boundary of Wortley township; as the Saviles had their own deer park at Tankersley they might have disputed the Wortley's right to hunt there. Hunting could clearly cause friction between the leading families in the neighbourhood. The heads of these families were quite prepared to take the law into their own hands and to use force to achieve their own ends.

Francis, the son of Thomas Wortley II, was educated at one of the Inns of Court and became a member of the Queen's Council of the North and a prominent JP. He was described by George, the sixth Earl of Shrewsbury, in 1582 as 'a gentylman bothe wise and of very good credytt in the country'. His son, Sir Richard Wortley (1561–1603), inherited the family estates in 1583 and rebuilt Wortley Hall three years later. His properties included the manors of Wortley, Hunshelf, Carleton, Newhall and Hoylandswaine in south Yorkshire, Beighton in Derbyshire, and Babworth and Ballome in Nottinghamshire, with other lands nearby. He was knighted in 1603, when James I arrived in York from Scotland, and upon his death in the same year he was buried in St George's chapel, Windsor. His widow took as her second husband William Cavendish, the son of Bess of Hardwick, and the future first Earl of Devonshire. The Wortleys were clearly an important local family who were accepted in the Earl of Shrewsbury's circle which was centred on Sheffield Manor Lodge.[25]

This Richard Wortley is the prime candidate in our attempt to identify the dragon of Wantley. He was keenly aware of his own status in society and was prepared to act in a high-handed manner to make his estate even grander. Marginal comments on an eighteenth-century map in the Wharncliffe muniments[26] show that in 1589 he enlarged the Old Park near his hall and that at about the same time he extended Wharncliffe Chase and enclosed a New Park within it. His actions met with fierce resistance.

The Troubles of the 1590s

Among the archives of the Wortley family are a collection of depositions from witnesses who were prepared to support a complaint made by the Wortleys to the Court of Chancery in 1594.[27] An astonishing series of charges were levelled against George Blount of More Hall, William Dickenson, senior and junior, Gilbert Dickenson, William Broadhead and Thomas Cock, relating to Wortley Park and Wharncliffe Chase from 1591 onwards. They and others were said to have broken the pales of Wortley Old Park to hunt there and to have overthrown a great stone wall that enclosed the New Park on Wharncliffe at Stead Springs Side and White Carr. On another occasion they were said to have hung up deer's flesh in the cockpit and the chapel yard at Wortley at night time with a 'libell or written paper therupon'. The conspirators were also said to have sworn a solemn oath of secrecy.

The principal witness for the Wortleys was Richard Lord, the vicar of Ecclesfield, who said:

> That hee heard that [Richard Wortley] had a great parte of his parke pale called Wortley Parke broken in peeces and pulled downe and ... had at severall times a greate parte of the wall of his chase called Warnecliff pulled down and overthrown, and ... had his deare dyvers tymes stolne beetwixte the firste of Auguste in the year of our Lord God 1592 and the feaste of Easter then next followinge. And allso heard that there weare little powles or sticks put upp in dyvers places within the Lordshipp of Wortley in the night season in forme of Gallowes, and deeres fleshe hanged thereuppon ... [he also] heard that there was a deares head sett upp in the portche of the Chappell att Wortley and a slanderous Libel fixed or sewed therunto.

The vicar's evidence was supported by that of Thomas Carr, a thirty year old yeoman from Tankersley, and by Roger Scott, a thirty-two year old husbandman of the parish of Ecclesfield, who added that Elizabeth, the wife of Gilbert Dickenson, had boasted of the illegal hunting and had criticised Raphe Broomhead for being the boldest man at the planning of the action but having the faintest heart when they arrived at the park pale.

Vicar Lord went on to say that 'Gilbert Dycconson, William Bromehead, and Raphe Bromehead are persons suspected for many disorders and misdemenors' within the parish of Ecclesfield:

> In the nighte tyme as the wearyinge or killinge of this deponent's tythe Lambes there for twoe yeares together, the cuttinge awaye of the tayles of A horse and mare of his this deponent's save some small parte wherein hanged dead horse heades and other bones, and saith that the said horse and mare came soe disfigured frome the said Gilbert Dicconson's howse, and further this deponent saith that there was a horse of this deponent's and a mare of one Nathaniell Smithe's in the church-yeard of Ecclesfield which said horse and mare weare in the night tyme taken owte of the said churchyeard and throwen into a deep Colepitt where they dyed. And further saith that others had their horse tayles cutt and theire fettlocks pared and shorne in the night tyme, and others theire flax mowen downe in the night beeinge but half ripe, and their geese necks writhen and killed and laid together beefore theire dores, and others had theire sheepe barrs cutt in peeces in the nighte, and

Ecclesfield Church. The scene of some of the troubles of the 1590's. This photograph was taken before the churchyard was altered in 1842.

another had his ram or tupp taken owte of his sheepe fowld and killed in the night tyme and the head and genitalls cutt of and sett uppon a maypole with a lewd and fylthy libell fixed to the same and others have had theire stone walles overthrowen and others theire dogges and swyne killed. And this deponent saith that hee never knew or heard of the like displeasures and misdemenors to bee committed or donne in any other place of all that cuntryee.

Local people, he claimed, were afraid to give evidence against these bully boys. He had obtained a warrant from the Quarter Sessions ordering the good behaviour of Gilbert Dickenson, William Broomhead, Henry Wainwright and Thomas Scargill. They had promised that 'they would henceforth bee good and honeste neighbours unto him ... but did not promise that hee ... should never have the like displeasure donne unto him againe'.

Twenty-seven people were named in the charges levelled by Richard Wortley. Many of them can be identified as members of families that resided within the neighbouring Lordship of Hallamshire, which shared a boundary with Wharncliffe Chase. On the whole, the defendants belonged to yeomen and minor gentry families which had long been resident on their estates. The Broomheads, Wilsons and Scargills, for example, had been there for over two hundred years. Some of the principal defendants were the trusted servants of the Earl of Shrewsbury, Lord of Hallamshire, the mightiest nobleman north of the Trent. William Dickenson, senior (1540–1606), had been bailiff of the earl's estates in Sheffield, Derbyshire, Worksop and Staffordshire since 1574; he lived in the High Street in Sheffield where he had built a house in 1575. His sons, Gilbert, William and Francis were also employed by the Earls of Shrewsbury and were each styled 'gentleman'. Francis (who was not involved in this dispute) lived at Rotherham, William, junior, lived at Shiregreen in the parish of Ecclesfield, and Gilbert resided at Barnes Hall in the same parish (close to Wharncliffe Chase) before moving a mile or so to Housley Hall upon the death of his father-in-law.[28]

A letter that Gilbert Dickenson wrote to George, the sixth earl, welcoming him home in 1585,

William Dickenson's house. This (demolished) timber-framed house in Sheffield's High Street was built for the bailiff of Hallamshire, whose family were leading opponents of the Wortleys.

Wortley remains a small settlement where the ridgeway from Sheffield to Halifax crossed the salt way from Cheshire to Rotherham. The hall and park dominate the northern part of the township, while the chase occupied much of the south.

demonstrates his importance in the Shrewsbury circle.[29] He was probably named after Gilbert Talbot, the seventh Earl of Shrewsbury, who succeeded his father in 1590 (and his brother Francis was probably named after the fifth earl). The Dickensons were clearly a family with power and influence in the locality. Gilbert Dickenson was prepared to abuse this power at an early age; in 1580, long before the troubles on Wharncliffe, he was brought before a JP and ordered to give security to keep the peace towards one Thomas Heywood. The Earls of Shrewsbury turned a blind eye to this sort of aggressive behaviour. They were frequently in contention with local people and local institutions. Gilbert Dickenson failed to get possession of the Ecclesfield Feoffees' estate for George Talbot but he managed to grab the estate of the Bradfield Feoffees.[30]

The Earls of Shrewsbury had a large deer park at Sheffield and an extensive chase in the Rivelin valley. One of the Dickensons was the keeper of Sheffield Park until 1596.[31] The creation of Richard Wortley's New Park on Wharncliffe Chase immediately beyond Hallamshire probably caused much comment, especially if it were thought that Wortley had exceeded his rights. The Dickensons must have felt confident of the support of the Earl of Shrewsbury, who was a much more powerful figure than Richard Wortley. The conspirators no doubt felt that right as well as might was on their side. They had a genuine grievance to excuse their hooliganism.

They may also have felt justified in the use of the violence which they directed against the Vicar of Ecclesfield. The disfigurement of his horses sounds like an ancient ritual insult. Acrimony over the collection of tithes seems to have fuelled the outrages which were committed there. The Revd Joseph Hunter wrote circumspectly: 'Lord appears in the court-rolls of the manor of Sheffield under circumstances which do not dispose favourably to the manner in which he sustained the clerical character'.[32] All had seemed well when he came to Ecclesfield in 1585. He had been presented to the living by the sixth Earl of Shrewsbury and had immediately leased the right to collect the small tithes – the tithes of wool and lambs – in the chapelry of Bradfield to Gilbert Dickenson.[33] It is not clear how their relationship turned sour but a quarrel over tithes seems likely to have been the major cause. Lord died in 1600 and was buried in Ecclesfield churchyard, where his (later) memorial may still be seen.[34] His will makes no reference to doles for the poor or any other charitable bequest, which is surprising for a parish priest.

Feelings about tithes were also running high in the parish of Penistone, a few miles to the north, where, as we have seen, Richard Wortley was trying to increase his profits by demanding a return to the old system of collecting in kind rather than by the fixed sum of money whose value had been undermined by inflation. The dispute began to smoulder in 1587 and flared up five years later, at the very time that George Blount, Gilbert Dickenson and others had broken into the Old Park at Wortley and the New Park in Wharncliffe Chase. George Blount was the only person actively to oppose Richard Wortley in both causes.[35]

Richard Wortley tried at first to enforce his claims before the ecclesiastical court at York. In 1587 he brought Henry Burdett of Denby, gentleman, there and two years later he used the same tactic with Francis Bosville of Gunthwaite, gentleman (the ancestor of the Godfrey Bosville who corresponded with Bishop Percy about *The Dragon of Wantley*).[36] In 1595 the whole question of the payment of tithes in the parish of Penistone was heard in the Court of the Exchequer before Lord Burghley, the chancellor, who found in favour of the defendants.[37] Thus the matter seemed to be resolved, but eight years later, with Burghley dead, a new king on the throne, and a recently-endowed knighthood to give him confidence Sir Richard Wortley tried again, this time bringing Lionel Rolleston of Penistone, gentleman, before the ecclesiastical court at York.[38] This Lionel Rolleston was a former 'Captain of foot in Ireland' who had married Francis Bosville's widow and was living at Gunthwaite. He was thus the leading gentleman in the parish and a JP for the West Riding. The parishioners quickly rallied to Rolleston's support. George Blount and Matthew Burdett, gentlemen, with ninety-four others, pledged mutual help if Wortley should act against any one of them. The original agreement is no longer amongst the Bosville archives (as it was when Godfrey Bosville corresponded with Bishop Percy), but Joseph Hunter saw a transcript that was made by John Wilson of Broomhead Hall. Hunter noted that

The eighteenth-century Wortley Hall stands on the site of its medieval predecessor within Wortley Old Park.

Wortley Hall. The eighteenth-century hall of Edward Wortley-Montague.

almost all the signatories were yeomen and that about half of them could not write their names. Was George Blount the leading organiser of this resistance as Godfrey Bosville suggested?[39] As we have seen, he was the only man who was involved in both the tithe and the hunting disputes. He lived at More Hall and seems to have been cast in the ballad as the hero who slew the dragon.

Sir Richard Wortley died in 1603, the year of the renewed battle over tithes, at the age of forty-two. The dragon had been truly slain. Did his neighbours really rejoice so much at the news of his death that one of them adapted an old tale about a dragon for their amusement? The heat of the controversies in which Wortley had been involved does make this year the likeliest date of composition. We do not know who wrote it but perhaps it was a musician in the employment of the Earl of Shrewsbury at Sheffield Manor Lodge, who knew the Dickensons and perhaps Blount and who would have known the stories about what happened at Wharncliffe. 'Musick and singing men' were in attendance at the funeral of Gilbert Talbot, the seventh Earl of Shrewsbury, in 1616, and he and his father before him are known to have had their own 'players'.[40] Despite its crudity, the ballad is far too sophisticated in its allusions to have been composed by any local person outside this circle.

Sir Richard Wortley was buried not in South Yorkshire but in St George's Chapel, Windsor. His Latin epitaph[41] speaks of the many virtues which should be attached to his memory. Instead, he is remembered as the Dragon of Wantley.

The Aftermath of the Troubles

Sir Richard Wortley's son, Francis, was only twelve when his father died. In 1610 he was knighted, the following year he became a baronet, and in time he acquired a reputation as a classical scholar. He was a fervent Royalist in the Civil War, as a result of which his estates were sequestered and he was imprisoned in the Tower of London, where he died. His son and namesake was the last of the family in the male line but the estates passed through an illegitimate daughter and subsequently through other heiresses. Later owners were known by the names of Wortley-Montagu and Stuart-Wortley. Edward Wortley-Montagu, the husband of the famous Lady Mary, rebuilt Wortley Hall in three campaigns from 1731 to his death thirty years later. He also largely rebuilt Wortley Church in its present form, the inn opposite and the old lodge at Wharncliffe (which was rebuilt again in the nineteenth century).[42] In 1826 James Archibald Stuart-Wortley was made the first baron Wharncliffe; fifty years later his successor was made the first Earl of Wharncliffe. The present earl is an American who lives in Maine. Wortley Hall is a Labour Educational and Holiday Centre.

The death of Sir Richard Wortley did not bring the disputes to an end. In 1629 thirteen men 'armed and arraied with swordes daggors pitchforkes pikestaves axes spades and other weapons' met at Hoylandswaine in the night time 'in forcible and warlike manner' and destroyed the new hedges and ditches that the Wortleys had constructed to enclose part of the commons.[43] In 1647 Nicholas Greaves was brought before the Quarter Sessions for hunting red and fallow deer in the chase at Wharncliffe.[44] The following year Ralph Greaves of Bolsterstone, yeoman, was charged with killing a doe in New Park after a chase with greyhounds; nine other local men, including a priest and several yeomen, were charged with killing forty deer in the same park and several others were charged with killing another thirty deer. They confessed their actions, but claimed that as Nicholas Greaves owned a one-eighth share, they were not guilty of any offence. The JPs treated them lightly, for they were fined only the value of the deer, but Sir Francis Wortley won his case.

The troubles were over, but thanks to *The Dragon of Wantley* the aggression of the Wortleys was never forgotten. In 1831 Joseph Hunter wrote, 'Within my remembrance, a perfect acquaintance with its nineteen double stanzas was a necessary accomplishment of the successors to the ancient minstrelsy of England, who attended the village festivals in this neighbourhood'.[45] At that time, two hundred deer roamed over Wharncliffe. A few still graze there today.

NOTES

Chapter One: The Hallamshire Countryside

1. W Fraser, ed., *Early Yorkshire Charters*, III (Edinburgh, 1916), p. 6.
2. The most accessible modern version is M L Faull and M Stinson, eds, *Domesday Book: Yorkshire* (Phillimore, Chichester, 1986).
3. J E A Jolliffe, 'Northumbrian Institutions', *English Historical Review*, XLI (1926), pp. 1–42.
4. A H Smith, *The Place–Names of the West Riding of Yorkshire* (Cambridge: English Place–Names Society, 1961), p. 245.
5. 'Yorkshire Fines, 1246–1272', *Yorkshire Archaeological Society Record Series*, LXXXII (1932), p. 148.
6. Sheffield Archives, Bright 1.
7. D Hey, 'Yorkshire's Southern Boundary' in *Essays on Northern History in Honour of Maurice W Beresford*, Northern History, XXXVII (2000), pp. 31–47. Jeffreys' map was reprinted by Harry Margary of Lympne Castle, Kent, in 1973, with introductory notes by J B Harley and J C Harvey; a copy can be seen in Sheffield Archives. The 1791 edition of Burdett's map was reprinted in 1975 by by the Derbyshire Archaeological Society, with an explanatory introduction by J B Harley, D V Fowkes and J C Harvey.
8. Smith, I, p. 235.
9. Ibid., 1, pp. 197, 201.
10. G N Garmonsway, ed., *The Anglo–Saxon Chronicle* (London, 1978), pp. 60–61.
11. Smith, ed., 1, p. 137.
12. K Cameron, *The Place–Names of Derbyshire* (Cambridge: English Place–Name Society, 1959), I, p. 12.
13. Smith, ed., I, p. 300.
14. Ibid., 1, p. 235.
15. Ibid., p. 101; for a discussion of *halgh* see M Gelling and A Cole, *The Landscape of Place–Names* (Stamford, 2000), pp. 123–33.
16. T W Hall, 'Waltheof and the Aula in Hallam' in *South Yorkshire Historical Sketches* (Sheffield, 1931), part 1.
17. A. L. Armstrong, 'Sheffield Castle', *Transactions of the Hunter Archaeological Society*, IV, pt I (1930), pp. 7–27.
18. D Hey, *The Fiery Blades of Hallamshire: Sheffield and Its Neighbourhood, 1660–1740* (Leicester, 1991), pp. 15–36, 50–51.
19. D. Hey, 'The Establishment of the Cutlers' Company' in C. Binfield and D. Hey, eds, *Mesters to Masters: A History of the Company of Cutlers in Hallamshire* (Oxford, 1997), pp. 12–25.
20. D Hey, *A History of Sheffield* (Lancaster, 1998), pp. 10–17.
21. B English, ed., *Yorkshire Hundred and Quo Warranto Rolls, 1274–1294* (Yorkshire Archaeological Society Record Series, CLI, 1996), p. 278.
22. E Curtis, 'Sheffield in the Fourteenth Century: Two Furnival Inquisitions', *Transactions of the Hunter Archaeological Society*, I, pt I (1914), pp. 31–58.
23. J G Ronksley, ed., *An Exact and Perfect Survey and View of the Manor of Sheffield, with other Lands, by John Harrison, 1637* (Sheffield, 1908).

24. J Evelyn, *Silva, or a Discourse on Forest Trees*, (ed. A. Hunter, 1801), II, pp. 206–11.
25. Sheffield Archives, Bright 24; M. Jones, *The Making of the South Yorkshire Landscape* (Barnsley, 2000), pp. 52–61.
26. *Pipe Roll, 30 Henry II*, p. 100.
27. D V Fowkes and G R Potter, eds, *William Senior's Survey of the Estates of the First and Second Earls of Devonshire* (Derbyshire Record Society, XIII, 1988).
28. J A Sheppard, 'Pre–Conquest Yorkshire: fiscal carucates as an index of land exploration', *Transactions of the Institute of British Geographers*, 65 (1975), pp. 67–78.
29. Ronksley, *op. cit.*
30. "Customs of the Manor of Sheffield', *Transactions of the Hunter Archaeological Society*, II, pt 4 (1924), pp. 371–73.
31. D Hey, *The Rural Metalworkers of the Sheffield Region* (Leicester, 1972).
32. Hey, *Fiery Blades*, pp. 50–52.
33. Revd A S Gatty, 'Records of the Court Baron of the Manor of Sheffield', *Transactions of the Hunter Archaeological Society*, I, pt 4 (1918), pp. 257–329.
34. T W Hall, *A Descriptive Catalogue of Sheffield Manorial Records* (Sheffield, 1926), p. 40.
35. English., p. 278; Revd J Hunter, *Hallamshire* (ed. Revd A Gatty, London, 1869), pp. 403–4; C Drury, 'The Sembly Quest', *Transactions of the Hunter Archaeological Society*, III, pt 2 (1926), pp. 105–111.
36. G Scurfield, 'Seventeenth–Century Sheffield and its Environs', *Yorkshire Archaeological Journal*, 58 (1986), pp. 147–71, reconstructs maps from Harrison's survey. See also C F Innocent, 'The Field System of Wigtwizzle', *Transactions of the Hunter Archaeological Society*, II, pt 4 (1924), pp. 276–78.
37. East Yorkshire Record Office, Beverley, DDBM / 14 / 8, 9.
38. A S Gatty, *op. cit.*
39. Curtis, pp. 31–53.
40. E Miller, ed., *The Agrarian History of England and Wales, III, 1350–1500* (Cambridge, 1991) provides the national background.
41. Hall, *Sheffield Manorial Records*, p. 24.
42. A H Thomas, 'Some Hallamshire Rolls of the Fifteenth Century', *Transactions of the Hunter Archaeological Society*, II, pt 1 (1920), pp. 65–79, pt 2 (1921), pp. 142–58, pt 3 (1922), pp. 225–45.
43. Ronksley, *op. cit.*
44. Sheffield Archives, C158: 'A Survey of Lands belonging to the Mannor of Sheffield, 1611'.
45. M Spray and D J Smith, 'The Rise and Fall of Holly in the Sheffield Region', *Transactions of the Hunter Archaeological Society*, X, pt 4 (1977), pp. 239–51; Hey, *Fiery Blades*, pp. 25–26; Thomas, *op. cit.*; Sheffield Archives, ACM S376.
46. Ronksley, *op. cit.*; Scurfield, *op. cit.* There are no early documentary references to the name Bar Dike.
47. J Kenworthy, *The Early History of Stocksbridge and District* (Deepcar, privately published in parts): 'Langsett' (1915), pp. 24–25; 'The Town Fields and Commons of Hunshelf, Langsett and Waldershelf' (1917), pp. 11–18; C. Paulus, *The Manor and Parish of Ecclesall* (Sheffield, 1927); Sheffield Archives, enclosure awards.
48. This paragraph is based on Hey, *Fiery Blades*, Binfield and Hey, *Mesters to Masters* and D Crossley, *et al.*, eds, *Water Power on the Sheffield Rivers* (Sheffield, 1989).

Chapter Two: Ecclesfield Priory and the Abbey of St Wandrille

1. R T Timson, *The Cartulary of Blyth Priory*, Thoroton Society Record Series, XXVII (1973), p. lxi.
2. Sir C Clay, ed., *Early Yorkshire Families*, Yorkshire Archaeological Society Record Series, CXXXV (1973), pp. 53–56 outlines what is known about the de Louvetots and questions the belief that Roger was succeeded by his nephew Richard, suggesting instead that William was Roger's son; Revd J Hunter, *South Yorkshire: The History and Topography of the Deanery of Doncaster*, II (London, 1831), p. 185. A list of twenty vicars of Sheffield is provided in A H Thompson and C T Clay, eds, *Fasti Parochiales*, II, Yorkshire Archaeological Society Record Series, CVII (1943), pp. 54–55.

3. Hunter, p. 185; P Hanks and F Hodges, *A Dictionary of Surnames* (Oxford, 1888), p. 197. A display board at Fourneville says that the place was known as Furnvilla in 1070 and as Fournevilla by the sixteenth century. On the origins of Norman families that settled in England, see L C Loyd, *The Origins of Some Anglo–Norman Families*, Harleian Society, 103 (1951) and P H Reaney, *The Origin of English Surnames* (London, 1967), pp. 68–74.
4. Revd J Eastwood, *History of the Parish of Ecclesfield* (London, 1862), pp. 56–62.
5. Y Poncelet, 'Les possessions anglaises de l'Abbaye de Saint–Wandrille', *Annales de Normandie*, May 1987, no. 2, pp. 149–72.
6. J W Clay, ed., *Yorkshire Church Notes, 1619–1631, by Roger Dodsworth*, Yorkshire Archaeological Society Record Series, XXXIV (1904), pp. 4–9.
7. A H Thompson and C T Clay, eds, *Fasti Parochiales*, I, Yorkshire Archaeological Society Record Series, LXXXV (1933), pp. 95–106; Eastwood, p. 114.
8. T W Hall, *A Descriptive Catalogue of Early Charters relating to Lands in and near Sheffield* (Sheffield, 1938), p. 4.
9. Eastwood, p. 96.
10. A H Thompson and C T Clay, eds, *Fasti Parochiales*, II, Yorkshire Archaeological Society Record Series, CVII (1943), p.113.
11. Eastwood, pp. 100–1.
12. Eastwood, p. 150.
13. Eastwood, p. 511.
14. Eastwood, p. 95, quoting the chartulary of St Wandrille's Abbey. The document is dated 1141 by the old calendar, 1142 by modern reckoning.
15. Poncelet, *op. cit.*
16. Revd A Gatty, *A Life at One Living* (London, 1884), p. 10.
17. *Fasti Parochiales*, I, p. 100, where it is suggested that *decanus* might signify rural dean.
18. Eastwood, pp. 81–83.
19. B English, ed., *Yorkshire Hundred and Quo Warranto Rolls, 1274–1294*, Yorkshire Archaeological Society Record Series, CLI (1996), p. 42.
20. T W Hall, *Descriptive Catalogue of the Wheat Collection* (Sheffield, 1920), pp. 5–7.
21. T W Hall, *South Yorkshire Historical Sketches* (Sheffield, 1931), pp. 16–61.
22. Eastwood, pp. 101–4.
23. Poncelet, *op. cit.*
24. Eastwood, pp. 85, 102.
25. Eastwood, p. 85.
26. M. Barley, *Houses and History* (London, 1986), p. 137.
27. The silence of the editors of *Fasti Parochiales* on this matter surely signifies their disagreement with Eastwood.
28. *Fasti Parochiales*, I, p. 101.
29. Eastwood, p. 100.
30. *Fasti Parochiales*, I, p. 102.
31. He was also described as prior in 1287; Eastwood, pp. 99, 104–8.
32. Eastwood, pp. 108–10. No one can be identified in the lay subsidy return of 1297 as the farmer of the Rectory Manor or of Woolley Grange. The prior and other clergymen would have been exempted from that tax.
33. Eastwood, p. 492.
34. W Brown and A H Thompson, eds, *The Register of William Greenfield, Archbishop of York, 1306–1315*, II , Surtees Society, 149 (1934), pp. 97–100, and V, 153 (1938), pp. xviii and 205.
35. *Calendar of Miscellaneous Inquisitions, 1348–1377*, no. 1003.
36. Eastwood, pp. 111–16.
37. Eastwood, pp. 122–23.
38. *Fasti Parochiales*, I, p. 102. Robert was therefore living in the Priory, not in a parsonage–house. He was described in 1328 as lately prior, guardian or rector.
39. Eastwood, pp. 312–13; *Fasti Parochiales*, I, pp. 102–4.
40. The title of a cleric with a Master's degree.
41. The title of a priest who was not a University graduate.

42. *The Returns of the Poll Tax for the West Riding of Yorkshire, 1379*, Yorkshire Archaeological and Topographical Society, 5 (1882).
43. *Fasti Parochiales*, I, p. 104.
44. *Victoria County History of Warwickshire*, II (1908), pp. 83–86.
45. T W Hall, *South Yorkshire Historical Sketches* (Sheffield, 1931), p. 28. Revd A S Gatty, *Registers of Ecclesfield Parish Church ... also the Churchwardens' Accounts* (London, 1878), pp. 148–49, note, and p. 155, note.
46. J Caley and J Hunter, eds, *Valor Ecclesiasticus* (London: Record Commission, six volumes, 1810–34).
47. *Fasti Parochiales*, I, 104–6.
48. *Transactions of the Hunter Archaeological Society*, I, pt 4 (1918), p. 267.
49. A S Gatty, ed., *Registers*, p. 154 notes a bequest of 26s 8d from Sir Thomas Clark.
50. References to the Prior in the court rolls of the Rectory Manor in 1519 (Henry Wilson) and 1538 (John Bochard) are to the Prior of St Anne's, Coventry; T W Hall, *South Yorkshire Historical Sketches* (Sheffield, 1931), pp. 27, 31 and 50.
51. Eastwood, 131, 154.
52. Eastwood, 131–32.
53. E G W Bill, ed., *A Calendar of the Shrewsbury Papers in the Lambeth Palace Library*, Derbyshire Archaeological Society Record Series, 1 (1966), p. 168 records an agreement of 20 February 1609 by which Nicholas Shircliffe of Ecclesfield granted to the Earl of Shrewsbury his right and title in Woolley Grange and woods, for the term of years for which he held it.
54. J G Ronksley, ed., *An Exact and Perfect Survey and View of the Manor of Sheffield with other Lands, by John Harrison, 1637* (Sheffield, 1908).
55. In 1451 'one acre of land near the water-mill of the lord prior' was recorded in a Rectory Manor court roll; T W Hall, *South Yorkshire Historical Sketches* (Sheffield, 1931), p. 30.
56. Eastwood, p. 137.
57. See the reconstruction of this and other farms in G Scurfield, 'Seventeenth-Century Sheffield and its Environs', *Yorkshire Archaeological Journal*, 58 (1986), pp. 147–71.
58. D Hey, ed., *The Hearth Tax Returns for South Yorkshire, Ladyday 1672* (Sheffield, 1991).
59. The full inventory is reproduced in D Hey, *The Village of Ecclesfield* (Huddersfield, 1968), pp. 115–16.
60. The date 1866 is embossed on the rainwater heads. For plans and drawings at the time of the restoration see Revd A Gatty, *St.Wandrille's Abbey* (Sheffield, 1887).
61. Eastwood, pp. 88, 140–42; Gatty, *St Wandrille's Abbey*; P F Ryder, 'Ecclesfield Priory', 'Report of the Royal Archaeological Institute's Summer Meeting at Wentworth Woodhouse', *The Archaeological Journal*, 138 (1980).
62. I am grateful to David Banham for guiding me around Ecclesfield Priory on many occasions during the years that he lived there.

Chapter Three: The Hallamshire Gentry and their Halls

1. J G Ronksley, ed., *An Exact and Perfect Survey and View of the Manor of Sheffield with other Lands, by John Harrison, 1637* (Sheffield, 1908).
2. Quoted by Revd J Eastwood, *History of the Parish of Ecclesfield* (London, 1862), p. 357. The 'Earl of Salop' was George, sixth Earl of Shrewsbury.
3. Revd J Hunter, *South Yorkshire; History and Topography of the Deanery of Doncaster*, II (London, 1831), pp. 46, 436; Eastwood, pp. 355–56. The surnames Reineville and Laci were derived from settlements in Calvados department, Normandy.
4. W Brown, ed., *Yorkshire Lay Subsidy 25 Edwardi I*, Yorkshire Archaeological Society Record Series, 16 (1894), pp. 72–76, 86–87.
5. *The Returns of the Poll Tax for the West Riding of Yorkshire, 1379* Yorkshire Archaeological and Topographical Society, 5 (1882).
6. Eastwood, p. 356.
7. D Hey, *The Fiery Blades of Hallamshire: Sheffield and its Neighbourhood, 1660–1740* (Leicester, 1991), pp. 32–33.

8. Hunter, *South Yorkshire*, II, p. 55.
9. J Guest, *Historic Notices of Rotherham* (Worksop, 1879), pp. 203, 452; D Hey, ed., *The Hearth Tax Returns for South Yorkshire, Ladyday 1672* (Sheffield, 1991).
10. Revd J Hunter, *Hallamshire* (ed. Revd A Gatty, London, 1869), pp. 340–42.
11. Sheffield Archives, WWM MP 46; John Gelley's map (1725); Thomas Jeffreys' map of Yorkshire (1772).
12. Eastwood, pp. 440–44; Hunter, *South Yorkshire*, II, p.5.
13. B English, ed., *Yorkshire Hundred and Quo Warranto Rolls, 1274–1294*, Yorkshire Archaeological Society Record Series, CLI (1996), p. 42; Eastwood, pp. 464–48.
14. Hunter, *South Yorkshire*, II, pp. 196–97.
15. D Hey, 'Penistone Market and Cloth Hall' in B Elliott, ed., *Aspects of Barnsley*, V (Barnsley, 1998), pp. 173–88; Hunter, *South Yorkshire*, II, pp. 194–96.
16. P F Ryder, 'Midhope Chapel' and 'Old Courthouse' in 'Report of the Royal Archaeological Institute Summer Meeting at Wentworth Woodhouse', *The Archaeological Journal*, 138 (1980).
17. Eastwood, pp. 436–40. The 1867 plan is inserted in my copy of Eastwood's history.
18. C Giles, *Rural Houses of West Yorkshire, 1400–1830* (London: Royal Commission on Historical Monuments, 1986), p. 21.
19. Unless otherwise stated, the following information about local families is taken from the computer database of medieval records held at The National Centre for Cultural Tradition, The University of Sheffield. These medieval records are taken from the transcripts in the early *Transactions of the Hunter Archaeological Society* and in the various catalogues of Sheffield records published by T Walter Hall.
20. Revd A Gatty, *A Life at One Living* (London, 1884), pp. 70–74; Eastwood, p. 415.
21. Revd A S Gatty, ed., *Registers of Ecclesfield Parish Church ... also the Churchwardens' Accounts* (London, 1878), pp. 148–49, note, and p. 155, note.
22. Hunter, *Hallamshire*, pp. 446–47.
23. D Hey and J Unwin, eds, *The Cutlers of Hallamshire, 1624–1699* (Sheffield, 1993), pp. 123–30.
24. W F Webster, ed., *Nottinghamshire Hearth Tax, 1664: 1674*, Thoroton Society Record Series, XXXVII (1988); D G Edwards, *Derbyshire Hearth Tax Assessment, 1662–70*, Derbyshire Record Society, VII (1982).
25. G Redmonds, *Yorkshire Surnames Series, pt I: Bradford & District* (Lepton, 1990), pp. 50–51, and personal communication. For the landholding connections, see Hunter, *South Yorkshire*, II, p. 78 and E W Crossley, *The Preceptory of Newland*, Yorkshire Archaeological Society Record Series, LXI (1920), pp. 1–83. The other circumstantial evidence includes the common occupation of smith and the use of the Christian name Peter. It is not clear from which of the two Steads the surname was derived, if they do have a single origin.
26. University of Leeds, Brotherton Library, Wilson collection, CLIX.
27. Hunter, *South Yorkshire*, II, p. 193; T W Hall, *Descriptive Catalogue of the Wheat Collection* (Sheffield, 1920), pp. 5–7.
28. P H Reaney and R M Wilson, *A Dictionary of English Surnames* (Oxford, revised edn, 1997), p. 64.
29. Hunter, *Hallamshire*, pp. 353–59, 417–18; P Roebuck, *Yorkshire Baronets, 1640–1760* (Oxford, 1980).
30. D Wilson, *A History of the Wilson Family of Broomhead* (Sheffield, privately printed, 1991).
31. T W Hall, *Material for the History of Wincobank, Sheffield, 1523 to 1750* (Sheffield, 1922); Borthwick Institute of Historical Research, York: wills and inventories.
32. Revd. J Hunter, *Familiae Minorum Gentium*, 5 vols (Harleian Society, 1895), pp. 1062–67.
33. Ibid., pp. 814–16.
34. Eastwood, pp. 431–33.
35. A few other gabled halls were erected in the seventeenth century, at Darnall, Fulwood, Owlerton, Stumperlowe and Wigtwizzle.

Chapter Four: The Lost Place-Names and Failed Surnames of Hallamshire

1. J Morris, ed., *Domesday Book: Yorkshire*, I (Chichester, 1986), section 10W.
2. A H Smith, ed., *The Place-Names of the West Riding of Yorkshire*, 1 (Cambridge: English Place-Name Society, 1961), pp. 209–10.
3. The documentary references to surnames quoted here and below are taken from the computer database of local medieval records held at the National Centre for English Cultural Tradition, The University of Sheffield. This database has been compiled from the transcripts of records in the first two volumes of the *Transactions of the Hunter Archaeological Society* and from the printed catalogues of archives published by T Walter Hall.
4. Marie-Thérèse Morlet, *Dictionnaire étymologique des noms de famille* (Paris, 1991), p. 501.
5. P F Ryder, 'Five South Yorkshire Timber-Framed Houses', *Yorkshire Archaeological Journal*, 59 (1987), pp. 51–82.
6. Smith, p. 212.
7. T W Hall, *A Descriptive Catalogue of Early Charters relating to Lands in and near Sheffield* (Sheffield, 1938), pp. 14–15.
8. South Yorkshire Archaeology Service, survey by Peter Ryder, 1984.
9. J G Ronksley, ed., *An Exact and Perfect Survey and View of the Manor of Sheffield with other Lands, by John Harrison, 1637* (Sheffield, 1908).
10. Smith, pp. 210–11.
11. W Brown, ed., *Yorkshire Lay Subsidy 25 Edwardi I*, Yorkshire Archaeological Society Record Series, 16 (1894); Smith, p. 213.
12. R E Leader, *A History of the Company of Cutlers in Hallamshire*, II (Sheffield, 1906).
13. Smith, p. 196.
14. Smith, p. 213.
15. T W Hall, *Material for the History of Wincobank, Sheffield, 1523 to 1750* (Sheffield, 1922).
16. D Hey, ed., *The Hearth Tax Returns for South Yorkshire, Ladyday 1672* (Sheffield, 1991).
17. Revd J Eastwood, *History of the Parish of Ecclesfield* (London, 1862), p. 416.
18. Smith, pp. 249–51; Revd A S Gatty, ed., 'Records of the Court Baron of the Manor of Sheffield', *Transactions of the Hunter Archaeological Society*, I, pt 3 (1918), p. 308; T W Hall, ed., *A Descriptive Catalogue of Sheffield Manorial Records* (Sheffield, 1926), p. 249.
19. Smith, p. 211.
20. See note 9.
21. Smith, pp. 192–93. For the distribution of people bearing the surname Ashurst, see D Hey, 'The Local History of Family Names', *The Local Historian*, 27, no. 4 (1997), supplement, p. vi.
22. Smith, pp. 228–29.
23. Smith, p. 243.
24. Smith, p. 232.
25. C A Ramsker, 'Pre-Register Genealogy and a Lost Place-Name', *The Local Historian*, 10, no. 5 (1973), pp. 227–33.

Chapter Five: Hallamshire Farming Families

1. This chapter draws on evidence contained in the computer database of local medieval manorial records at the National Centre for English Cultural Tradition, The University of Sheffield. I thank the various members of The Names Project Group (listed in the Preface) for their help in tracing the history of these families.
2. M Gelling and A Cole, *The Landscape of Place-Names* (Stamford, 2000), p. 103.
3. The Kents were recorded on thirty-six occasions in local medieval records, and on only one occasion (in 1408, at Birley) was the name written as 'de Kent'. It is well known that such forms were sometimes scribal errors.
4. P F Ryder, 'Five South Yorkshire Timber-Framed Houses', *Yorkshire Archaeological Journal*, 59 (1987), pp. 51–82.

5. *Vernacular Architecture*, 24 (1993), pp. 43–44, 25 (1995), pp. 41–42; personal communication from Ruth Morgan, 1988; J Harvey, ed., *Dronfield Then: 1530–1640* (Dronfield, 1980), pp. 84–7.
6. S O Addy, *The Evolution of the English House* (revised edn, London, 1933); C F Innocent, *The Development of English Building Construction* (Cambridge, 1916).

Chapter Six: Rivelin Chase and Hallam Moors

1. J E Bartlett, 'The Excavation of a Barrow at Lodge Moor, Sheffield, 1954–55', *Transactions of the Hunter Archaeological Society*, VII, pt 6 (1957), pp. 321–30 and A H Henderson, 'The Excavation of a Barrow Remnant at Lodge Moor, Sheffield, 1956–57', pp. 331–37.
2. G H B Ward, 'Hallam and Ughill Moors', *Sheffield Clarion Ramblers' Handbook* (1950–51), pp. 125–51, says that after the great fire on Hallam Moor in July 1868 navvies constructing the Bradfield reservoirs (Agden, 1869, Strines 1871) made a trench across the moor, from the Black Clough south towards Foul Hole. See also the remarks of the Revd A Gatty in his edition of Revd J Hunter, *Hallamshire* (1869), p. 460.
3. Sheffield Archives, ACM S 60. Inscriptions on the rock base of Stanedge Pole include 'HH 1697' [i.e. Hallamshire and Hathersage], and 'H' [on the Hathersage side]. The base of Moscar Cross was re-discovered by Terry Howard in 1998.
4. J B Wheat, 'Garret Gleanings', *Transactions of the Hunter Archaeological Society*, IV, pt 1 (1930), pp. 49–56. Wheat suggested a date of c.1270 for the charter, but the grant is identical in form and purpose to the one quoted in note 12, below, which appears to date from the last years of the thirteenth century and to be contemporary with Sheffield's town charter of 1297.
5. Sheffield Archives, Ronksley, 1153.
6. Revd J Hunter, *Hallamshire* (ed. Revd A Gatty, London, 1869), pp. 18–19.
7. Sheffield Archives, ACM S 60. G H B Ward's suggestions that Sevenstones was the prehistoric stone circle near Hordron Edge and that Broad Rake was the trench do not fit.
8. Sheffield Archives, ACM S 70.
9. B English, ed., *Yorkshire Hundred and Quo Warranto Rolls, 1274–1294*, Yorkshire Archaeological Society Record Series, CLI (1996), pp. 124–25.
10. J G Ronksley, ed., *An Exact and Perfect Survey and View of the Manor of Sheffield with other Lands, by John Harrison, 1637* (Sheffield, 1908). See G Scurfield, 'Seventeenth-Century Sheffield and its Environs', *Yorkshire Archaeological Journal*, 58 (1986), pp. 147–71 for a meticulous reconstruction of the map which probably accompanied the survey, but which has since been lost.
11. M Gelling, *Place-Names in the Landscape* (London, 1984), pp. 191–92 suggests a meaning for firth of 'land overgrown with brushwood, scrub on the edge of forest'. The previously accepted meaning was simply 'wood'. In the fourteenth century Welsh *ffridd* meant 'barren land'. G Redmonds, *Yorkshire Surnames Series, part one: Bradford & District* (Lepton, 1990), p. 21 says that 'firth' came to refer more specifically to an area of forest or free chase. The surname Firth is prolific in West Yorkshire.
12. Hunter, *Hallamshire* , pp. 55–56. The name Bell Hagg is thought to have been derived from a former beacon on this prominent hill; A H Smith, ed., *The Place-Names of the West Riding of Yorkshire*, I (Cambridge: English Place-Name Society, 1961), p. 193.
13. A H Thomas, 'Some Hallamshire Rolls of the Fifteenth Century', *Transactions of the Hunter Archaeological Society*, II, part I (1920), pp. 65–79. The accounts also mention sales of wood, charcoal and tiling-stones, and a quarry for grindstones. T W Hall, *A Descriptive Catalogue of Sheffield Manorial Records* (Sheffield, 1926), p. 45 notes that in 1441 'Henry Wrasteler, forester of the Ryvelynge' presented fifteen people at the manor court for 'pannage of swine in Ryvelyng'. E Curtis, 'Sheffield in the Fourteenth Century: Two Furnival Inquisitions', *Transactions of the Hunter Archaeological Society*, I, pt I (1914), pp. 31–53; 1332 'pannage of the woods of Ryvelyngden'. *Cf.* T W Hall, *A Descriptive Catalogue of Sheffield Manorial Records*, II (Sheffield, 1928), p 2: Thomas Beamount and William Burton were fined for felling and carrying away 'two loads of green wood of the lord, out of Le Firth of Revelinge'; Sheffield Archives, Ronksley collection, 4165: verdict of Sheffield manor court, 1723: 'For putting cattle

upon the commons called Riveling Wood, having no common right to do so, a fine of £1.19s.11d. For any persons putting cattle on the said common of Riveling Wood not an inhabitant of the Liberty of Stannington, Moorwood, Hallam and Fulwood, a fine of £1.19s.11d. For burning bracking on the above Common, not having a right to do so, a fine of 6s.8d.'.

14. S O Addy, *Historical Memorials of Beauchief Abbey* (Sheffield, 1878), pp. 37, 53; S Pegge, *An Historical Account of Beauchief Abbey* (London, 1801), p. 157; Hunter, *Hallamshire*, 30, 162.
15. D Postles, 'Rural Economy on the Grits and Sandstones of the South Yorkshire Pennines, 1086–1348', *Northern History*, XV (1979), pp. 1–19.
16. J R Wigfull, 'Extracts from the Note-Book of William Dickenson', *Transactions of the Hunter Archaeological Society*, II, pt II (1921), pp. 189–200.
17. i.e. sufficient grazing for eight cows. *Cf.* E Curtis, 'Sheffield in the Fourteenth Century: Two Furnival Inquisitions', *Transactions of the Hunter Archaeological Society*, I. pt I (1914), pp. 31–53: 1383 'At the Moor and Ryvelyngden two parcels of pasture with wood and deer living there with hunting for the same, £4'.
18. A laund was a grassy plot in a deer park or chase. Our modern word 'lawn' is derived from it. The a.r.p. measurements are in acres, roods [four to an acre], and perches [forty to a rood].
19. Sheffield Archives, Bright 24.
20. J Evelyn, *Silva, or a Discourse on Forest Trees* (ed. A Hunter, London, 1801), pp. 206–11.
21. Sheffield Archives, ACM S 284.
22. University of Leeds, Brotherton Library, Wilson collection, vol. CLIX, p. 79.
23. Sheffield Archives, Ronksley, 159/12084, ACM S 158, 282, 376, 377; C Jackson, ed., *The Diary of Abraham de la Pryme*, Surtees Society, LIV (1870), p. 165; Historical Manuscripts Commission, 29: *Portland Manuscripts*, VI (1901), pp. 143–46; M Spray and D J Smith, 'The Rise and Fall of Holly in the Sheffield Region,' *Transactions of the Hunter Archaeological Society*, X, pt 4 (1977), pp. 239–51.
24. Sheffield Archives, ACM S 60; *Sheffield Clarion Ramblers' Handbook* (1950–51), pp. 138–41.
25. Local Studies Department, Sheffield Central Library, *Sheffield Register* of 8 September 1787. Acts of Parliament allowed enclosure when the owners of about three-quarters of the land were in favour.
26. Sheffield Archives, ACM S 70.
27. J B Wheat, pp. 50–51.
28. Local Studies Department, Sheffield Central Library.
29. *Sheffield Clarion Ramblers' Handbook* (1950–51), p. 142.
30. *Sheffield Clarion Ramblers' Handbook* (1948–49), pp. 86–93.
31. J Cass, 'Water Supply', in C Binfield *et al.*, *The History of the City of Sheffield, 1843–1993*, II (Sheffield, 1993), pp. 118–129; Cass, 'The Rivelin Tunnel, 1903–1910', *Transactions of the Hunter Archaeological Society*, 18 (1995), pp. 60–74. The pillar alongside the conduit was one of the sighting towers erected to plan the route of the tunnel which brings water over four miles from Ladybower to the lower Rivelin reservoir.
32. *The Compact Oxford English Dictionary*, p. 714.
33. J V Beckett, *The Aristocracy in England, 1660–1914* (Oxford, 1986), p. 342; G E Mingay, ed., *The Agrarian History of England and Wales, VI: 1750–1850* (Cambridge, 1989), p. 924.
34. P B Munsche, *Gentlemen and Poachers: the English Game Laws, 1671–1831* (Cambridge, 1981), pp. 8, 173–74.
35. Munsche, p. 35.
36. Revd J Hunter, *South Yorkshire: the History of the Deanery of Doncaster*, II (London, 1831), p. 183.
37. G Walker, *The Costume of Yorkshire* (London, 1814), plates IV, XX and XXXII.
38. *Agrarian History*, VI, p. 925; Munsche, p. 36.
39. R Carr, 'Country Sports', in G E Mingay, ed., *The Victorian Countryside*, II (London, 1981), chapter 34, pp. 475–76, 482–83.
40. *Sheffield Clarion Ramblers' Handbook* (1955–56), p. 78.
41. J N Dransfield, *History of Penistone* (Penistone, 1906), p. 512.
42. *Hallamshire*, pp. 11–12.
43. *Sheffield Clarion Ramblers' Handbook* (1950–51), p. 144.
44. Dransfield, p. 510; *Sheffield Clarion Ramblers' Handbook* (1962–63), pp. 55–63.
45. The quarry was used for roofing slates until the 1880s or 1890s.

46. M H F Chaytor, *The Wilsons of Sharrow: The Snuff-Makers of Sheffield* (Sheffield, 1962).
47. *Sheffield Clarion Ramblers' Handbook* (1955–56), pp. 76–78.
48. A particularly fine example can be seen on a huge rock on Eyam Moor (O.S. reference 218785), which is illustrated in W Wood, *The History and Antiquities of Eyam*, 6th edition (1865), p. 33. Wood thought that the basin had been carved out, but it is probably natural, especially as it is the only one. The initials IB are inscribed on the west side of the rock.
49. J Radley, 'Some New Rock Basins in the Rivelin Valley', *Transactions of the Hunter Archaeological Society*, VIII, part 4 (1962), pp. 234–35; J Radley, 'Rock Basins on Hallam Moors: the Answer', *Transactions of the Hunter Archaeological Society*, X, part 1 (1964), p. 35; R Doncaster, 'A Note on Rock Basins in the Rivelin Valley,' *Transactions of the Hunter Archaeological Society*, 13 (1984), p. 23.
50. A Yates, 'George Broomhead's First Job', *Dark Peak News*, Autumn 1992, pp. 9–11. I would like to thank Alan Yates for his encouragement and support in locating the basins.

Chapter Seven: Millstones on the Moors

1. L H Butcher, 'Archaeological Remains on the Wharncliffe–Greno Upland, South Yorkshire', *Transactions of the Hunter Archaeological Society*, VII, pt I (1957), pp. 38–39. P Rahtz and K Sheridan, 'Tamworth', *Current Archaeology*, 29 (1971), pp. 164–68 notes the discovery of a quern made of millstone grit at a Middle Saxon mill site at Tamworth. See also D L Farmer, 'Millstones for Medieval Manors', *Agricultural History Review*, 40 (1992), pp. 98–103, and H S A Fox, 'The Millstone Makers of Medieval Dartmoor', *Devon and Cornwall Notes and Queries*, 37 (1995), pp. 153–57.
2. They are found within the gridlines SK 23 to 29 easting and SK 72 to 87 northing. For a gazetteer of sites see G Tucker, 'Millstone Making in the Peak District of Derbyshire', *Industrial Archaeology*, VIII, no. I (1985), pp. 42–58.
3. H Egan, *The Millstone Industry in the Peak District* (dissertation for the Certificate of Local History, University of Sheffield, 1985). The newer stones seem to date from the later nineteenth century until the abandonment of the trade in the 1920s.
4. D Hey, *Packmen, Carriers and Packhorse Roads* (Ashbourne, 2001), p. 101.
5. G R Potter and M Walton, 'A Fragment of a Compotus Roll of the Manor of Sheffield, 1479–80', *Transactions of the Hunter Archaeological Society*, VI, pt I (1944), p. 22.
6. R Meredith, 'Millstone Making at Yarncliff in the reign of Edward IV', *Derbyshire Archaeological Journal*, CI (1981), pp. 102–6.
7. J P Polak, 'The Production and Distribution of Peak Millstones from the Sixteenth to the Eighteenth Centuries', *Derbyshire Archaeological Journal*, CVII (1987), pp. 55–72; an admirable survey of the history of the industry.
8. R Blome, *Britannia* (London, 1673), pp. 75, 257; J Houghton, *A Collection for Improvement of Husbandry and Trade*, II, no. 44 (London, 1692); Hey, *Packmen*, p. 102. The Bawtry parish register records the burial in 1699 of 'Mr. Daniel Sullery senr. A trader in Mill stones'. He paid tax on seven hearths in 1672; D Hey, ed., *The Hearth Returns for South Yorkshire, Ladyday 1672* (Sheffield, 1991), p. 18.
9. M Plant, 'A Scythe-Stone Industry on Beeley Moor', *Derbyshire Archaeological Journal*, LXXXVIII (1968), pp. 98–100. The terms 'millstone' and 'grindstone' were often used ambiguously.
10. Leeds University, Brotherton Library, Wilson collection, CLIX f. 79 and 80. The Ordnance Survey still mark 'Millstone Hole' at SK 270868, by Rivelin Dams.
11. M Davies-Shiel, *Watermills of Cumbria* (Clapham, 1978), p. 86; R. Entwistle, *Holymoorside, Past and Present* (Chesterfield, 1976), p. 48.
12. F W Steer, *Farm and Cottage Inventories of Mid-Essex, 1635 to 1749* (Chichester, 1969), p. 215.
13. Davies-Shiel, p. 86.
14. Sheffield Archives, ACM S376; Lichfield Joint Record Office, wills and inventories, B/C/11; Revd J Hunter, *Familiae Minorum Gentium* (Harleian Society, 5 vols, 1895), p. 126.

15. D G Edwards, ed., *Derbyshire Hearth Tax Assessments, 1662–70*, Derbyshire Record Society, VII (1982), pp. 75–76.
16. F Nixon, *Industrial Archaeology of Derbyshire* (Newton Abbot, 1969), p. 259; D M Palliser, *The Age of Elizabeth* London, 1983), p. 261; Sheffield Archives, Cammell deeds, 68 to 78.
17. E Darwin, *Botanic Garden, Economy of Vegetation* (London, 1795); Revd W Bingley, *Useful Knowledge: or a Familiar Account of the Various Productions of Nature, vol. I: Minerals*, fourth edn (London, 1825), pp. 44–45.
18. T Tomlinson, *Querns, Millstones and Grindstones made in Hathersage and District* (Hathersage, 1981); information collected by the late Richard Doncaster and quoted in Tucker, *op. cit.*
19. D Defoe, *A Tour through the Whole Island of Great Britain,* (London: Everyman edition, 1962), II, p. 176.
20. Information provided by the late Tom Tomlinson.
21. I owe this reference to Mrs Margaret Sterland.
22. Lichfield Joint Record Office, wills, B/C/11. I owe this reference to Mrs Kathleen Battye. Very few millstones have any such initials on them to denote ownership. Some abandoned, dome-shaped millstones, which appear to be seventeenth or eighteenth century in date, can be found on Froggatt Edge and Gardom's Edge with 'W' carved on them in the old-fashioned manner by which the central strokes crossed.
23. C Morris, ed., *The Journeys of Celia Fiennes* (London, 1947), pp. 54, 170, 238.
24. Revd J Hunter, *Familiae Minorum Gentium* (Harleian Society, 5 vols, 1895), p. 341.
25. Leeds University, Brotherton Library, Wilson collection, CLIX, f. 94–95.
26. Sheffield Archives, ACM S378, f. 117.
27. Information from the late Tom Tomlinson.
28. Sheffield Archives, Tibbitts, 413/9.
29. Revd W W Skeat, ed., *The Book of Husbandry, by Master Fitzherbert, 1534* (London, 1882), p. 29.
30. A Hopkinson, *Study of a Village: Killamarsh, 1535–1750* (dissertation for the Certificate in Local History, University of Sheffield, 1984); Yorkshire Archaeological Society, Duke of Leeds collection, DD5/5/155.
31. *Journal of the House of Commons*, XIX (1718–21), p. 230.
32. Defoe, II, p. 181.
33. Sheffield Archives, Bagshawe collection, 313, printed in R Meredith, 'Hathersage Affairs, 1720–35', *Transactions of the Hunter Archaeological Society*, XI (1981), pp. 14–27.
34. Polak, *op. cit.*
35. J Farey, *General View of the Agriculture of Derbyshire*, I (London, 1811), p. 221; S Glover, *Directory of the County of Derbyshire* (Derby, 1827–29), p. 25; W White, *Sheffield Directory* (Sheffield, 1833), p. 425.
36. Public Record Office, H.O. 107/2148, R.G. 9/2543, R.G. 10/3632, also available on microfilm in the Local Studies Department, Sheffield Central Library.
37. B Robinson, *Walls across the Valley: the building of the Howden and Derwent Dams* (Cromford, 1993).
38. Information from Mr Robert Vernon. B Hudson, *Through Limestone Hills* (Sparkford, Yeovil, 1989), p. 80 has a photograph of a train-load of millstones, ready to leave for Norway, *c.* 1900, in the stone yard of Stancliffe Estates Company, Darley Dale.

Chapter Eight: Beauchief Abbey

1. K Cameron, *The Place-Names of Derbyshire*, II (Cambridge: English Place-Name Society, 1959), p. 208.
2. H M Colvin, *The White Canons in England* (Oxford, 1951); J Burton, *Monastic and Religious Orders in Britain, 1000–1300* (Cambridge, 1994), pp. 55–60.
3. R R Darlington, *The Cartulary of Darley Abbey*, 2 vols (Kendal, 1945); A Saltman, *The Cartulary of Dale Abbey* (Derbyshire Archaeological Society Record Series, 2, 1957).
4. S O Addy, *Historical Memorials of Beauchief Abbey* (Sheffield, 1878), pp. 138–43; J Caley and J Hunter, eds, *Valor Ecclesiasticus*, six vols (London: Record Commission, 1810–34).
5. R Meredith, 'Beauchief Abbey and the Pegges', *Derbyshire Archaeological Society*, 87 (1967), pp. 86–126.

6. M Chatfield, *Churches the Victorians Forgot* (Ashbourne, 1979), pp. 155–57.
7. The results of the excavations were never fully published. See W H Elgar, 'Beauchief Abbey', *Transactions of the Hunter Archaeological Society*, III (1929), pp. 162–64.
8. Addy, p. 135.
9. Now kept at Weston Park Museum, Sheffield.
10. C J Morroney, 'More than meets the Eye? A Preliminary Discussion of the Archaeological Remains of Beauchief Abbey and Park', *Review of Archaeology in South Yorkshire, 1993–94* (Sheffield, 1994), pp. 60–67; R Harte and C Morroney, 'Two Way Traffic: the Importance of Beauchief Abbey as a Case Study for the Premonstratensian Order in England', *Review of Archaeology in South Yorkshire, 1994–95* (Sheffield, 1996), pp. 81–88; A V Smith, *Beauchief Abbey: Notes on the Layout and Remains – the Abbey and Surrounding Area* (Sheffield, privately printed, 1993).
11. Sheffield Archives, Fairbank, BEA 1.
12. British Library, Mss Cotton, Caligula A. viii, ff. 4–27.
13. Addy, chapters III and V.
14. Sheffield Archives, MD 3414; D Hey, L Howarth and D Luscombe, eds, *Beauchief Abbey Cartulary* (Derbyshire Record Society, forthcoming).
15. A pedigree of the Chaworth family is given in S Pegge, *An Historical Account of Beauchief Abbey* (London, 1801), p. 20.
16. Pegge, pp. 226–27.
17. Addy, pp. 29–32; H Armitage, *Chantrey Land* (London, 1910), pp. 32–36.
18. Addy, p. 116.
19. C Platt, *The Monastic Grange in Medieval England* (London, 1969).
20. Pegge, appendices 5 and 10; Addy, pp. 138–43.
21. Ordnance Survey map reference, SK 285799.
22. SK 273783.
23. SK 284854. For further details of the granges see Hey, Howarth and Luscombe (forthcoming).
24. SK 312680.
25. SK 444791, SK 425547, SK 459623.
26. Pegge, p. 189.
27. D Crossley *et al.*, eds, *Water Power on the Sheffield Rivers* (Sheffield University, 1989), pp. 95–102.
28. *c.* SK 320807.
29. SK 324813.
30. SK 336833.
31. Addy, pp. 57, 136.
32. Addy, chapter V; Colvin, pp. 396–97.
33. Pegge, pp. 217–18.
34. C B Andrewes, ed., *The Torrington Diaries*, II (London, 1935), pp. 25–26.

Chapter Nine: The Dragon of Wantley

1. M Gregson, *Portfolio of Fragments relative to the History and Antiquities, Topography and Genealogies of the County Palatine and Duchy of Lancaster*, ed. J Harland (London, third edn, 1869), pp. 151–52. Gregson claimed, incorrectly, that the hero of the ballad was from More Hall in the Lancashire hundred of West Derby.
2. *The Dramatick Works of Henry Carey* (London, 1743).
3. Carey gave Phillips the nickname Namby-Pamby, which has passed into general use.
4. J J Cartwright, ed., *The Wentworth Papers, 1705–1739* (London, 1883), p. 539: Lady Strafford, 19 January 1738: 'We was at Covent Garden Play House last Night, my mother was so good as to treat us with it, and the Dragon of Wantcliff was the farce. I like it vastly and the musick is excessive pretty, and tho' it is a burlesque on the opera yet Mr. Handel owns he thinks the tunes very well composed. I conclude your lordship will go to it as soon as you come to town, for every body generally commends it and it has been acted 36 times already, and they are always pretty full'.

5. Revd J Hunter, *Hallamshire: The History of the Parish of Sheffield* (ed. Revd A Gatty, London, 1869), p. 478.
6. J Simpson, *British Dragons* (London, 1980), pp. 118–19.
7. G Grigson, *The Penguin Book of Ballads* (Harmondsworth, 1975), p. 13. See also T Watt, *Cheap Print and Popular Piety, 1550–1640* (Cambridge, 1991). Randal Taylor's version of the ballad included a tune, but ballads were set to different tunes at various times.
8. *A Ballet of the Manner of the Killing of the Serpent in Sussex, September 1614*. I am grateful to Dr Helen Weinstein for her helpful comments on the registration of ballads at Stationers' Hall.
9. Quoted in H B Wheatley, ed., *Reliques of Ancient English Poetry ... by Thomas Percy, DD, Bishop of Dromore* (London, 1827), III, p. 279.
10. The typical folk legend elements used in *The Dragon of Wantley* include spiky armour, the dragon's invulnerability except in one spot, victory by an unheroic trick, close tie-in with topography and with local landowners, and possibly the conversation between hero and dragon. I am grateful to Dr Simpson for her helpful comments.
11. Hunter, *Hallamshire*, pp. 478–79. Despite his interest in the ballad, Hunter surprisingly makes no comment on the heraldic dragon.
12. Quoted in Rev. J Hunter, *South Yorkshire*, II, (London, 1831), p. 331. Roger Dodsworth noted (some time between 1619 and 1631): 'In Wharncliffe (a chase of Sir Frauncis Wortley's) on a great stone nere the Lodge, wherin are cut 3 seates or chaires, in which rocke are ingraven thes wordes: Pray for the saule of Sir Thomas Wortelay, knight for the King's Body to Edward the fourthe, Richard third, Harry the VII and VIII, howes saules God pardon which Thomas causyd a house to be mad for this cas ne mydes of Wernclif for his pleasor and to her the hartes' bel, in the yere of our lord a thousand CCCCCX'. He also observed that in the chase were 'read and fallow deare and roo', but he made no mention of the dragon legend; J W Clay, ed., *Yorkshire Church Notes, 1619–31 by Roger Dodsworth*, Yorkshire Archaeological Society Record Series, XXXIV (1904), pp. 16 and 88.
13. Wheatley, ed., *Reliques*, p. 281. The same correspondent claimed that in the lodge he saw 'the picture of the Dragon and Moor of Moor-hall'. If the Wortleys had such a picture, this supports the suggestion that the ballad was based on an older story. The correspondent was recalling a visit that he had made forty years previously.
14. D Hey, ed., *The Hearth Tax Returns for South Yorkshire, Ladyday 1672* (Sheffield, 1991), p. 91. Nor were any of the eighty-six householders in the township of Wortley named Matthew. A Mrs Northall was taxed on four hearths in the adjoining township of Grenofirth and a Mr Northall was one of the Duke of Norfolk's woodwards in the early eighteenth century. A memorial in Wortley Church commemorates William Bland, keeper of Wharncliffe, who died in 1642.
15. *Notes and Queries*, third series, IX (London, 1866), p. 29.
16. Wheatley, ed., *Reliques*, p. 283.
17. Hunter, *South Yorkshire*, II, p. 338. See Public Record Office, E/310/178/34–23 for the case in the Court of Exchequer (1595). For the dispute before the Ecclesiastical Court at York see Borthwick Institute of Historical Research, York, CP. G. 2384, CP. H. 285, 286, 1280, 1281. See also Hull University Library, DDBM/7/4 and Sheffield Archives, Wh. M. 93.
18. Hunter, *South Yorkshire*, II, p. 332; M Craven, *A Derbyshire Armory*, Derbyshire Record Society, XVII (1991), p.19. A George Blount, gentleman, was one of the lessees of Conisbrough Park in 1634 (Public Record Office, C3/409/39).
19. D Hey, 'The Parks at Tankersley and Wortley', *Yorkshire Archaeological Journal*, 47 (1975), pp. 109–19; Hunter, *South Yorkshire*, II, pp. 308–9. In 1379 Elizabeth, the widow of Nicholas of Wortley, chivaler, was assessed at 20s poll tax, one of the highest rates in the wapentake of Staincross.
20. Hunter, *South Yorkshire*, II, pp. 310–14.
21. *Ibid.*, p. 329. Hunter commented that, 'The inscription has suffered something by its long exposure to the weather, from which, however, it is now protected. In the seventh line there is a various reading in copies which were taken when it was more legible than at present. Some have it "for this case in mydyst of"; and it is impossible to decide from the present appearance of the stone what may be the true reading'. See note 12 for Roger Dodsworth's reading in the first half of the seventeenth century, the earliest inscription that we have.
22. *Ibid.*, pp. 330–1; Hunter, *Hallamshire*, p. 3, note.

23. L H Butcher, 'Archaeological Remains on the Wharncliffe-Greno Upland, South Yorkshire', *Transactions of the Hunter Archaeological Society*, VII, pt I (1950), p. 38. The survey also yielded much evidence of Mesolithic and Romano-British settlement.

24. W Brown, ed., *Yorkshire Star Chamber Proceedings*, Yorkshire Archaeological Society Record Series, XLI (1909), pp. 178–81.

25. Hunter, *South Yorkshire*, II, p. 316; Sheffield Archives, Wh. 70. On 1 May 1589 the Earl of Shrewsbury wrote to the Lord Chancellor, attempting to arbitrate in a dispute between Richard, the son and heir of Francis Wortley, deceased, and his widow, who had remarried; see E G W Bill, *A Calendar of the Shrewsbury Papers in the Lambeth Palace Library*, Derbyshire Archaeological Society Record Series, 1 (1966), p. 56.

26. Sheffield Archives, Wh. M. Maps 2.

27. Sheffield Archives, Wh. M. 48; transcribed in Revd J Eastwood, *History of the Parish of Ecclesfield* (London, 1862), pp. 493–507. See also, Bill, ed., p.108, quoting a letter from the Earl of Shrewsbury to the Lord President of the Council of the North, dated 22 September 1593, about the imprisonment of Raufe Broumhedd at York, on the suit of [?] Wortley, both being parties to a suit concerning bastardy in the Star Chamber. Bill, ed., p. 176 quotes a letter from Richard Wortley to Edward Talbot at Pontefract, dated 25 January 1593, thanking him for his efforts to secure a reconciliation between Wortley and the Earl of Shrewsbury. Wortley defended his behaviour in commencing a suit against Edward Savile, in serving a process on Mr William Dickenson, in arresting Mr Linacre in the liberty of Scarsdale, and in the matter of the insolent speeches allegedly used by his servant Watts.

28. Eastwood, *Ecclesfield*, pp. 36, 73–75, 162, 314–17, 439; Revd A S Gatty, *Registers of Ecclesfield Parish Church, Yorkshire from 1558 to 1619* (London, 1878), p. 19, note. A connection between George Blount and Gilbert and William Dickenson is revealed by an indenture of 1608, which names all three in a complicated transaction concerning More Hall and George's illegitimate son, Charles Blunt alias Heptenstall. See T W Hall, *Descriptive Catalogue of the Wheat Collection* (Sheffield, 1920), p. 140.

29. Hunter, *Hallamshire*, p. 97.

30. R Meredith, ed., *Calendar of the Arundel Castle Manuscripts* (Sheffield City Libraries, 1965), Talbot Letters, 2/43; Hunter, *Hallamshire*, p. 73.

31. Talbot Letters, 2/144.

32. Hunter, *Hallamshire*, p. 431. The reference in the court rolls could not be traced by Eastwood, nor can it be found today.

33. Sheffield Archives, ACM SD416.

34. Eastwood, *Ecclesfield*, pp. 188–90; Gatty, *Registers*, p. 139, note. Lord's descendants were buried in the same grave as late as 1729.

35. Sheffield Archives, Wh. M. 93. The defendants had the active support of Mr John Savile, lord of the manor of Thurlstone within the parish of Penistone.

36. Borthwick Institute of Historical Research, York, CP. G. 2264, 2266, 1637; Hull University Library, DDBM/7/4. The case was transferred to the Court of Common Pleas.

37. Hunter, *South Yorkshire*, II, pp. 332, 338; Public Record Office, E310/178/34–23.

38. Borthwick, CP. H. 285, 286. The case involved tithes of oats, rye, wheat and hay in Gunthwaite.

39. Lady Macdonald of the Isles, *The Fortunes of a Family* (Edinburgh, 1927), pp. 58–59; Hunter, *South Yorkshire*, II, pp. 332, 338.

40. E D Mackerness, *Somewhere Further North: A History of Music in Sheffield* (Sheffield, 1974), pp. 3–5. See also T Watt, *Cheap Print and Popular Piety, 1500–1640* (Cambridge, 1991), p. 30 on the professional troupes of interlude players who travelled from one noble household to another.

41. Sheffield Archives, Wh. M. 103 (4).

42. *The Journal of Mr John Hobson, late of Dodworth Green*, Surtees Society, LXV (1875), p. 253: '31 May 1726: At Warncliffe lodge, where they are erecting a new building, within which they bury underground a stone with an inscription now illegible, said to be, Pray for the soul of Sir Richard Wortley, who builded a lodge here in the year 1510'.

43. Sheffield Archives, Wh. M. 23.

44. Sheffield Archives, Wh. M. 49.

45. Hunter, *South Yorkshire*, II, p. 331.

BIBLIOGRAPHY

1. Documentary Sources

Sheffield Archives: Arundel Castle S60, S70, S158, S282, S284, S376, S377, S378, SD 416, C158: 'A Survey of Lands belonging to the Mannor of Sheffield, 1611'; Bagshawe 313; Bright 1, 24; Cammell deeds, 68 to 78; Fairbank, BEA 1; Miscellaneous, MD 3414; Ronksley, 159/12084, 1153; Tibbitts 413/9; Wharncliffe M. 23, 46, 48, 49, 93.103 (4), maps 2; John Gelley's map (1725).

Local Studies Department, Sheffield Central Library: Sheffield Register of 8 September 1787.

Public Record Office, E310/178/34-23, H.O. 107/2148, R.G. 9/2543, R.G. 10/3632.

British Library, Mss Cotton, Caligula A. viii, ff. 4-27.

Borthwick Institute of Historical Research, York: wills and inventories; C.P. G. 1637, G 2264, G 2266, G 2384, C.P. H. 285, 286, 1280, 1281.

Lichfield Joint Record Office, wills and inventories, B/C/11.

South Yorkshire Archaeology Service, survey by Peter Ryder, 1984.

Leeds University, Brotherton Library, Wilson collection, CLIX f. 79 and 80.

Yorkshire Archaeological Society, Duke of Leeds collection, DD5/5/155.

East Yorkshire Record Office, Beverley, DDBM / 14 / 8, 9.

Hull University Library, DDBM/7/4

Thomas Jeffreys's map of Yorkshire (1772) was reprinted by Harry Margary of Lympne Castle, Kent, in 1973, with introductory notes by J. B. Harley and J. C. Harvey; a copy can be seen in Sheffield Archives. The 1791 edition of Burdett's map was reprinted in 1975 by by the Derbyshire Archaeological Society, with an explanatory introduction by J. B. Harley, D. V. Fowkes and J. C. Harvey.

The computer database of medieval records relating to Hallamshire is held at The National Centre for Cultural Tradition, The University of Sheffield. These medieval records are taken from the transcripts in the early *Transactions of the Hunter Archaeological Society* and in the various catalogues of Sheffield records published by T. Walter Hall.

2. Original Sources in Print

S. O. Addy, *Historical Memorials of Beauchief Abbey* (Sheffield, 1878).

C. B. Andrewes, ed., *The Torrington Diaries*, II (London, 1935).

A Ballet of the Manner of the Killing of the Serpent in Sussex, September 1614.

E. G. W. Bill, ed., *A Calendar of the Shrewsbury Papers in the Lambeth Palace Library*, Derbyshire Archaeological Society Record Series, 1 (1966).

Revd W. Bingley, *Useful Knowledge: or a Familiar Account of the Various Productions of Nature, vol. I: Minerals*, fourth edn (London, 1825).

R. Blome, *Britannia* (London, 1673).

W. Brown, ed., *Yorkshire Lay Subsidy 25 Edwardi I*, Yorkshire Archaeological Society Record Series, 16 (1894).

W. Brown, ed., *Yorkshire Star Chamber Proceedings*, Yorkshire Archaeological Society Record Series, XLI (1909).

W. Brown and A. H. Thompson, eds, *The Register of William Greenfield, Archbishop of York, 1306-1315*, II, Surtees Society, 149 (1934) and V (1938).

Calendar of Miscellaneous Inquisitions, 1348-1377, no. 1003.

J. Caley and J. Hunter, eds, *Valor Ecclesiasticus* (London: Record Commission, six volumes, 1810-34).

K. Cameron, *The Place-Names of Derbyshire*, I (Cambridge: English Place-Name Society, 1959).

J. J. Cartwright, ed., *The Wentworth Papers, 1705-1739* (London, 1883).

Sir C. Clay, ed., *Early Yorkshire Families*, Yorkshire Archaeological Society Record Series, CXXXV (1973).

J. W. Clay, ed., *Yorkshire Church Notes, 1619-1631, by Roger Dodsworth*, Yorkshire Archaeological Society Record Series, XXXIV (1904).

E. W. Crossley, 'The Preceptory of Newland', *Yorkshire Archaeological Society Record Series*, LXI (1920), pp. 1-83.

E. Curtis, 'Sheffield in the Fourteenth Century: Two Furnival Inquisitions', *Transactions of the Hunter Archaeological Society*, I, pt I (1914), pp. 31-58.

'Customs of the Manor of Sheffield', *Transactions of the Hunter Archaeological Society*, II, pt 4 (1924), pp. 371-73.

R. R. Darlington, *The Cartulary of Darley Abbey*, 2 vols (Kendal, 1945).

E. Darwin, *Botanic Garden, Economy of Vegetation* (London, 1795).

D. Defoe, *A Tour through the Whole Island of Great Britain*, (London: Everyman edition, 1962).

The Dramatick Works of Henry Carey (London, 1743).

D. G. Edwards, *Derbyshire Hearth Tax Assessment, 1662-70*, Derbyshire Record Society, VII (1982).

B. English, ed., *Yorkshire Hundred and Quo Warranto Rolls, 1274-1294* (Yorkshire Archaeological Society Record Series, CLI, 1996).

J. Evelyn, *Silva, or a Discourse on Forest Trees*, II, (ed. A. Hunter, 1801).

J. Farey, *General View of the Agriculture of Derbyshire*, I (London, 1811).

M. L. Faull and M. Stinson, eds, *Domesday Book: Yorkshire* (Phillimore, Chichester, 1986).

D. V. Fowkes and G. R. Potter, eds, *William Senior's Survey of the Estates of the First and Second Earls of Devonshire*, Derbyshire Record Society, XIII (1988).

W. Fraser, ed., *Early Yorkshire Charters*, III (Edinburgh, 1916).

G. N. Garmonsway, ed., *The Anglo-Saxon Chronicle* (London, 1978).

Revd A.S. Gatty, *Registers of Ecclesfield Parish Church ... also the Churchwardens' Accounts* (London, 1878).

Revd A. S. Gatty, 'Records of the Court Baron of the Manor of Sheffield', *Transactions of the Hunter Archaeological Society*, I, pt 4 (1918), pp. 257-329.

S. Glover, *Directory of the County of Derbyshire* (Derby, 1827-29).

M. Gregson, *Portfolio of Fragments relative to the History and Antiquities, Topography and Genealogies of the County Palatine and Duchy of Lancaster*, ed. J. Harland (London, third edn, 1869).

T. W. Hall, *Descriptive Catalogue of the Wheat Collection* (Sheffield, 1920).

T.W. Hall, *Material for the History of Wincobank, Sheffield, 1523 to 1750* (Sheffield, 1922).

T.W. Hall, *A Descriptive Catalogue of Sheffield Manorial Records* (Sheffield, 1926).

T. W. Hall, *A Descriptive Catalogue of Sheffield Manorial Records*, II (Sheffield, 1928).

T. W. Hall, *A Descriptive Catalogue of Early Charters relating to Lands in and near Sheffield* (Sheffield, 1938).

D. Hey, ed., *The Hearth Tax Returns for South Yorkshire, Ladyday 1672* (Sheffield, 1991).

D. Hey and J. Unwin, eds, *The Cutlers of Hallamshire, 1624-1699* (Sheffield, 1993).

D. Hey, L. Howarth and D. Luscombe, eds, *Beauchief Abbey Cartulary* (Derbyshire Record Society, forthcoming).

Historical Manuscripts Commission, 29: *Portland Manuscripts*, VI (1901).

J. Houghton, *A Collection for Improvement of Husbandry and Trade*, II, no. 44 (London, 1692).

C. Jackson, ed., *The Diary of Abraham de la Pryme*, Surtees Society, LIV (1870).

The Journal of Mr John Hobson, late of Dodworth Green, Surtees Society, LXV (1875).

Journal of the House of Commons, XIX (1718-21).

R. Meredith, ed., *Calendar of the Arundel Castle Manuscripts* (Sheffield, 1965).

C. Morris, ed., *The Journeys of Celia Fiennes* (London, 1947).

Notes and Queries, third series, IX (London, 1866).

Pipe Roll, 30 Henry II.

G. R. Potter and M. Walton, 'A Fragment of a Compotus Roll of the Manor of Sheffield, 1479-80', *Transactions of the Hunter Archaeological Society*, VI, pt I (1944), p. 22.

The Returns of the Poll Tax for the West Riding of Yorkshire, 1379, Yorkshire Archaeological and Topographical Society, 5 (1882).

J. G. Ronksley, ed., *An Exact and Perfect Survey and View of the Manor of Sheffield, with other Lands, by John Harrison, 1637* (Sheffield, 1908).

A. Saltman, *The Cartulary of Dale Abbey*, Derbyshire Archaeological Society Record Series, 2 (1957).

Revd W. W. Skeat, ed., *The Book of Husbandry, by Master Fitzherbert, 1534* (London, 1882).

A. H. Smith, *The Place-Names of the West Riding of Yorkshire* (Cambridge: English Place-Names Society, 1961).

F. W. Steer, *Farm and Cottage Inventories of Mid-Essex, 1635 to 1749* (Chichester, 1969).

A. H. Thomas, 'Some Hallamshire Rolls of the Fifteenth Century', *Transactions of the Hunter Archaeological Society*, II, pt 1 (1920), pp. 65-79, pt 2 (1921), pp. 142-58, pt 3 (1922), pp. 225-45.

A. H. Thompson and C. T. Clay, eds, *Fasti Parochiales*, I, Yorkshire Archaeological Society Record Series, LXXXV (1933); II, CVII (1943).

R. T. Timson, *The Cartulary of Blyth Priory*, Thoroton Society Record Series, XXVII (1973).

G. Walker, *The Costume of Yorkshire* (London, 1814).

W. F. Webster, ed., *Nottinghamshire Hearth Tax, 1664: 1674*, Thoroton Society Record Series, XXXVII (1988).

H. B. Wheatley, ed., *Reliques of Ancient English Poetry ... by Thomas Percy, D.D., Bishop of Dromore*, III (London, 1827).

W. White, *Sheffield Directory* (Sheffield, 1833).

J. R. Wigfull, 'Extracts from the Note-Book of William Dickenson', *Transactions of the Hunter Archaeological Society*, II, pt II (1921), pp. 189-200.

Yorkshire Fines, 1246-1272', *Yorkshire Archaeological Society Record Series*, LXXXII (1932).

3. Books

S. O. Addy, *The Evolution of the English House* (revised edn, London, 1933).

H. Armitage, *Chantrey Land* (London, 1910).

M. Barley, *Houses and History* (London, 1986).

J. V. Beckett, *The Aristocracy in England, 1660-1911* (Oxford, 1986).

C. Binfield *et al.*, *The History of the City of Sheffield, 1843-1993*, II (Sheffield, 1993).

C. Binfield and D. Hey, eds, *Mesters to Masters: A History of the Company of Cutlers in Hallamshire* (Oxford, 1997).

J. Burton, *Monastic and Religious Orders in Britain, 1000-1300* (Cambridge, 1994).

M. Chatfield, *Churches the Victorians Forgot* (Ashbourne, 1979).

M. H. F. Chaytor, *The Wilsons of Sharrow: The Snuff-Makers of Sheffield* (Sheffield, 1962).

H. M. Colvin, *The White Canons in England* (Oxford, 1951).

M. Craven, *A Derbyshire Armory*, Derbyshire Record Society, XVII (1991).

D. Crossley, *et al.*, eds, *Water Power on the Sheffield Rivers* (Sheffield, 1989).

M. Davies-Shiel, *Watermills of Cumbria* (Clapham, 1978).

J. N. Dransfield, *History of Penistone* (Penistone, 1906).

Revd J. Eastwood, *History of the Parish of Ecclesfield* (London, 1862).

H. Egan, *The Millstone Industry in the Peak District* (dissertation for the Certificate of Local History, University of Sheffield, 1985).

R. Entwistle, *Holymoorside, Past and Present* (Chesterfield, 1976).

Revd A. Gatty, *A Life at One Living* (London, 1884).

Revd A. Gatty, *St.Wandrille's Abbey* (Sheffield, 1887).

M. Gelling, *Place-Names in the Landscape* (London, 1984).

M. Gelling and A. Cole, *The Landscape of Place-Names* (Stamford, 2000).

C. Giles, *Rural Houses of West Yorkshire, 1400-1830* (London: Royal Commission on Historical Monuments, 1986).

G. Grigson, *The Penguin Book of Ballads* (Harmondsworth, 1975).

J. Guest, *Historic Notices of Rotherham* (Worksop, 1879).

T. W. Hall, *South Yorkshire Historical Sketches* (Sheffield, 1931).

P. Hanks and F. Hodges, *A Dictionary of Surnames* (Oxford, 1888).

J. Harvey, ed., *Dronfield Then: 1530-1640* (Dronfield, 1980).

D. Hey, *The Village of Ecclesfield* (Huddersfield, 1968).

D. Hey, *The Rural Metalworkers of the Sheffield Region* (Leicester, 1972).

D. Hey, *Packmen, Carriers and Packhorse Roads*, second edn (Ashbourne, 2001).

D. Hey, *The Fiery Blades of Hallamshire: Sheffield and Its Neighbourhood, 1660-1740* (Leicester, 1991).

D. Hey, *A History of Sheffield* (Lancaster, 1998).

A. Hopkinson, *Study of a Village: Killamarsh, 1535-1750* (dissertation for the Certificate in Local History, University of Sheffield, 1984).

B. Hudson, *Through Limestone Hills* (Yeovil, 1989).

Revd J. Hunter, *Hallamshire* (ed. Revd A. Gatty, London, 1869).

Revd J. Hunter, *South Yorkshire: The History and Topography of the Deanery of Doncaster*, II (London, 1831).

Revd J. Hunter, *Familiae Minorum Gentium*, 5 vols (Harleian Society, 1895).

C.F. Innocent, *The Development of English Building Construction* (Cambridge, 1916).

J. Kenworthy, *The Early History of Stocksbridge and District* (Deepcar, privately published in parts): 'Langsett' (1915); 'The Town Fields and Commons of Hunshelf, Langsett and Waldershelf' (1917).

R. E. Leader, *A History of the Company of Cutlers in Hallamshire*, II (Sheffield, 1906).

L. C. Loyd, *The Origins of Some Anglo-Norman Families*, Harleian Society, 103 (1951).

Lady Macdonald of the Isles, *The Fortunes of a Family* (Edinburgh, 1927).

E. D. Mackerness, *Somewhere Further North: A History of Music in Sheffield* (Sheffield, 1974).

E. Miller, ed., *The Agrarian History of England and Wales, III, 1350-1500* (Cambridge, 1991).

Marie-Thérèse Morlet, *Dictionnaire étymologique des noms de famille* (Paris, 1991).

M. Jones, *The Making of the South Yorkshire Landscape* (Barnsley, 2000).

G.E. Mingay, ed., *The Victorian Countryside*, 2 vols (London, 1981).

G. E. Mingay, ed., *The Agrarian History of England and Wales, VI: 1750-1850* (Cambridge, 1989).

P. B. Munsche, *Gentlemen and Poachers: the English Game Laws, 1671-1831* (Cambridge, 1981).

F. Nixon, *Industrial Archaeology of Derbyshire* (Newton Abbot, 1969).

D. M. Palliser, *The Age of Elizabeth* (London, 1983).

C. Paulus, *The Manor and Parish of Ecclesall* (Sheffield, 1927).

S. Pegge, *An Historical Account of Beauchief Abbey* (London, 1801).

C. Platt, *The Monastic Grange in Medieval England* (London, 1969).

P. H. Reaney, *The Origin of English Surnames* (London, 1967).

P. H. Reaney and R. M. Wilson, *A Dictionary of English Surnames* (Oxford, revised edn, 1997).

G. Redmonds, *Yorkshire Surnames Series, pt I: Bradford & District* (Lepton, 1990).

B. Robinson, *Walls across the Valley: the building of the Howden and Derwent Dams* (Cromford, 1993).

P. Roebuck, *Yorkshire Baronets, 1640-1760* (Oxford, 1980).

'Report of the Royal Archaeological Institute's Summer Meeting at Wentworth Woodhouse', *The Archaeological Journal,* 138 (1980).

Sheffield Clarion Ramblers' Handbook (1948-49), (1950-51), (1955-56) and (1962-63).

J. Simpson, *British Dragons* (London, 1980).

A. V. Smith, *Beauchief Abbey: Notes on the Layout and Remains — the Abbey and Surrounding Area* (Sheffield, privately printed, 1993).

T. Tomlinson, *Querns, Millstones and Grindstones made in Hathersage and District* (Hathersage, 1981).

Vernacular Architecture, 24 (1993) and, 25 (1995).

Victoria County History of Warwickshire, II (1908).

T. Watt, *Cheap Print and Popular Piety, 1550-1640* (Cambridge, 1991).

D. Wilson, *A History of the Wilson Family of Broomhead* (Sheffield, privately printed, 1991).

W. Wood, *The History and Antiquities of Eyam*, sixth edition (1865).

4. Articles

A. L. Armstrong, 'Sheffield Castle', *Transactions of the Hunter Archaeological Society*, IV, pt I (1930), pp. 7-27.

J. E. Bartlett, 'The Excavation of a Barrow at Lodge Moor, Sheffield, 1954-55', *Transactions of the Hunter Archaeological Society*, VII, pt 6 (1957), pp. 321-30.

L. H. Butcher, 'Archaeological Remains on the Wharncliffe-Greno Upland, South Yorkshire', *Transactions of the Hunter Archaeological Society*, VII, pt I (1957), pp. 38-39.

J. Cass, 'The Rivelin Tunnel, 1903-1910', *Transactions of the Hunter Archaeological Society*, 18 (1995), pp. 60-74.

R. Doncaster, 'A Note on Rock Basins in the Rivelin Valley,' *Transactions of the Hunter Archaeological Society*, 13 (1984), p. 23.

C. Drury, 'The Sembly Quest', *Transactions of the Hunter Archaeological Society*, III, pt 2 (1926), pp. 105-111.

W. H. Elgar, 'Beauchief Abbey', *Transactions of the Hunter Archaeological Society*, III (1929), pp. 162-64.

D. L. Farmer, 'Millstones for Medieval Manors', *Agricultural History Review*, 40 (1992), pp. 98-103.

H. S. A. Fox, 'The Millstone Makers of Medieval Dartmoor', *Devon and Cornwall Notes and Queries*, 37 (1995), pp. 153-57.

R. Harte and C. Morroney, 'Two Way Traffic: the Importance of Beauchief Abbey as a Case Study for the Premonstratensian Order in England', *Review of Archaeology in South Yorkshire, 1994-95* (1996), pp. 81-88.

A. H. Henderson, 'The Excavation of a Barrow Remnant at Lodge Moor, Sheffield, 1956-57', *Transactions of the Hunter Archaeological Society*, VII, pt 6 (1957), pp. 331-37.

D. Hey, 'The Parks at Tankersley and Wortley', *Yorkshire Archaeological Journal*, 47 (1975), pp. 109-19.

D. Hey, 'The Local History of Family Names', *The Local Historian*, 27, no. 4 (1997), supplement.

D. Hey, 'Penistone Market and Cloth Hall' in B. Elliott, ed., *Aspects of Barnsley*, V (Barnsley, 1998), pp. 173-88.

D. Hey, 'Yorkshire's Southern Boundary' in *Essays on Northern History in Honour of Maurice W. Beresford, Northern History*, XXXVII (2000), pp. 31-47.

C. F. Innocent, 'The Field System of Wigtwizzle', *Transactions of the Hunter Archaeological Society*, II, pt 4 (1924), pp. 276-78.

J. E. A. Jolliffe, 'Northumbrian Institutions', *English Historical Review*, XLI (1926), pp. 1-42.

R. Meredith, 'Beauchief Abbey and the Pegges', *Derbyshire Archaeological Society*, 87 (1967), pp. 86-126.

R. Meredith, 'Hathersage Affairs, 1720-35', *Transactions of the Hunter Archaeological Society*, XI (1981), pp. 14-27.

R. Meredith, 'Millstone Making at Yarncliff in the reign of Edward IV', *Derbyshire Archaeological Journal*, CI (1981), pp. 102-6.

C. J. Morroney, 'More than meets the Eye? A Preliminary Discussion of the Archaeological Remains of Beauchief Abbey and Park', *Review of Archaeology in South Yorkshire, 1993-94* (1994), pp. 60-67.

M. Plant, 'A Scythe-Stone Industry on Beeley Moor', *Derbyshire Archaeological Journal*, LXXXVIII (1968), pp. 98-100.

J. P. Polak, 'The Production and Distribution of Peak Millstones from the Sixteenth to the Eighteenth Centuries', *Derbyshire Archaeological Journal*, CVII (1987), pp. 55-72.

Y. Poncelet, 'Les possessions anglaises de l'Abbaye de Saint-Wandrille', *Annales de Normandie* (May 1987), no. 2, pp. 149 72.

D. Postles, 'Rural Economy on the Grits and Sandstones of the South Yorkshire Pennines, 1086-1348', *Northern History*, XV (1979), pp. 1-19.

J. Radley, 'Some New Rock Basins in the Rivelin Valley', *Transactions of the Hunter Archaeological Society*, VIII, part 4 (1962), pp. 234-35.

J. Radley, 'Rock Basins on Hallam Moors: the Answer', *Transactions of the Hunter Archaeological Society*, X, part 1 (1964), p. 35.

P. Rahtz and K. Sheridan, 'Tamworth', *Current Archaeology*, 29 (1971), pp. 164-68

C. A. Ramsker, 'Pre-Register Genealogy and a Lost Place-Name', *The Local Historian*, 10, no. 5 (1973), pp. 227-33.

P. F. Ryder, 'Five South Yorkshire Timber-Framed Houses', *Yorkshire Archaeological Journal*, 59 (1987), pp. 51-82.

G. Scurfield, 'Seventeenth-Century Sheffield and its Environs', *Yorkshire Archaeological Journal*, 58 (1986), pp. 147-71.

J. A. Sheppard, 'Pre-Conquest Yorkshire: fiscal carucates as an index of land exploration', *Transactions of the Institute of British Geographers*, 65 (1975), pp. 67-78.

M. Spray and D. J. Smith, 'The Rise and Fall of Holly in the Sheffield Region', *Transactions of the Hunter Archaeological Society*, X, pt 4 (1977), pp. 239-51.

G. Tucker, 'Millstone Making in the Peak District of Derbyshire', *Industrial Archaeology*, VIII, no. I (1985), pp. 42-58.

J. B. Wheat, 'Garret Gleanings', *Transactions of the Hunter Archaeological Society*, IV, pt 1 (1930), pp. 49-56.

A. Yates, 'George Broomhead's First Job', *Dark Peak News*, (Autumn 1992), pp. 9-11.

INDEX

Place-names in and near Hallamshire

Sheffield, Ecclesfield and Bradfield are referred to throughout.

Family Names